The
Handbook
for the
New Legal Writer

ASPEN COURSEBOOK SERIES

The
Handbook
for the
New Legal Writer

JILL BARTON
Professor of Legal Writing
University of Miami School of Law

RACHEL H. SMITH
Professor of Legal Writing
University of Miami School of Law

Wolters Kluwer
Law & Business

Published by Wolters Kluwer Law & Business in New York.

Wolters Kluwer Law & Business serves customers worldwide with CCH, Aspen Publishers, and Kluwer Law International products. (www.wolterskluwerlb.com)

To contact Customer Service, e-mail customer.service@wolterskluwer.com, call 1-800-234-1660, fax 1-800-901-9075, or mail correspondence to:

Wolters Kluwer Law & Business
Attn: Order Department
PO Box 990
Frederick, MD 21705

Design and book composition by Keithley & Associates, Inc.

Printed in the United States of America.

1 2 3 4 5 6 7 8 9 0

ISBN 978-1-4548-3144-0

Library of Congress Cataloging-in-Publication Data

Barton, Jill, (professor) author.
  The handbook for the new legal writer / Jill Barton, Professor of Legal Writing, University of Miami School of Law, Rachel H. Smith, Professor of Legal Writing, University of Miami School of Law.
     p. cm. — (Aspen coursebook series)
  Includes bibliographical references and index.
  ISBN 978-1-4548-3144-0 (alk. paper)
1. Legal composition—United States. I. Smith, Rachel H., (professor) author.
II. Title.
  KF250.B38 2014
  808.06´634—dc23

                                                    2014008446

About Wolters Kluwer Law & Business

Wolters Kluwer Law & Business is a leading global provider of intelligent information and digital solutions for legal and business professionals in key specialty areas, and respected educational resources for professors and law students. Wolters Kluwer Law & Business connects legal and business professionals as well as those in the education market with timely, specialized authoritative content and information-enabled solutions to support success through productivity, accuracy and mobility.

Serving customers worldwide, Wolters Kluwer Law & Business products include those under the Aspen Publishers, CCH, Kluwer Law International, Loislaw, Best Case, ftwilliam.com and MediRegs family of products.

CCH products have been a trusted resource since 1913, and are highly regarded resources for legal, securities, antitrust and trade regulation, government contracting, banking, pension, payroll, employment and labor, and healthcare reimbursement and compliance professionals.

Aspen Publishers products provide essential information to attorneys, business professionals and law students. Written by preeminent authorities, the product line offers analytical and practical information in a range of specialty practice areas from securities law and intellectual property to mergers and acquisitions and pension/benefits. Aspen's trusted legal education resources provide professors and students with high-quality, up-to-date and effective resources for successful instruction and study in all areas of the law.

Kluwer Law International products provide the global business community with reliable international legal information in English. Legal practitioners, corporate counsel and business executives around the world rely on Kluwer Law journals, looseleafs, books, and electronic products for comprehensive information in many areas of international legal practice.

Loislaw is a comprehensive online legal research product providing legal content to law firm practitioners of various specializations. Loislaw provides attorneys with the ability to quickly and efficiently find the necessary legal information they need, when and where they need it, by facilitating access to primary law as well as state-specific law, records, forms and treatises.

ftwilliam.com offers employee benefits professionals the highest quality plan documents (retirement, welfare and non-qualified) and government forms (5500/PBGC, 1099 and IRS) software at highly competitive prices.

MediRegs products provide integrated health care compliance content and software solutions for professionals in healthcare, higher education and life sciences, including professionals in accounting, law and consulting.

Wolters Kluwer Law & Business, a division of Wolters Kluwer, is headquartered in New York. Wolters Kluwer is a market-leading global information services company focused on professionals.

To our anchors:
Rudy, Dan, and Eric

Summary of Contents

Contents

Preface

Welcome to *The Handbook for the New Legal Writer*—a new kind of legal writing textbook that is grounded in the realities of modern law practice.

The *Handbook* provides step-by-step instruction on how to write effective legal documents. We begin with objective writing in the form of office memos. Later, we move to persuasive writing through trial motions and appellate briefs. Then, we cover other forms of legal communication, including correspondence via letter, email, and instant message. We also describe how to draft judicial opinions and prepare for oral argument.

At every step, the *Handbook* uses annotated examples of realistic legal documents prepared by the authors, skilled practitioners, and judges to show—rather than tell—students how to be successful legal writers. Because it is designed to be the only textbook students need to excel in their first-year legal writing programs, the *Handbook* also includes chapters on legal research, *Bluebook* citation, and writing tools, including grammar, punctuation, plain language, and style.

The *Handbook* uses the term "anchors" throughout the text to show students how to analyze legal questions. If the best answer in law school is, "It depends," then we finish the answer by stating, "It depends on the anchors." Anchors are the facts, rules, and reasons that the answer to a legal question depends upon. We coined this term as a tool to help students understand how to read and synthesize legal authorities and how to analyze a client's legal problem.

We hope that by offering clear direction and pertinent examples, the *Handbook* will be an accessible, trustworthy, and valuable guide for the new legal writer.

Anchors aweigh!

Jill and Rachel
March 2014

Acknowledgments

We are fortunate to be part of a talented and creative team of legal writing professors at the University of Miami School of Law. Their feedback and support over the two years that we developed this book provided us with an invaluable foundation. This book is richer because of their careful reading, class testing, and collaborative spirit. Thanks go to Ellen Ross Belfer, Terri Doud, Alyssa Dragnich, Christina M. Frohock, Jennifer Hill, Peter Nemerovski, Shara Kobetz Pelz, Rachel Stabler, Annette Torres, and Cheryl E. Zuckerman.

Additionally, we are grateful to the students at the University of Miami School of Law, whose thoughtful questions helped us make the *Handbook* more effective for its audience. We especially appreciate the efforts of our research assistants: Olivia Kelman, Candice Manyak, Christine Tudor, and Daniel Zailskas. We also greatly appreciate the administrative assistance provided by Mercy Hernandez and Sylvia Hernandez. And we owe great thanks to our supportive administrators: Dean Patricia D. White and Vice Dean Patrick O. Gudridge.

We appreciate the efforts of everyone at Aspen Publishers, especially Sarah Hains, Christine Hannan, and Carol McGeehan. They helped us transform our idea about teaching legal writing in a novel way into this book. In addition, the anonymous Aspen reviewers, who examined early drafts of the *Handbook*, provided us with many valuable comments that helped us shape the book. Thanks also goes to Jay Harward at Newgen North America.

We owe a great debt to our colleagues in the national legal writing commnity; their encouragement and enthusiasm continue to inspire us. We are especially privileged to have learned from Judy Popper, Rosi Schrier, Wanda Temm, and Barbara Wilson.

We also want to express our admiration and appreciation for the legal writers whose excellent work provided examples for this book: U.S. Supreme Court Chief Justice John G. Roberts and Associate Justices Sandra Day O'Connor, Antonin Scalia, Anthony M. Kennedy, Clarence Thomas, Ruth Bader Ginsburg, Samuel Alito, and Elena Kagan; U.S. Circuit Court of Appeals Chief Judge Alex Kozinksi, U.S. District Judge Steven D. Merryday, Judge Kevin G. Ross of the Minnesota Court of Appeals, and Judge Vance E. Salter of the Florida Third District Court of Appeal; and attorneys Howard K. Blumberg, Conal Doyle, Gregory G. Garre, Brian Koukoutchos, Kenneth W. Starr, Kathleen Sullivan, and Laurence Tribe. We know their words will continue to inspire our students, as they have inspired us.

The
Handbook
for the
New Legal Writer

part I

Reading and Writing Like a Lawyer

chapter 1

Introduction to Legal Writing

To be a lawyer is to be a writer. Most lawyers write every single day that they practice law. On a given day, the average attorney can be expected to write or edit any number of documents that vary widely in form, style, and purpose. Even a new lawyer is responsible for understanding how to prepare a vast range of documents, including memos, briefs, letters, and emails. This book will guide you with step-by-step instructions for how to prepare each of these types of common legal documents.

Legal documents can generally be divided into two categories: (1) objective documents and (2) persuasive documents. Objective and persuasive documents serve different purposes, have different audiences, and require the legal writer to adapt to different formats and writing styles. The type of document that you will prepare in a given situation depends upon the purpose of the document and its intended audience.

1. OBJECTIVE DOCUMENTS

The purpose of an objective legal document is to inform, advise, and counsel. An objective document analyzes a legal issue to predict the most likely outcome.

The typical objective document is an office memorandum that applies the relevant law to the client's facts. Objective memos are used to analyze the legal consequences of a particular situation, the likelihood that a legal claim will be successful, the advisability of a legal strategy, and many other legal questions. The conclusion of an objective legal document is usually similar to the following statement:

The court will likely hold that _____ because _____.

The most common objective documents are office memos, judicial opinions, and advice emails. Because an objective document is expected to accurately advise the reader, the analysis in an objective document must be scrupulous, balanced, and reliable.

2. PERSUASIVE DOCUMENTS

The purpose of a persuasive legal document is to argue, convince, and induce action. A persuasive document analyzes a legal issue to persuade the reader of the correct outcome.

The typical persuasive document is a motion that asks the court to grant some particular relief to the writer's client. The conclusion of a persuasive legal document is usually similar to the following statement:

The Court should grant the requested relief because _____.

The most common persuasive documents are trial motions, responses, replies, and appellate briefs, which the writer directs to the court. Opposing counsel reviews and responds to the papers, and both sides typically draft letters and emails to opposing counsel. Because a persuasive document is intended to persuade the reader, the analysis in a persuasive document must be logical, credible, and compelling.

Law students and lawyers write both objective and persuasive documents. Both types of documents require a careful legal analysis. The next chapter will show you how to approach your legal analysis, beginning with how to read and understand the authorities that will allow you to analyze your legal question. Then, Chapter 5 will introduce you to the common format for both objective and persuasive documents.

chapter 2

Reading and Understanding Authorities

1. READING CONSTITUTIONS AND STATUTES

The right to speak freely, the right to bear arms, the right against unreasonable searches and seizures—all are rights guaranteed by the U.S. Constitution—with some carefully worded limitations. These limitations have been subject to debate for centuries. While some argue that the Constitution is a living, breathing document with a meaning that evolves over time, others advocate for a plain language interpretation. But even the most careful reader will strain to understand the plain meaning of the Constitution. As an example, consider the meaning of the Second Amendment, which citizens have argued over since before it was ratified in 1791:

> A well regulated Militia, being necessary to the security of a free State, the right of the people to keep and bear Arms, shall not be infringed.

The centuries-old language raises some questions: What is a well-regulated Militia? Why is the clause "being necessary to the security of a free State" offset by commas? And what does the term "Arms" include?

When reading constitutions and statutes, every word, every comma, and every clause matters. You will need to carefully consider the meaning of each term and punctuation mark. Take care to look for terms, including "and," "or," "unless," "except," "not," "if," "may," "must," "shall," and "provided that," which impact the meaning of the words around them.

When reading statutes, you also need to consider the overall organization of the body of laws. Statutes are typically organized by topic into numerical titles or subject codes. For instance, federal statutes contained within the U.S. Code are organized into 51 titles, from Title 1—General Provisions to Title 51—National and Commercial Space Programs. Some state statutes are organized into subject codes organized alphabetically. For example, the California statutes contained within the California Code are arranged into 29 subject codes, from Business and Professions to Welfare and Institutions. Federal and state statutes are then divided within the titles or subject codes into subtitles, chapters, sections, and subsections.

When you search for a statute on a particular legal question, keep in mind that more than one statute or statutory section might apply. For instance, suppose you need to defend a client against a littering charge in Arizona. To find the littering statute(s), you would begin by reviewing the list of titles in the Arizona Revised Code. Your search would reveal the following hierarchy:

Title 13 Criminal Code
→ Chapter 16 Criminal Damage to Property
→ 13-1601 Definitions
→ 13-1602 Criminal damage; classification
→ 13-1603 Criminal littering or polluting; classification
→ 13-1604 Aggravated criminal damage; classification
→ 13-1605 Aggregation of amounts of damage

You will likely quickly recognize that Section 1603 applies:

A. A person commits criminal littering or polluting if such person without lawful authority does any of the following: 1. Throws, places, drops or permits to be dropped on public property or property of another which is not a lawful dump any litter, destructive or injurious material which he does not immediately remove.[1]

A careful reading shows that Section 1603 describes the littering conduct prohibited. You would notice that the statute criminalizes "any" of the listed actions and repeatedly uses "or." You would also notice that the statute appears to include exceptions if the person acts with "lawful authority" or "immediately remove[s]" the litter. But a few terms in the statute, including "litter" and "destructive or injurious material" are open to interpretation. Section 1601 helpfully provides a definition of "litter," which you would use in interpreting the statute.

In this chapter, unless the context otherwise requires:
3. "Litter" includes any rubbish, refuse, waste material, offal, paper, glass, cans, bottles, organic or inorganic trash, debris, filthy or odoriferous objects, dead animals or any foreign substance of whatever kind or description, including junked or abandoned vehicles, whether or not any of these items are of value.[2]

But because Section 1601 does not define "destructive or injurious material," you would have to use case law to see how courts have interpreted the term. You would also want to use case law to understand how courts have interpreted the definition in Section 1601 and how they have applied the language of Section 1603 to the actions of defendants in specific cases.

This reading of an Arizona statute shows that you must consider the context of each statute you analyze because related statutes often define key terms. It also shows that legislative bodies regularly use dense, complicated

---

1. Ariz. Stat. §13-1603(A)(1) (2013).
2. *Id.* §13-1601(3).

language that might leave room for debate. Your task as a new legal reader is to carefully analyze the plain language in a constitutional or statutory provision so you can understand its precise meaning.

2. READING AND BRIEFING A CASE

Reading a case is different than reading a novel or newspaper article. You might have to read a case several times before you understand it. Cases often involve complex legal issues, archaic language, unfamiliar terms, and confounding analyses. Your job as a lawyer when reading a case is to figure how and why the court reached its decision. You can start by identifying the eight key parts of a case:

1. Case name and citation
2. Procedural history
3. Issue(s)
4. Facts
5. Rule(s)
6. Reasoning
7. Holding(s)
8. Order or disposition

These eight key parts of a case form the basis of a "case brief." A case brief is a document you create for your own use where you identify each of these key parts. Preparing a case brief allows you to read the case carefully and record your analysis. This record guarantees that you will have noticed and extracted the most important parts of the case, and it preserves your understanding of the case so you can come back to it later and not have to analyze the case from scratch. As a law student, you will write countless case briefs. As a lawyer, you will probably develop your own shorthand for briefing cases, but you will always need to identify the following key parts of any case you read.

A. Case Name and Citation

The case name identifies the parties in the case. The citation provides information regarding the volume, case reporter, and page where the case has been published, the court that decided the case, and the year of decision. The citation is the primary information a lawyer uses to locate a case. See Chapter 42 for details on how to write citations according to the preferred format in *The Bluebook: A Uniform System of Citation* (Columbia Law Review Ass'n et al. eds., 19th ed. 2010).

B. Procedural History

The procedural history describes the case's progress through the legal system. The procedural history will tell you how the case arrived at the court that wrote the opinion you are reading.

C. Issue(s)

The issue is a summary of the legal question that the opinion is intended to answer. It is usually a combination of the law and facts that gave rise to the dispute before the court. Some cases address multiple issues.

D. Facts

The facts are those facts that are legally significant to the issue that the court is deciding.

E. Rule(s)

The rules are the general legal principles that the court applies to the facts of the case to reach its decision. Usually, the rules come from statutes or other cases.

F. Reasoning

The reasoning is the analytical process the court follows to reach its decision. The reasoning describes how the court applied the rules to the facts to determine the appropriate outcome. Identifying the reasons that support the court's resolution of the issue is crucial to understanding a case.

This book identifies these reasons as "anchors." Anchors are the grounds or bases of a court's decision. The court might state the anchors explicitly, or the court might use wording that is less direct. As a result, you will need to carefully read and understand an opinion to fully identify the anchors that motivated a court's decision. Chapter 3 describes anchors in more detail and discusses how to use the anchors from multiple cases to answer new legal questions.

G. Holding(s)

The holding is the court's answer. It states the court's resolution of the specific issues before it. The holding briefly describes how the court applied the rule to the specific facts of the case. When a case addresses multiple issues, there will be multiple holdings: one for each issue.

H. Order or Disposition

The order or disposition is the court's instruction for what should happen in the case procedurally in light of the court's decision.

When you write a case brief, it's important to begin to digest the information you read and highlight in an opinion. Case briefs need to be concise, even for opinions that are dozens of pages long. The case brief should summarize and synthesize the information from the opinion. Although most cases include all eight key parts, cases rarely (if ever) describe each part concisely and in order. Moreover, cases often include information that is not directly relevant to the court's decision or the reason you are reading the case.

In the following case, the plaintiff sued a circus company for negligence after a circus bear frightened the plaintiff's horse while on a public street. The eight key parts of the case and the anchors are identified in the margin. A sample case brief follows on page 13.

BOSTOCK-FERARI AMUSEMENT CO. v. BROCKSMITH
73 N.E. 281 (Ind. Ct. App. 1905) [3]

*This is the **case name and citation**. Bostock-Ferari Amusement Co. is the defendant and Brocksmith is the plaintiff. The citation abbreviates the North Eastern (N.E.) Reporter and includes the volume (73) and page number (281). Ind. Ct. App. is the correct Bluebook abbreviation for the Appellate Court of Indiana. 1905 is the year the case was decided.*

Opinion

The complaint alleges that the plaintiff, while driving in his buggy, was injured in consequence of his horse taking fright from the sight of a bear walking along a public street of the city of Vincennes. The action was begun in the circuit court of Knox county, and, upon change of venue, tried in the circuit court of Sullivan county. The court rendered judgment upon the verdict of the jury in favor of appellee for $750.

The complaint was in three paragraphs. The first was dismissed, and the cause was tried upon the amended second and third paragraphs, to which a general denial was filed. The errors relied upon are the action of the court in overruling demurrers to the said second and third paragraphs, respectively, of the complaint, and overruling appellant's motion for a new trial. Among the reasons set out in the motion for a new trial are that the verdict was contrary to the law, and was not sustained by sufficient evidence.

*The first two paragraphs describe the case's **procedural history**, which are the legal steps that led to this appeal.*

The question of the sufficiency of the second paragraph of complaint is not entirely free from doubt, but we conclude that each of said paragraphs is sufficient to withstand a demurrer.

It is sought to maintain an action for damages resulting from the fright of a horse at the sight of a bear, which its keeper and owner was leading along a public street for the purpose of transporting it from a railroad train by which it had been carried to Vincennes to the point in Vincennes at which the bear was to be an exhibit, as a part of appellant's show. It is not claimed, either by allegation or proof, that the show was in itself unlawful; and there is no pretense that the transporting of the bear from one place to another for the purpose of exhibition was unlawful, or in itself negligence. The case is therefore one of the fright of a horse merely at the appearance of the bear while it was being led along the street, was making no noise or other demonstration, and was in the control of its keeper. It appears without contradiction from the evidence that when the horse took fright the bear was doing nothing except going with his keeper. He was muzzled. He had a ring in his nose, to which a chain was attached. It was strong enough to hold and control him. He had

*These three sentences describe the central **issue** in the case. A good case brief will concisely summarize the legal question and reference the relevant facts and law.*

*This section includes most of the key **facts**. A case brief should summarize the key facts, focusing on the facts that are legally significant.*

---

3. Note that the citations in this opinion and the citations in the examples provided throughout this book have been edited to conform to *Bluebook* style.

around his neck a collar about two inches wide and one-half inch thick, to which also was attached a chain. The keeper had both chains in his hand when the accident occurred. The chain connected with the ring in his nose was small. The one connected with his collar was large. It was for the purpose of chaining him at night when he was alone. The chains were strong enough to control the bear. The animal was characterized by the witnesses who knew him as "gentle," "kind," and "docile." His keeper testified that he had never known him to be mean or growl. He testified, also, that he never knew of a bear scaring a horse; that shortly before the accident the keeper met two ladies in a buggy, and their horses did not scare. He was described as of pretty good size and brown. One witness said he was a "large, ugly looking brown bear." When a person is injured by an attack by an animal feræ naturæ, the negligence of the owner is presumed, because the dangerous propensity of such an animal is known, and the law recognizes that safety lies only in keeping it secure. 2 Am. & Eng. Ency. Law 351(2d Ed.). In the case before us the injury did not result from any vicious propensity of the bear. ⚓ He did nothing but walk in the charge of his owner and keeper, Peter Degeleih. He was being moved quietly upon a public thoroughfare for a lawful purpose. ⚓

> This is the first of two major rules from the case.

> The most important parts of the court's **reasoning** are highlighted in gray throughout this opinion. Most courts detail step-by-step the rationale for their decision.

We have given the facts that are not controverted. There is also evidence tending strongly to support the claim made by appellant that appellee was guilty of negligence proximately contributing to his injury. Appellant also earnestly argues—supporting its argument with references to recognized authorities—that the owner and keeper of the bear was an independent contractor. But the disposition which we think should be made of the appeal makes it unnecessary to consider these questions. The liability of the appellant must rest on the doctrine of negligence. The gist of the action as claimed by appellee is the transportation of the bear, with knowledge that it was likely to frighten horses, without taking precaution to guard against fright. An animal feræ naturæ, reduced to captivity, is the property of its captor. 2 Black. Comm. 391, 403; 4 Black. Comm. 235, 236. The owner of the bear had the right to transport it from one place to another for a lawful purpose, and it was not negligence per se for the owner or keeper to lead it along a public street for such purpose. *Scribner v. Kelley*, 38 Barb. 14 (N.Y. Sup. Ct. 1862); *Macomber v. Nichols*, 34 Mich. 212 (1876); Ingham on Law of Animals, 230. The conducting of shows for the exhibition of wild or strange animals is a lawful business. The mere fact that the appearance of a chattel, whether an animal or an inanimate object, is calculated to frighten a horse of ordinary gentleness, does not deprive the owner of such chattel of his lawful right to transport its property along a public highway. *Macomber v. Nichols*, supra; *Holland v. Bartch*, 120 Ind. 46 (1889); *Wabash, etc., Co. v. Farver*, 12 N. E. 296 (Ind. 1887); *Gilbert v. Flint, etc.*, 16 N. W. 868 (Mich. 1883); *Piollet v. Simmers*, 106 Pa. 95 (1854). One must use his own so as not to unnecessarily injure another, but the measure of care to be employed in respect to animals

> This is the first part of the court's two-part **holding**. The holding is similar to the rule, but the rules are stated generally and the holding is stated in a way that is specific to this case.

> This is the second major **rule**.

and other property is the same. It is such care as an ordinarily prudent person would employ under similar circumstances. ⏺ This is not inconsistent with the proposition that, if an animal feræ naturæ attacks and injures a person, the negligence of the owner or keeper is presumed. The evidence is that the horse was of ordinary gentleness, but this fact would not deprive the appellant of the right to make proper use of the street. If the bear had been carelessly managed, or permitted to make any unnecessary noise or demonstration, it would have been an act of negligence. It is not uncommon for horses of ordinary gentleness to become frightened at unaccustomed sights on the public highway. The automobile, the bicycle, the traction engine, the steam roller, may each be frightful to some horses, but still they may be lawfully used on the public streets. King David said, "An horse is a vain thing for safety." Modern observation has fully justified the statement. A large dog, a great bull, a baby wagon, may each frighten some horses, but their owners are not barred from using them upon the streets on that account. Nor, under the decisions, would the courts be warranted in holding that the owner of a bear, subjugated, gentle, docile, chained, would not, under the facts shown in the case at bar, be permitted to conduct the homely brute along the public streets, because of his previous condition of freedom. In *Scribner v. Kelley*, supra, the court said: "It does not appear that the elephant was at large, but, on the contrary, that he was in the care and apparently under the control of a man who was riding beside him on a horse; and the occurrence happened before the passage of the act of April 2, 1862, regulating the use of public highways. There is nothing in the evidence to show that the plaintiff's horse was terrified because the object he saw was an elephant, but only that he was frightened because he suddenly saw moving upon a highway crossing upon which he was traveling, and fully 100 feet from him, a large, animate object, to which he was unaccustomed. Non constat that any other moving object of equal size, and differing in appearance from such as he was accustomed to see, might not have inspired him with similar terror. The injury which resulted from his fright is more fairly attributed to a lack of ordinary courage and discipline in himself than to the fact that the object which he saw was an elephant." ⏺

It is alleged in the complaint that the bear was an object likely to frighten a horse of ordinary gentleness, which fact the appellant well knew. There is no evidence that the bear was an object likely to frighten horses of ordinary gentleness, nor that the appellant knew that the bear was an object likely to frighten horses of ordinary gentleness. ⏺ The evidence shows, so far as the observation of the keeper and the appellant is stated and gave information, that he had not frightened horses.

The learned counsel for appellee insist that the appellant was negligent in not having had the proper number of persons in charge of the bear to give warning of the danger; citing *Bennett v. Lovell*, 12 R. I. 166 (1878).

In that case the plaintiff and his wife were thrown from their wagon and injured in consequence of their horse taking fright from some tubing and machinery which had been left upon a public highway by the defendant, who was carrying the same for the use of the city waterworks. The court held that one who left such an object on the highway without proper precaution cannot be said to be using the due care he ought to use. The court indulges in dicta by way of illustration to the effect that a person moving an animal which, from its appearances, noise, or offensiveness, is calculated to frighten human beings, without taking precautions by having a sufficient number of persons in charge of it to warn others of the danger, and, if need be, to aid them in passing it, or who leaves such an object on the highway without proper precaution, cannot be said to be using that due care he ought to use, etc. The facts are not analogous with those in the case at bar. The appellant used the public highway. The animal was gentle, was securely in the control of his keeper, and is — This sentence is the second part of the court's **holding**. not shown to have been an animal which, from its appearance, noise, or other offensiveness, was calculated to frighten horses. The facts upon the question of negligence are undisputed, and that question is therefore to be determined by the court as a matter of law.

The judgment is reversed, with instruction to sustain appellant's motion — This is the court's **order**. for a new trial.

1. **Case name and citation:** *Bostock-Ferari Amusement Co. v. Brocksmith*, 73 N.E. 281 (Ind. Ct. App. 1905).

2. **Procedural history:** The plaintiff sued the bear owner for negligence and won $750 at the trial court. The defendant appeals the denial of its motion for a new trial.

3. **Issue:** Is the owner of a wild animal, like a bear, liable for negligence if the injury suffered is not the result of any vicious propensity of the wild animal?

4. **Facts:** The plaintiff was injured while driving a horse-drawn buggy after his horse was scared when it saw a bear being walked along a public street. The bear's owner was lawfully transporting the bear from the train to an exhibit where it would be on display. The bear was muzzled, chained, and controlled by its owner. The bear was characterized by those who knew it as "gentle," "kind," and "docile."

5. **Rules:**
   a. When a person is injured in an attack by a wild animal, the negligence of the owner is presumed.
   b. An owner must employ a measure of care that an ordinarily prudent person would employ under similar circumstances so that he does not unnecessarily injure another.

6. **Reasoning:** The fact that the appearance of a wild animal may frighten a horse of "ordinary gentleness" does not mean that the owner of the animal does not have the "lawful right to transport its property along a public highway." The bear in this case was like an automobile, bicycle, traction engine, steam roller, large dog, great bull, or baby wagon—all of which may frighten a horse, but are allowed on public streets. The holding fits with the rule that the owner of a wild animal that attacks and injures a person is presumed to be negligent because this bear did not attack anyone. The court compared this case to *Scribner v. Kelley*, where a horse was frightened by the sight of an elephant, not because it was an elephant, but because it was a large object moving ahead of the horse, which the horse had never seen before. The court distinguished a case where a horse had been frightened by tubing and machinery that had been left by the side of the road, because in leaving the tubing and machinery by the road, the defendant in that case had not exercised due care.

7. **Holding:** The defendant was not negligent because it had the right to transport the bear "from one place to another for a lawful purpose," and the bear was gentle, under the control of his keeper, and not the type in "its appearance, noise, or other offensiveness," that would frighten horses.

8. **Order:** The judgment was reversed with an instruction to sustain the defendant's motion for a new trial.

chapter 3

It Depends on the "Anchors"

The law typically doesn't offer easy answers. The best answer to a legal question is often, "It depends." A lawyer's job is to figure out what the answer depends upon. The *Handbook* uses the term "anchors" to describe the facts, rules, and reasons your answer depends on. Now, you can start your legal analysis with this simple answer to your legal question: "It depends on the anchors."

The anchors are the reasons why a court decided a particular legal question the way it did. The anchors are the grounds or bases of a court's decision on your specific issue. The anchors can be the relevant parts of a constitution or statute or they can be key facts or minor rules from case law. By identifying the anchors and applying them to the facts from your legal question, you can effectively analyze most legal questions.

As you read cases to help answer your legal question, carefully consider how the court addressed your issue. To identify the anchors, consider which facts, rules, or reasons were especially relevant. The court might state the anchors explicitly, or the court might use wording that is less direct—especially if your legal question is not the primary issue in an opinion. As a result, you will need to carefully read and understand an opinion to fully identify the anchors that motivated a court's decision.

Reading, briefing, and analyzing cases to identify the anchors requires more than just note taking. As you read multiple relevant cases, you will be able to compare the anchors among them to gain a deeper understanding of your legal issue. Effective legal analysis requires you to achieve a sophisticated understanding of a relevant area of law. This process requires you to synthesize and summarize your understanding of multiple authorities, rather than merely regurgitating and repeating your notes and case briefs.

1. IDENTIFYING THE ANCHORS

The case about the bear and the horse has five anchors, which are listed here in the order that they appear. The anchors are noted throughout the opinion with the ⚓ symbol.

1. The bear did not have a "vicious propensity."
2. The bear was under its keeper's control as it "moved quietly upon a public thoroughfare for a lawful purpose."
3. The bear was securely under its keeper's control, which showed that the owner employed a "measure of care" to not unnecessarily injure another.
4. A lack of ordinary courage and discipline in the horse can be more to blame than the fact that the horse was surprised to see a large animal on the street.
5. There was no evidence that the owner knew that the bear was likely to frighten horses of ordinary gentleness.

This list summarizes the reasons that motivated the court's decision making. As you reread the list of anchors and compare it to the opinion on pages 9-12 where the anchors are marked, you will notice that the anchors appear throughout the court's opinion. Further, the court states some anchors more than once—sometimes using different language—and combines its discussion of some of the anchors.

2. SYNTHESIZING THE ANCHORS

After you identify the anchors in a case, you should understand how the court reached its decision in that case. When you are asked to analyze a legal question to solve a client's problem, you will likely need to read more than one relevant case. You will, therefore, need to create a list of anchors synthesized from multiple cases. In addition, to answer the client's question, you will need to tailor your list of anchors to address the client's specific legal question.

For instance, suppose your client was bicycling down a neighborhood sidewalk at dawn when a rooster crowed from a fence post a few feet away and spooked her, causing her to fall. She wants to know whether she can recover damages from the rooster's owner for negligence because the rooster was on a neighbor's fence when it scared her. The *Bostock-Ferari* case will help you answer her question, along with *Scribner*,[1] which it cited. In your search for more recent cases, you also find *Thompson v. Lee*,[2] which affirmed a verdict against a motorcyclist who collided with an escaped cow on a highway.

To answer your client's question, you should start by reading and briefing each case. Next, you should review each case to identify the anchors that are relevant to the legal question before you. Here, the question is whether the owner of a noisy rooster that flew to a neighbor's fence is negligent.

Start by listing the anchors from each case that address your legal question.

---

1. 38 Barb. 14 (N.Y. Sup. Ct. 1862).
2. 402 N.E. 1309 (Ind. Ct. App. 1980).

BOSTOCK-FERARI AMUSEMENT CO. v. BROCKSMITH

1. The bear did not have a "vicious propensity."
2. The bear was under its keeper's control as it "moved quietly upon a public thoroughfare for a lawful purpose."
3. The bear was securely under its keeper's control, which showed that the owner employed a "measure of care" to not unnecessarily injure another.
4. A lack of ordinary courage and discipline in the horse can be more to blame than the fact that the horse was surprised to see a large animal on the street.
5. There was no evidence that the owner knew that the bear was likely to frighten horses of ordinary gentleness.

SCRIBNER v. KELLY

6. The defendants did not know their elephant was dangerous and would frighten the plaintiff's horse.
7. The horse was not injured by any action of the elephant; instead, the horse was frightened because it lacked ordinary courage when it saw a large, unfamiliar object traveling 100 feet in front of him.

THOMPSON v. LEE

8. Cows are not normally dangerous or ferocious.
9. The owner did not have any reason to believe that this cow was abnormally dangerous or vicious.
10. The owner did not know the cow had escaped.

Once you have a list of the anchors from each of the relevant cases, you can develop a synthesized list, which combines common anchors from different cases. A review of the anchors above reveals that the courts had two broad reasons for their decisions. First, the courts examined the nature of the animal that allegedly caused injury, and second, the courts analyzed whether the animals' owners exercised the necessary level of care. From this understanding, you can create a synthesized list of the anchors to help answer your client's question about the rooster owner's negligence:

1. Whether the animal had a propensity to be vicious or frightening (Anchors 1 and 8) and whether the injured party had the propensity to frighten easily (Anchors 4 and 7).
2. Whether the owner took care to keep the animal contained and did not know of a vicious propensity or escape. (Anchors 2, 3, 5, 6, 9, and 10).

These anchors are referenced in different ways throughout the courts' opinions. Each reference to an anchor gives you new insight into how the courts made their decisions, and it helps you identify what is most relevant in answering your legal question. By identifying the anchors and synthesizing the list of anchors that address your legal question, you will reach the level of understanding that is necessary for you to effectively analyze and write about a legal question.

chapter 4

Understanding Hierarchy of Authority

When you are presented with a legal question, the first step is to identify the relevant authorities. Some authorities are law, and some authorities comment on the law. The authorities that make up the governing law are called "primary" authorities. Authorities that comment on the law are called "secondary" authorities or secondary sources. This chapter will explain how to identify the authorities that will help you answer your legal question. Because all authorities are not equal, this chapter also will explain the hierarchy among them.

Principles of Hierarchy of Authority

- Primary authorities are law; secondary sources comment on the law.
- Primary authorities are either federal or state law.
- The hierarchy of authority is (1) constitutions, (2) statutes, (3) case law, and (4) regulations.
- The hierarchy of case law determines whether a case is binding or non-binding on a legal issue.
- Whether a case is binding or non-binding on a new legal issue depends on (1) what jurisdiction's law applies to the issue and (2) which courts from that jurisdiction have the power to bind other courts.

---

1. PRIMARY AUTHORITIES

Primary authorities include constitutions, statutes, cases, regulations, ordinances, and other government rulings. All of these authorities will not apply to every legal question, so understanding the differences between primary authorities and their relative rank or hierarchy is important.

Primary authorities fall into one of two categories: They are federal law or state law. For example, an opinion from the U.S. District Court for the District of Massachusetts is a federal authority because it comes from a federal court. Likewise, the Constitution of the Commonwealth of Massachusetts is a state authority because it is the governing document for the state government of Massachusetts.

A. The Hierarchy of Primary Authorities

In both federal and state law, a simple hierarchy applies (see Figure 4.1). First, constitutions are the highest authority and preempt all other law. A county government cannot enact a regulation that conflicts with the state constitution—and if a county does so, a court would overturn the regulation.

Statutes enacted by Congress and state legislatures are second in the hierarchy of primary authorities. Case law—at the third level—includes the opinions from courts of all levels. Courts will often be called upon to interpret statutory and constitutional provisions and to determine whether statutes are in conflict with the constitution. Finally, the lowest level includes government regulations, rulings, and ordinances. Local environmental regulations and traffic ordinances are included in this fourth level.

B. The Hierarchy of Case Law

Case law is the type of primary authority that lawyers most often use to analyze legal questions. Even if a constitution or statute applies, lawyers will use case law to interpret the provisions. The usefulness of a particular case to your legal question is determined by the hierarchy of case law, which depends on what type of court issued the opinion and where that court is situated in the American judicial system.

i. Court System Structure

Courts are broadly divided into two systems: federal courts and state courts. There is one system of federal courts, and every state has its own system

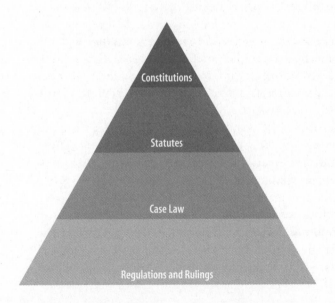

Figure 4.1

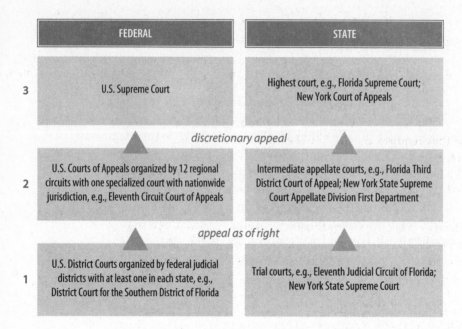

Figure 4.2

of state courts. The federal and state court systems share a similar tiered structure although the names that states use to describe the courts at each level vary.[1]

To understand the differences between the courts, consider how a lawsuit usually progresses through the federal court system. First, a lawyer files a lawsuit in a trial court, called a U.S. District Court, before a single judge. Next, the losing party in the trial court can appeal as of right to an intermediate appellate court, called a U.S. Court of Appeals, where the case will be decided by a panel of judges. Then, the losing party can ask the highest court—the U.S. Supreme Court—which has a panel of Justices, to exercise its discretion to review the case.

Many states have a three-tiered structure like the federal courts, but some states have no intermediate appellate level court. Some states have specialized courts for certain cases based on subject matter, a tier below the trial court level that handles small claims, or a combination of these structures. Figure 4.2 depicts the three-tiered court structure.

Some trial courts and most of the intermediate appellate and highest courts issue written opinions explaining their reasoning and decisions. Those opinions are the cases that you will read and rely upon to do your legal analysis.

ii. Jurisdiction

The term "jurisdiction" means the authority of a court to exercise its power over the subject matter and parties in a case. Jurisdiction also describes the

---

1. Refer to the courts' websites to learn the specific names for the courts in your state. You may also consult Table 1 in *The Bluebook*.

geographic area over which a court exercises its power. Both of these meanings are important for understanding the hierarchy of case law.

a. Authority

Federal courts have the authority to decide cases that raise a federal question or satisfy the requirements for diversity jurisdiction.[2] Under diversity jurisdiction, a federal court can decide a case that doesn't raise a federal question—meaning a case that requires the application of state law—when the parties are from different states and the amount in controversy exceeds $75,000.[3] A federal court can also use its discretion to exercise supplemental jurisdiction over a state law claim that is closely related to a claim over which it has jurisdiction.[4]

Most state trial courts have the authority to decide cases that arise within their borders, including disputes governed by state and federal law. Some state courts, however, are limited by subject matter, including courts that decide only criminal, probate, or family law cases.

b. Area

All federal courts do not apply the same law, just as all state courts do not apply the same law. Instead, courts apply the law of a specific geographic area or jurisdiction. The federal courts are divided into 94 judicial districts, which are organized into 12 regional circuits. Each regional circuit has a court of appeals that decides cases appealed from the district courts in that circuit. The federal courts within a circuit apply the law of that circuit to federal law issues. For example, the District Court for the Southern District of Florida is in the Eleventh Circuit, so it applies Eleventh Circuit law to federal law issues.

Figure 4.3 shows the geographic division of the federal circuits. In addition to the 11 numbered circuits, the D.C. Circuit covers the District of Columbia and the Federal Circuit Court of Appeals has nationwide jurisdiction over specialized subject matter, including patents, trademarks, and international trade.

State courts usually apply their own law to state law issues. State courts, however, may apply the law of another state to an issue in certain situations, including a contractual agreement by the parties to be bound by the law of another state.

iii. Binding and Non-Binding Cases

Stare decisis is a Latin phrase that means "to stand by things decided."[5] In practice, stare decisis describes the policy of American courts to follow the precedents established by earlier cases.

---

2. In addition, the federal system has courts that specialize by subject matter, including courts that handle bankruptcy or tax cases.

3. 28 U.S.C. §1332(a)(1) (2012).

4. 28 U.S.C. §1367 (2012).

5. *Black's Law Dictionary* (9th ed. 2009).

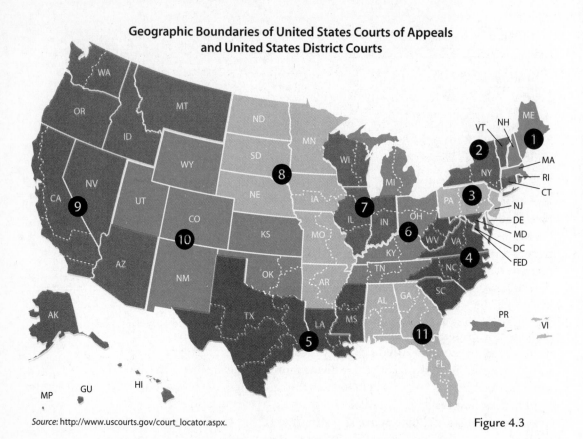

Geographic Boundaries of United States Courts of Appeals and United States District Courts

Source: http://www.uscourts.gov/court_locator.aspx.

Figure 4.3

The precise impact that an earlier precedent will have on a later case depends on whether it is binding or non-binding. A binding precedent is one that a court is required to follow. These cases are also referred to as "mandatory" authorities. A non-binding precedent is one that a court may consider, but is not required to follow. These cases are also called "persuasive" authorities.

Before you can decide the outcome of a legal question, you have to determine which precedents are binding and which are not. Determining whether a case is binding for your particular legal issue requires you to answer the following two questions:

1. What jurisdiction's law applies to my legal issue?
2. Which courts from that jurisdiction have the power to bind the court in my case?

a. What Jurisdiction's Law Applies?

First, you need to determine which specific jurisdiction's law governs your legal issue. If your legal question is one of federal law, any case that applies the law of the relevant federal circuit is potentially binding. Similarly, for state law questions, any case that applies the law of the relevant state is potentially binding.

When trying to identify binding authorities on your issue, keep in mind that a federal court can hear a case involving a state law issue and a state court can hear a case involving a federal claim. For instance, suppose a California resident wants to sue someone who lives in Nevada to quiet title on a piece of land in California. On the basis of diversity jurisdiction, the California resident may sue the Nevada resident in federal court on a state adverse possession claim. Because the adverse possession claim will be decided under California law, any case that applies California state law is potentially a binding case.

b. Which Courts Are Binding?

Next, you will need to determine which particular courts have the power to bind the court in your case. A court is bound by the decisions of higher courts from the jurisdiction that supplies the applicable law. This is known as "vertical stare decisis."

For example, if you are dealing with a state law issue in a case in a state trial court in Florida, decisions of the state intermediate appellate courts[6] and the Florida Supreme Court are binding, and decisions of the state trial courts and federal courts are non-binding (see Figure 4.4).

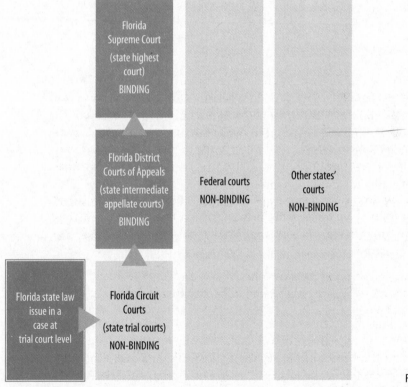

Figure 4.4

---

6. In some states, a trial court is bound only by the decisions of the appellate court to which its decisions are appealed. *See, e.g., In re Quirk*, 705 So. 2d 172, 181 n.17 (La. 1997).

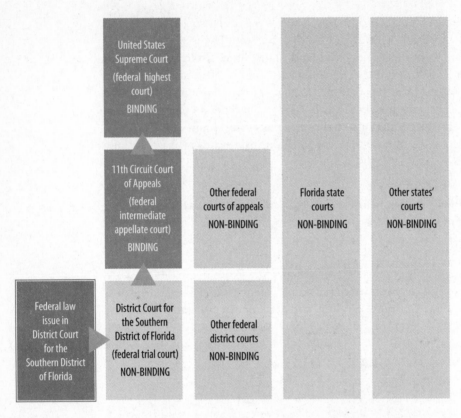

Figure 4.5

Similarly, if you are dealing with a federal law issue in a case in the District Court for the Southern District of Florida, decisions of the Eleventh Circuit Court of Appeals and the U.S. Supreme Court are binding. Decisions of the district courts in Florida, federal courts in other circuits, and state courts are non-binding (see Figure 4.5).

In addition to a court's obligation to follow the decisions of higher courts from the applicable jurisdiction, courts also have a policy that they follow their own previous decisions. This policy is known as "horizontal stare decisis." A highest level court, however, can overrule itself. For instance, the U.S. Supreme Court famously overruled its 1896 decision in *Plessy v. Ferguson* with the landmark decision of *Brown v. Board of Education* in 1954.

Following this policy, decisions of a federal court of appeals bind that court as well as the district courts in that circuit. A federal court of appeals decision can be overruled by the U.S. Supreme Court or the court of appeals sitting *en banc*, which is when a case is reheard by all (or most) of the judges, rather than a three-judge panel. Thus, if you are dealing with a federal law issue in a case that has been appealed to the Fourth Circuit Court of Appeals from the District Court for the Eastern District of Virginia, decisions of the U.S. Supreme Court and the Fourth Circuit Court of Appeals are binding. Decisions of federal district courts, other federal courts of appeals, and state courts are non-binding (see Figure 4.6).

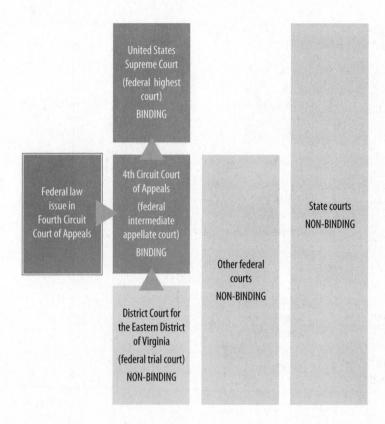

Figure 4.6

Some states do not follow the policy of horizontal stare decisis. For example, in Illinois, an intermediate appellate court is bound only by decisions of the highest court; it is not obligated to follow a decision by another state intermediate appellate court.[7]

When a federal court applies state law or a state court applies federal law, only decisions of the highest court from the applicable jurisdiction are binding. Consider the adverse possession case, where the California resident wants to sue the Nevada resident in federal court in California. When the California resident files suit, the case will be at the trial court level. Because the federal district court will apply state law, the only binding authority will be decisions of the California Supreme Court. Decisions of the California intermediate appellate courts and trial courts will be persuasive, but they are not binding on the federal district court. Also, federal court decisions, even if they apply California law, will be non-binding, but they may be highly persuasive (see Figure 4.7).

A court is not bound by decisions from lower courts or any court outside the applicable jurisdiction. So a court in the Eleventh Circuit is not bound by court rulings from the Second Circuit, and a court in New Hampshire is not bound by court rulings in Vermont (unless the New Hampshire court is applying Vermont law).

---

7. *O'Casek v. Children's Home & Aid Soc'y*, 892 N.E.2d 994, 1006 (Ill. 2008).

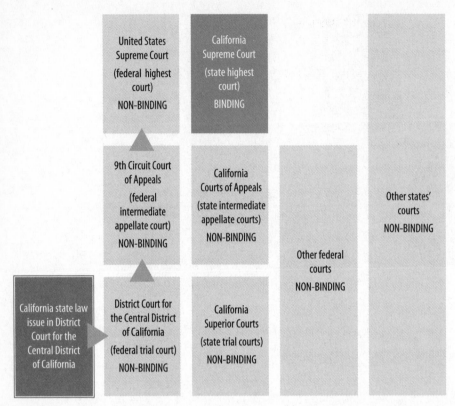

Figure 4.7

When analyzing a legal question, identify and use binding authorities when they are available. But keep in mind that your legal analysis may involve a combination of binding and non-binding precedent when there is not sufficient binding authority directly on point. And if your legal question involves a case of first impression in your jurisdiction, you will have to rely entirely on persuasive authorities because no binding authorities exist.

2. SECONDARY AUTHORITIES

Primary authorities are the law, while secondary authorities comment on the law. Secondary sources include legal encyclopedias, treatises, Restatements, and law review articles. You can read them to gain an understanding of the particular area of law relevant to your legal issue. In general, you should not cite to secondary authorities in a legal memorandum or a persuasive document because they are not law.

chapter 5

The Format for Legal Analysis

1. CREAC

Written legal analysis is organized using a format known as "CREAC."[1] Each letter of CREAC stands for a necessary component of legal analysis:

C	=	Conclusion
R	=	Rule
E	=	Explanation
A	=	Analysis, Application, Argument
C	=	Conclusion

Using this structure, the legal writer begins and ends the analysis with the Conclusion on a particular legal issue. The beauty of the CREAC format is that it assures the reader that there will be no surprises because the writer provides the Conclusion at the outset. Further, the CREAC format requires the writer to identify and fully explain the relevant legal authorities before applying those authorities to the facts from the legal question. After doing so, the writer walks the reader through the law and analysis so that the reader understands the logical progression of the writer's thinking. CREAC thus helps guarantee that the writer's legal analysis is logically sound and meticulously supported.

CREAC is the preferred structure for most analytical legal documents, including memos, motions, briefs, and judicial opinions. Judges, lawyers, and legal writing professors all expect these documents to follow the CREAC format. Accordingly, this book will describe in detail and provide examples and instructions for how to write each of the CREAC components.

The following is an excerpt of a judicial opinion that is organized using the CREAC format. The annotations reflect each CREAC component. In the

---

1. This structure for legal analysis has also been identified as CRAC, CREXAC, and TREAT. These names all identify the same organizational format.

opinion, the plaintiff was injured by a dog and sought damages from the dog's owner. After the judge granted partial summary judgment, a jury awarded the plaintiff damages. The defendant appealed, arguing that the plaintiff had failed to prove scienter (which means having knowledge) and there were triable issues of fact on the issues of contributory negligence and assumption of risk.

KNAPP v. BALL
175 So. 2d 808 (Fla. Dist. Ct. App. 1965)

[Facts omitted.]

The trial judge was eminently correct in ruling that the defendant was — This is the court's **Conclusion**.
responsible for the injury which her dog inflicted on plaintiff, without
the need to show scienter. Section 767.01, Florida Statutes, provides: — This is the **Rule**. Here, the
"Owners of dogs shall be liable for any damage done by their dogs to court identifies the legal rule
sheep or other domestic animals or livestock, or to persons." *See Sweet* that governs the issue. The
v. Josephson, 173 So. 2d 444 (Fla. 1965); *Ferguson v. Gangwer*, 192 So. 196 authorities so the reader
(Fla. 1939); *Josephson v. Sweet*, 173 So. 2d 463 (Fla. Dist. Ct. App. 1964); knows where the rule comes
Vandercar v. David, 96 So. 2d 227 (Fla. Dist. Ct. App. 1957). from.

Liability of the owner of a dog for such injuries under Section 767.01 is
based on an obligation as an insurer rather than on negligence, and contributory negligence as such is not a defense. *See Vandercar*, 96 So. 2d at
229, wherein this court said:

> "But the fact that liability is imposed by statute [767.01], and not
> based on negligence, does not require rejection of an offered defense
> that the injured party incited and encouraged the dog's action which
> caused injury.

> "The rule established by the authorities is that while liability of an — This is the **Explanation**.
> owner of a dog is based on an obligation as insurer rather than on Here, the court explains the
> negligence, and contributory negligence as such is not a defense, meaning of the Rule using
> nevertheless, if an injured party unnecessarily and voluntarily puts case law.
> himself in the way to be hurt, knowing the probable consequences,
> he may be deemed to have assumed the risk and to have induced his
> injury."

Appellant's contention that there was a triable issue as to assumption of — This is the **Analysis**. Here, the
risk is without support in the record, and the trial judge was correct in court analyzes the facts of
concluding against the presence of such issue. this particular case by
applying the law and
The appellant and the appellee are sisters. At the time of this incident the explaining the reasoning
appellee was a social guest temporarily residing in her sister's home. As that led to the court's
pointed out in *Vandercar*, the defense of contributory negligence was not Conclusion.
available in this action on a liability imposed by statute and not based
on negligence. And the facts of the case were insufficient upon which to
invoke a defense of assumption of risk. It was not shown that appellee did

anything to incite or encourage the dog's actions which resulted in her injury. Her mere presence in the house as a guest did not amount to an assumption of risk of injury by the owner's dog, and the dog's prior actions were not shown to be such as to reasonably lead appellee to believe her continued presence would probably lead to her injury from that source.

Affirmed. ———————————————————————— This is the **Conclusion**. Here, the court repeats the Conclusion it has reached on the legal issue before it. In this opinion, the final Conclusion is very brief.

2. IRAC

A close relative of the CREAC format, known as IRAC, is the most common format for law school exams and the essays on the bar exam. IRAC includes the following components:

I   = Issue
R   = Rule
A   = Analysis, Application, Argument
C   = Conclusion

CREAC is merely an evolution of IRAC, and IRAC reflects the fact that the writer has not had time to think through the legal question and provide a conclusion. The fundamental difference between IRAC and CREAC is that under IRAC, the writer begins the analysis with an objective statement of the issue to be addressed, rather than the specific Conclusion the writer has reached after completing the analysis.

For example, in the case excerpt from *Knapp v. Ball*, the court begins its analysis with the Conclusion:

The trial judge was eminently correct in ruling that the defendant was responsible for the injury which her dog inflicted on plaintiff, without the need to show scienter.

Under the IRAC format, the writer would instead state the issue being analyzed without reaching a conclusion:

The issue before the court is whether the trial judge correctly ruled that the defendant was responsible for the injury that the defendant's dog inflicted on the plaintiff, without the need to show scienter.

Because the IRAC format allows the writer to outline the analysis before reaching a conclusion, it is useful when planning, organizing, and outlining documents that will ultimately follow the CREAC format. But aside from this difference between the initial Conclusion and an objective issue statement, the analysis under CREAC or IRAC will be the same.

Although the CREAC format explicitly builds in a more detailed explanation of the rules than the IRAC format, identified as the Explanation section, in practice the level of rule explanation required in a particular document depends on the nature of the legal issue being analyzed, not whether the writer is using CREAC or IRAC. With the CREAC structure in mind, the following chapters will describe how to write each CREAC component for both objective and persuasive documents.

part II

Objective Writing

chapter 6

Constructing CREAC in Objective Documents

Lawyers, clients, and judges need to understand both sides of a legal issue to make fair and objective decisions. Throughout your law school and legal career, you will be asked to answer legal questions that vary in scope and complexity. Clients will come to you with legal problems to solve. Supervising attorneys will call on you to assist in analyzing part or all of a legal dispute or transaction. If you work as a judicial intern or clerk, your judge will expect you to fairly evaluate both sides of a case to help resolve it.

The key to writing objectively is to fully and fairly examine both sides of the arguments surrounding your legal question and to make an honest prediction about the most likely result. This part of the *Handbook* will show you how to prepare each part of a CREAC analysis for your legal problem. Whether you need to summarize your analysis in a memorandum, judicial opinion, letter, or email, you can use the CREAC format to clearly and effectively explain your legal analysis.

chapter 7

Writing an Objective Conclusion

The first sentence of every CREAC is a Conclusion. The Conclusion statement provides a fitting topic sentence for the discussion of your legal question. The Conclusion should convey two pieces of information: (1) your answer to the legal question and (2) a reason for your answer.

Typically, the Conclusion is a single sentence that states the answer, then the word "because," and then the reason for the answer. Occasionally, for complex legal questions, you might need to write two or even three sentences to summarize your Conclusion. Giving the reader the answer to the legal question at the start is the best way to introduce the analysis that follows.

Writing an Objective Conclusion

1. Use an issue statement as a placeholder
2. Develop your legal question—the Question Presented
3. Develop your answer—the Brief Answer
4. State your conclusion and give a reason

---

1. STEP ONE: USE AN ISSUE STATEMENT AS A PLACEHOLDER

Even though the Conclusion is the first sentence of any CREAC, you usually cannot provide an educated answer to the legal question until you have written a draft of the Rule, Explanation, and Analysis sections. Thus, the first step in reaching your Conclusion is to identify the precise legal question you have been asked to answer. Because you need to analyze the relevant law and how the law applies to your facts before you can reach your Conclusion, you should start the draft of your document with a precise issue statement that can serve as a placeholder for the Conclusion. Be vigilant in identifying and narrowing your legal issue.

For instance, suppose you have been asked to analyze the broad question of whether your client's burglary conviction will be overturned on appeal.

After you analyze the relevant facts and law, you might realize that your client's appeal depends on only one element of burglary: whether he entered the "curtilage" of the home of the victim, Sam Perry. Your issue statement placeholder for this document could be the following:

The issue is whether Sam Perry's compound qualifies as curtilage.

Similarly, in a legal memorandum on a contract dispute involving whether a business owner had the intent to sell the business even though she made a pricing mistake in her offer, the Conclusion should hone in on the precise legal issue that will determine the outcome of the case. The precise legal issue is whether the owner made a binding offer. An effective issue statement placeholder for this memorandum could be as follows:

This case concerns whether Sandra Lee made a binding offer to sell her widget business to Graham Enterprises.

Note that the issue statements do not include any legally significant facts. At this stage of the writing process, the writer has not reviewed the relevant case law to determine the relevant anchors. Without a solid understanding of the relevant law and the anchors, the writer cannot identify which facts are legally significant. As a result, the issue statement merely states the precise legal question.

2. STEP TWO: DEVELOP YOUR LEGAL QUESTION— THE QUESTION PRESENTED

A. Identify the Anchors

At this point, you can begin unraveling the mystery behind your legal question. Review the relevant authorities and begin to list the anchors that justified the courts' decisions on your precise legal question.[1] Remember that the anchors are the grounds or bases of a court's decision. The court might state the anchors explicitly, or the court might use wording that is less direct. As a result, you will need to carefully read and understand an opinion to fully identify the anchors that motivated a court's decision relating to your legal question. After you identify the anchors, create a synthesized list of the anchors that are relevant to your precise legal question.

For example, burglary cases typically define the "curtilage" surrounding a home according to three anchors. Your synthesized list of the anchors for your analysis of the curtilage issue could be as follows:

1. Whether the area has an enclosure;
2. Whether the enclosure has openings for entering and exiting the property; and

---

1. Refer to Chapter 2, "Reading and Understanding Authorities"; Chapter 3, "It Depends on the 'Anchors'"; and Part VIII, "Research" for detailed instructions on finding relevant authorities.

3. Whether the enclosure is irregular, like sparse shrubs, or fortifying, like a privacy fence.[2]

B. Use the Anchors to Identify the Legally Significant Facts

The anchors break down the reasoning of the relevant cases into concrete parts, so they not only help you understand the nuances of the authorities, but they also guide you to identify the facts that will answer your question. These facts are your "legally significant facts."

With the curtilage anchors in mind, the kinds of facts that would be legally significant become obvious: (1) facts relating to the enclosure surrounding a property, (2) facts relating to openings or gaps in the enclosure, and (3) facts relating to the kind of enclosure.

Review the anchors and facts relating to your legal question. Pick out the facts that fit best with the anchors. You want to match up every legally significant fact to a relevant anchor. Keep in mind that you want to look at the legal question objectively, so try to identify facts that support each side of the argument for each anchor. For instance, in the curtilage analysis, that would mean identifying facts that could help you argue that the enclosure is—and is not—sufficient.

C. Follow the Under-Does-When Formula

A Question Presented is a formal statement of your specific legal issue and the most relevant facts. Questions Presented are common at the beginning of a legal memorandum because they give the reader an overview of your case.[3]

Questions Presented can be framed in several ways, but the most common format follows the "under-does-when" formula or a variation of it. This type of Question Presented has three parts:

1. The Question Presented begins with an introductory clause starting with "under," and it identifies the jurisdiction and the type of law.
2. The Question Presented then states the precise legal question using a verb, such as "does," "did," "can," "is," or "was." Because the Question Presented gives an overview of the case, it can refer to the parties involved generally or use specific names. Terms, including "buyer" and "seller," or "plaintiff" and "defendant," are common.
3. Finally, the Question Presented states two or more legally significant facts that are typically introduced with "when" or "where." Include the facts that are the most legally relevant for your legal question. Be precise when stating the facts and take care that you do not summarize the facts in a way that shows bias toward one conclusion. Also, list the facts in parallel construction.[4]

---

2. *See, e.g., State v. Hamilton*, 660 So. 2d 1038 (Fla. 1995).
3. Review the examples of legal memoranda following Chapter 16.
4. Refer to Chapter 19, "Grammar Principles for the New Legal Writer" for detailed instructions on parallel construction.

For the memo described previously, regarding whether the business owner made a binding offer to sell her business when she placed an ad with a pricing mistake, the following example uses a variation of the under-does-when structure:

The first part of the Question Presented provides the jurisdiction and the type of law.

Under New York contract law, did the owner of a widget business make a binding offer to sell her business when she placed an ad to sell her business, but she mistakenly priced the business for a fraction of its worth?

The second part provides the specific legal question.

The third part provides the most important legally significant facts. This Question Presented states the facts objectively, and it has facts that support a "yes" answer and a "no" answer to the question.

Judicial opinions also may begin with an objective statement of the issue that incorporates legally significant facts. These issue statements follow varying formats to seamlessly fit in with the opinion that follows. For example, Justice Antonin Scalia began *Florida v. Jardines* with the following:

> We consider whether using a drug-sniffing dog on a homeowner's porch to investigate the contents of the home is a "search" within the meaning of the Fourth Amendment.[5]

In a similar case that also involved a drug-sniffing dog, Justice Elena Kagan began the opinion by precisely framing the issue before the Court:

> In this case, we consider how a court should determine if the "alert" of a drug-detection dog during a traffic stop provides probable cause to search a vehicle.[6]

As these examples show, a good Question Presented or issue statement will introduce the reader to the precise legal question and provide some legally significant facts to put the dispute in context.

3. STEP THREE: DEVELOP YOUR ANSWER— THE BRIEF ANSWER

The Brief Answer logically follows the Question Presented in a legal memorandum. It provides a formal summary of your conclusion. The Brief

---

5. *Florida v. Jardines*, 133 S. Ct. 1409, 1413 (2013).
6. *Florida v. Harris*, 133 S. Ct. 1050, 1053 (2013).

Answer also has three parts, although it is typically broken up into two to five sentences.

1. The first sentence of the Brief Answer provides a direct answer to the question—either "yes" or "no." Your answer will often include a qualifying term, such as "probably," because no one can predict with absolute certainty how a court or jury will decide a particular case. The Brief Answer commonly begins with "probably yes" or "probably not."

2. The next one to two sentences briefly summarize the applicable law and anchors.

3. The final one to two sentences should summarize your analysis and conclusion. Be careful not to repeat the facts from the Question Presented; instead, your Brief Answer should explain how the facts fit with the law and how you reached your conclusion.

The following example contains the answer, two sentences summarizing the relevant law and anchors, and one sentence summarizing the writer's reasoning and conclusion.

Probably not. An advertisement is not an offer but a mere invitation to enter into a bargain. Even where a binding offer is made, the offeror can withdraw a mistaken offer if she exercised ordinary care, the other party was aware of the mistake, and enforcement of the offer would be unconscionable. Here, a court would likely find that no offer was made because the advertisement merely invited buyers to make an offer to buy the business, and forcing the offeror to accept the low price listed in the advertisement would likely be deemed unconscionable.

The Brief Answer begins with a direct answer and a qualifying term.

This part describes the most relevant law and anchors.

This summary of the analysis supports the Conclusion, applying the relevant law to the specific facts from the Question Presented.

4. STEP FOUR: STATE YOUR CONCLUSION AND GIVE A REASON

Once you have drafted the Question Presented and Brief Answer, you have the foundation for a strong Conclusion. All Conclusions should provide your answer to the legal question and a reason for your answer. You can start with the following format:

[answer to legal question] because [reason(s) supporting answer].

A Conclusion also might include the parties' names and the jurisdiction. Depending on your level of certainty, an objective Conclusion typically includes a qualifying term, such as "probably" or "likely."

The examples of the following Conclusions identify the precise legal issues, and they reference legally significant facts and anchors when giving the reason.

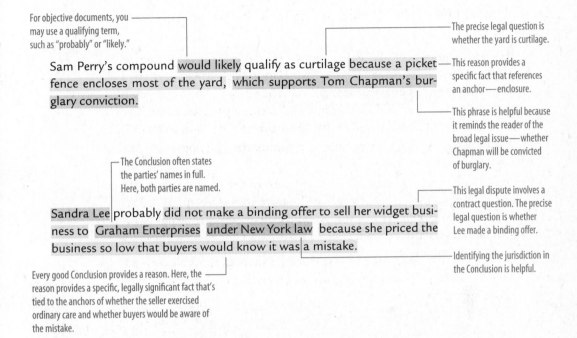

For objective documents, you may use a qualifying term, such as "probably" or "likely."

The precise legal question is whether the yard is curtilage.

Sam Perry's compound would likely qualify as curtilage because a picket fence encloses most of the yard, which supports Tom Chapman's burglary conviction.

This reason provides a specific fact that references an anchor—enclosure.

This phrase is helpful because it reminds the reader of the broad legal issue—whether Chapman will be convicted of burglary.

The Conclusion often states the parties' names in full. Here, both parties are named.

This legal dispute involves a contract question. The precise legal question is whether Lee made a binding offer.

Sandra Lee probably did not make a binding offer to sell her widget business to Graham Enterprises under New York law because she priced the business so low that buyers would know it was a mistake.

Identifying the jurisdiction in the Conclusion is helpful.

Every good Conclusion provides a reason. Here, the reason provides a specific, legally significant fact that's tied to the anchors of whether the seller exercised ordinary care and whether buyers would be aware of the mistake.

A strong Conclusion at the start of your legal document is helpful because it introduces your reader to the legal question and your answer. Most judicial opinions also begin and end with a Conclusion that details the legal issue and the answer; the Conclusion also may reference the law and legally significant facts. A judicial opinion's Conclusion will be authoritative and definite—unlike the Conclusion in a legal memorandum that may include a qualifying term. The following paragraph serves as Justice Kagan's opening Conclusion in *Florida v. Harris*. This format shows you that Conclusions may be written in various ways, depending on the purpose of your legal document, the complexity of the legal issue, and the certainty of your Conclusion.

The Conclusion begins with a precise statement of the issue.

In this case, we consider how a court should determine if the "alert" of a drug-detection dog during a traffic stop provides probable cause to search a vehicle. The Florida Supreme Court held that the State must in every case present an exhaustive set of records, including a log of the dog's performance in the field, to establish the dog's reliability. We think that demand inconsistent with the "flexible, common-sense standard" of probable cause. [7]

The second sentence provides key facts and the procedural history to put the dispute in context.

The Conclusion ends with the Court's answer and a reference to the supporting law.

---

7. *Id.* (citations omitted).

chapter 8

Writing an Objective Rule Section

While the Conclusion narrows your legal question, the Rule should be broad. The Rule section lays out the controlling law, beginning with the broadest and most important rule.

Writing an Objective Rule Section

1. Organize rules from general to specific
2. Include quotations of key language
3. Cite correctly

---

1. STEP ONE: ORGANIZE RULES FROM GENERAL TO SPECIFIC

When you write about a simple legal issue, the Rule could be a single sentence. For more complex questions, the Rule section could be a whole paragraph or more. Regardless of the complexity, the Rule section should be structured with the broadest, most general rule first. More specific rules will follow—to complete the Rule and Explanation sections.

A. Start with Constitutions and Statutes

When constitutions and statutes govern your question, they provide a logical starting point based on hierarchy of authority. The constitutional provision or statute is the broadest statement of the rule. Typically, when the Rule section is made up of a constitutional provision or statute, the rule Explanation section begins with case law that interprets the provision. A legal memorandum addressing the question of whether a suspension violated a student's free speech rights could begin like this:

> The suspension of a student who held a sign promoting illegal drug use at   — Conclusion
> a school-supervised event likely did not violate the student's free speech

40

rights. The state constitution guarantees that "[e]very person may freely — This Alaska constitutional
speak, write, and publish on all subjects, being responsible for the abuse provision provides the
of that right." Alaska Const. §5 (2002). broadest rule.

Similarly, Justice Scalia began the Rule section in *Florida v. Jardines* by quoting
key language from the Fourth Amendment.

The Fourth Amendment provides in relevant part that the "right of the — The Rule begins with the
people to be secure in their persons, houses, papers, and effects, against highest authority.
unreasonable searches and seizures, shall not be violated." The Amend-
ment establishes a simple baseline, one that for much of our history
formed the exclusive basis for its protections: When "the Government — The Rule then adds an
obtains information by physically intruding" on persons, houses, papers, explanatory statement from
or effects, "a 'search' within the original meaning of the Fourth Amend- case law.
ment" has "undoubtedly occurred." *United States v. Jones*, 132 S. Ct. 945,
950-51 n. 3 (2012).[1]

Questions governed by statutes will likewise begin with the statute—but
take note that more than one statute or statute section could apply. For
instance, in the example below, the legal question relates to burglary; more
specifically, it relates to whether the defendant entered the curtilage of a
home. The Rule section begins with the state burglary statute, which does not
reference curtilage, and continues with a second state statute that defines a
key term in the statute: dwelling.

The definition of dwelling provides the first reference to curtilage. The
structure of the Rule section, from broad to specific, shows the reader why
the legal question requires interpretation of the term curtilage. The second
statute would not make sense without the first, so the organization of the
Rule section is logical, beginning with the broad statute and then providing
the more specific definitional statute.

Sam Perry's compound would likely qualify as curtilage because a picket — Conclusion
fence encloses most of the yard, lending support to Chapman's burglary
conviction. Burglary means "entering or remaining in a dwelling, a struc- — This Rule section begins
ture, or a conveyance with the intent to commit an offense therein...." with the broad burglary
Fla. Stat. §810.02(b)(1) (2013). A "dwelling" includes a "building or statute about a "dwelling."
The second statute defines
conveyance...which has a roof over it and is designed to be occupied by "dwelling" and references
people lodging therein at night, together with the curtilage thereof." Fla. "curtilage."
Stat. §810.011(2) (2013).

Similarly, in the next example, two statutes apply. The first provides the
broad rule on adverse possession, so it begins the Rule section. The second
sentence logically follows because it defines a key part of the controlling statute: what "occupied" means under California adverse possession law.

Blackhurst can likely establish the "open and notorious" possession ele- — Conclusion
ment for an adverse possession claim. In California, adverse possession

---

1. *Florida v. Jardines*, 133 S. Ct. 1409, 1414 (2013).

is defined as follows: "Where it appears that there has been an actual *— This Rule section begins* continued occupation of land, under a claim of title, exclusive of any *with the controlling adverse* other right, but not founded upon a written instrument, judgment or *possession statute. The* decree, the land so actually occupied, and no other, is deemed to have *second sentence explains* been held adversely." Cal. Civ. Proc. Code §324 (2012). Land is "deemed *one key term: "occupied."* to have been possessed and occupied" only where "it has been protected by a substantial enclosure," and "has been usually cultivated or improved." *Id.* §325.

When no constitution or statute applies to your legal question, case law provides the starting point for the Rule section.

B. Outline Your Case Law

Rule sections that are made up of case law also should be organized from the broadest, most general rule to the more specific rules. A good place to start figuring out this organization is by reviewing your cases to see how the courts explain your rules. Courts typically reference the broadest rule first, so the structure of your Rule section will likely be similar to the structure found in the cases you are using.

Create an outline of your Rule section that follows one of your strongest cases, putting the broadest rule at the top and putting the more specific rule(s) below. Do the same outline with two more cases. The outlines should be comparable and provide you with a map for your Rule section.

i. Rule with Key Terms That Need to Be Defined

Your broadest rule might include legally significant terms that need to be defined and interpreted to answer your legal question. If so, your Rule section will begin with the overall rule, followed by more specific rules that define key terms:

Sam Johnson was not malicious or grossly negligent when he failed to *— Conclusion* warn others that the old oil well was next to the party tent because he believed the well posed no danger. A landowner who offers his land for *— This Rule section begins* recreation loses immunity if he is malicious or grossly negligent in failing *with the broad negligence* to warn others about a danger. *Lonergan v. May*, 53 S.W.3d 122, 127 (Mo. *rule. The next two sentences* Ct. App. 2001). Under Missouri law, malice requires actions "so reck- *help define two key terms:* less or wantonly and willfully in disregard of one's rights that a trier of *"malice" and "gross* fact could infer from such conduct bad faith." *Henderson v. United States,* *negligence."* 965 F.2d 1488, 1494 (8th Cir. 1992). Gross negligence equals "a reckless disregard for proper conduct" and can be demonstrated by "a conscious indifference" to others' safety. *Id.* at 1493-94.

ii. Legal Test with Elements

Perhaps your legal question involves one element of a multipart legal test. Generally, in an elements test, every element must be present for the rule to be satisfied. The rule stating the legal test would be the first sentence of your Rule section, and the rule describing the specific element or elements you will analyze would be next.

> The Court will likely dismiss Plaintiff's claim for intentional infliction of ——Conclusion
> emotional distress because Prudence Jones did not act outrageously when
> she asked Plaintiff to leave the store after he removed all of his clothes.
> The tort of intentional infliction of emotional distress has the following ——This broad rule states the
> four elements: (1) extreme and outrageous conduct; (2) intent to cause, legal elements.
> or disregard of a substantial probability of causing, severe emotional
> distress; (3) a causal connection between the conduct and the injury;
> and (4) severe emotional distress. *Howell v. N.Y. Post Co.*, 612 N.E.2d 699,
> 702 (N.Y. 1993). Outrageous conduct is "conduct exceeding all bounds ——This sentence describes the
> usually tolerated by decent society." *Id.* specific element that the
> memo will analyze.

iii. Factors Test

Your rule might involve a set of factors that courts should consider when applying the rule. A factors test differs from a legal test with elements because in a factors test, not every factor must be present for the rule to be satisfied. The rule stating the purpose of the test would be the first sentence of your Rule section, and the rules describing the relevant factors would follow.

> The Court will probably find that the trademarks are so similar that ——Conclusion
> the public is likely to be confused because both include the silhouette
> of a cat and the number nine. The Ninth Circuit applies the eight-factor ——This sentence states the
> *Sleekcraft* test to determine whether there is a likelihood of confusion. purpose of this factors test.
> *Jada Toys, Inc. v. Mattel, Inc.*, 518 F.3d 628, 633 (9th Cir. 2008). The eight ——This sentence lists the
> factors are as follows: (1) the strength of the mark; (2) the proximity of relevant factors, using
> the goods; (3) the similarity of the marks; (4) the evidence of actual con- parallel construction for
> fusion; (5) the marketing channels used; (6) the type of goods and the each factor.
> degree of care likely to be exercised by the purchaser; (7) the defendant's
> intent in selecting the mark; and (8) the likelihood of expansion of the
> product lines. *Id.; see also AMF Inc. v. Sleekcraft Boats*, 599 F.2d 341, 348-49
> (9th Cir. 1979).

When listing the elements or factors for a factors test, you should state each factor using parallel construction to enhance readability.[2]

iv. Balancing Test

Your main rule also might include a balancing test, where each part of the test needs to be described. The logical organization would be to start with the overall balancing test, then explain the parts of the test. Remember to

---

2. Refer to Chapter 19, "Grammar Principles for the New Legal Writer" for more guidance on parallel construction.

use your cases as a guide to develop the organizational structure of your Rule section.

> The Court will likely hold that the evidence is admissible under Federal —Conclusion
> Rule of Evidence 403 because any potential jury confusion can be mitigated by an instruction from the Court. Rule 403 requires a district court —This sentence describes the overall balancing test.
> to engage in balancing to determine whether the probative value of the
> evidence is "substantially outweighed" by the dangers listed in Rule
> 403, including unfair prejudice, confusion of the issues, misleading the
> jury, undue delay, waste of time, or needless presentation of cumulative
> evidence. Fed. R. Evid. 403. In balancing, "the proper equation places —This sentence further explains the parts of the test.
> on one side the maximum reasonable probative force for the offered evidence," while "the other side of the equation should include the likely
> prejudicial impact of the evidence." *Coleman v. Home Depot, Inc.*, 306 F.3d
> 1333, 1343 (3d Cir. 2002).

v. Rule with Exceptions

Your rule might be a rule that is limited by exceptions. The statement of the rule would be the first sentence of your Rule section, and the later sentences would describe the relevant exceptions.

> The Court is unlikely to hold that the warrantless search was unreason- —Conclusion
> able in this case because the firefighter was probably acting within the
> community caretaking exception. The Fourth Amendment guarantees the —These two sentences state the rule.
> "right of the people to be secure in their persons, houses, papers, and
> effects, against unreasonable searches and seizures." U.S. Const. amend
> IV. Generally, a search of private property without a warrant based upon
> probable cause is unreasonable. *Cady v. Dombrowski*, 413 U.S. 433, 439
> (1973). There are, however, exceptions to the warrant requirement, —These sentences describe the relevant exception to the rule.
> including searches the police undertake as part of their "community care-
> taking" function. *Id.* at 441. The community caretaking exception applies
> when law enforcement officers conduct a warrantless search as part of
> their caretaking function, "totally divorced from the detection, investiga-
> tion, or acquisition of evidence relating to any criminal statute." *Id.*

2. STEP TWO: INCLUDE QUOTATIONS OF KEY LANGUAGE

Once you have your rules organized in an outline from the broad to the specific, you can begin drafting the Rule section. Analyze the language of the rules to determine how much you want to quote directly and how much you want to paraphrase.

Generally, the key language from constitutions and statutes should be quoted directly. Our legal system has spent centuries interpreting the precise language of our Constitution and statutes, so using the exact language in your legal documents is key.

A writer may make a stylistic choice to quote only portions of a key provision or to use an ellipsis to cut out irrelevant parts. Consider the previous examples. Note how the writer quoted the most important parts of the relevant constitutional and statutory provisions while paraphrasing a small portion for readability.

On the other hand, Rule sections made up of case law will likely include fewer quotations. As you saw in the outline you made of your key cases, courts use different language to state the same rules. Unless a court states a rule in a particularly eloquent way or uses legal terms of art that are important to the meaning of the rule, you should usually try to rewrite and paraphrase the rules to fit your legal document. In the following Rule paragraph, Justice Samuel A. Alito quotes only key portions of the Court's previous decisions and paraphrases most of the rules to fit the case.

> We have said in a variety of contexts that "the government may not deny a benefit to a person because he exercises a constitutional right." *Regan v. Taxation with Representation of Wash.*, 461 U.S. 540, 545 (1983). In *Perry v. Sindermann*, 408 U.S. 593 (1972), for example, we held that a public college would violate a professor's freedom of speech if it declined to renew his contract because he was an outspoken critic of the college's administration. And in *Memorial Hospital v. Maricopa County*, 415 U.S. 250 (1974), we concluded that a county impermissibly burdened the right to travel by extending healthcare benefits only to those indigent sick who had been residents of the county for at least one year. Those cases reflect an overarching principle, known as the unconstitutional conditions doctrine, that vindicates the Constitution's enumerated rights by preventing the government from coercing people into giving them up.[3]

3. STEP THREE: CITE CORRECTLY

As a final step, check that you have provided a citation for each rule in your Rule section. Your readers will not be able to verify your analysis if they can't find the sources you cite. Failing to cite your sources correctly will undermine the usefulness and credibility of your Rule section.

In general, every sentence in the Rule and Explanation sections will have a citation. There are rare exceptions, such as when the writer includes a transition sentence that helps guide the reader through the Rule section but does not come from a controlling authority. Additionally, each citation should follow the preferred format detailed in *The Bluebook*. Proper *Bluebook* citation format is discussed in detail in Chapter 42.

---

3. *Koontz v. St. Johns River Water Mgmt. Dist.*, 133 S. Ct. 2586, 2594 (2013).

chapter 9

Writing an Objective Explanation Section

At this point, you have identified the major rule or rules for your legal document. Whether your rule is from a statute or a case or multiple statutes or cases, your next job is to explain what the rule[1] means. Looking at different fact patterns in cases and various courts' interpretations of the rule will help you explain the rule to your reader. Rule Explanation is a critical step because without it, the reader has no context for understanding how the language of the rule has been interpreted and applied by the courts.

Consider how unhelpful your document would be if you quoted a burglary statute with a confusing term like "curtilage," but you did not explain what curtilage means. Plenty of courts have examined the boundaries of curtilage in burglary cases, and you should use relevant case law to explain burglary, curtilage, and other related rules of law.

Your job in the Explanation section is—not surprisingly—to explain the rules to the reader in the easiest possible terms. Before you explain the rules, make sure you fully understand your cases. Read and reread your cases—you will discover new, relevant details each time. As you read them, try to identify the issues that impact a court's decision. Every opinion has at least one anchor that is the basis for the court's decision.

Use the anchors to guide your explanation of the relevant law. In burglary cases in Florida, for example, an offender can be convicted if he enters the curtilage surrounding a home. Courts often define curtilage according to three anchors: (1) whether the area has an enclosure; (2) whether the enclosure has openings for entering and exiting the property; and (3) whether the enclosure is irregular, like sparse shrubs, or fortifying, like a privacy fence.[2] This list of three anchors is synthesized from reading multiple relevant court opinions. The answer to a new legal question involving curtilage depends on how the facts of the question line up with one or more of these anchors.

For instance, if an offender steps past a single shrub to reach a property, a court would likely determine that he did not enter the curtilage of a home.

---

1. As described in Chapter 8, your Rule section will often involve multiple rules, but in this section, we will refer to the rule as singular for the sake of simplicity.

2. *See, e.g., State v. Hamilton*, 660 So. 2d 1038 (Fla. 1995).

The facts do not fit with the anchor that requires some sort of enclosure surrounding the property. But if an offender rappels over a ten-foot brick wall and breaks into a house, he might want to explore a plea agreement. The fact that he crossed over a well-fortified enclosure means that a conviction would be solidly anchored in the law.

The structure of your Explanation section depends on your purpose and your audience. For an objective legal document, such as a client advice email, judicial opinion, or office memorandum, your task is to thoroughly explain both sides of the law so you can justify your Conclusion. If you are writing an office memorandum that predicts the outcome of a dispute for a senior attorney, the attorney will need to understand the law that is favorable and unfavorable to the client before trusting your Conclusion. In the same way, a court would not want to give a one-sided view of the law in its opinions. The parties and the public expect fairness and a complete explanation of the law.

Writing an Objective Explanation Section

1. Focus on your question
2. Understand the big picture
3. Use cases to describe your anchors

---

1. STEP ONE: FOCUS ON YOUR QUESTION

Keep in mind that the Explanation should explain only the rule that applies to the question you have been asked to answer. Many cases address more than one issue, which will require you to focus your Explanation on only the relevant parts of the cases.

For instance, suppose your supervisor asks you to analyze whether a client made a valid offer to sell her business in a contract dispute. Relevant cases will analyze whether a party made a valid offer, but they also might analyze other elements and issues, such as whether a party accepted the offer or whether a party had the legal capacity to enter into a binding contract. Relevant cases also might address additional causes of action. Your job is to identify the parts of the cases that relate to your precise question—whether the client made a valid offer.

2. STEP TWO: UNDERSTAND THE BIG PICTURE

To write your Explanation section, you will need to understand the applicable law so well that you feel like an expert. A good starting place is to identify and understand a seminal case that relates to your legal issue. The next logical step is to identify, read, and digest the cases that have fact patterns comparable (or contrastable) to the facts in your legal question. Reading cases where the courts have detailed the background and reasoning that led to their decisions is also helpful. Try to understand the "big picture" legal framework that relates to your legal issue.

As you read and reread your relevant cases, make sure to identify the anchors that determine the courts' decisions. If you were researching the question of whether your client made a valid offer, you would want to understand why one case held that a valid offer was made and why another case held that no valid offer was made.

For most legal issues, you will rely on multiple cases to understand the big picture. One case is rarely enough to explain what a rule means, to understand how it has been interpreted, and to identify the anchors that the courts have used to apply the rule. Your task in the Explanation is to extract and synthesize this information from multiple cases.

Remember that you can be creative when choosing applicable cases to use in your Explanation. The facts from your legal question do not have to match up perfectly to the cases. For the question of whether your client made a valid offer to sell her business, any applicable case dealing with "offer" could work well in your Explanation, even if it deals with the offer to sell a car or a circus. The key would be to identify binding cases where the courts analyzed the language and actions that demonstrated—or failed to demonstrate—an offer being made.

3. STEP THREE: USE CASES TO DESCRIBE YOUR ANCHORS

A. Start with a Broad Topic Sentence

Once you understand the body of law that relates to your legal question, think about how you can most logically explain the anchors to your reader. Explanation paragraphs should begin with a topic sentence to help guide the reader through the Explanation. A topic sentence should provide substantive information, such as providing a conclusion, summarizing a major point, or introducing the paragraph's subject. The purpose of a topic sentence is to help your reader understand the information you are about to convey.

Most Explanation sections will start with broad statements about the law and then provide more specific details and reasoning to explain the broad statements. The organization is comparable to an upside-down triangle—the broad statements are at the top giving the big picture and the more specific details follow. This Explanation paragraph by Chief Justice John G. Roberts is a perfect example of an upside-down triangle.

> Our cases make clear that students do not "shed their constitutional rights to freedom of speech or expression at the schoolhouse gate." *Tinker v. Des Moines Indep. Cmty. Sch. Dist.*, 393 U.S. 503, 506 (1969). At the same

— This topic sentence introduces the general principle that students have First Amendment rights.

time, we have held that "the constitutional rights of students in public —The first part of this sentence
school are not automatically coextensive with the rights of adults in other uses a transition to qualify
settings," *Bethel Sch. Dist. No. 403 v. Fraser*, 478 U.S. 675, 682 (1986), and the first rule, explaining that
students' rights are subject to
that the rights of students "must be 'applied in light of the special charac- special limits.
teristics of the school environment,'" *Hazelwood Sch. Dist. v. Kuhlmeier*, 484
U.S. 260, 266 (1988) (quoting *Tinker*, 393 U.S. at 506).[3] —This part explains a specific
limitation.

B. Illustrate Your Anchors

Providing a broad summary of one of the anchors is an excellent place to start
your Explanation. An Explanation paragraph may start with a topic sentence
that broadly describes one or more anchors. Then, the rest of the sentences
in the paragraph should include specific facts, holdings, and reasoning from
relevant cases that explain and illustrate the anchor or anchors described in
the topic sentence.

For example, remember that Florida courts define curtilage in burglary
cases according to the following anchors:

1. Whether the area has an enclosure;
2. Whether the enclosure has openings for entering and exiting the property; and
3. Whether the enclosure is irregular, like sparse shrubs, or fortifying, like
a privacy fence.[4]

A student writing a memo on a curtilage question could logically organize
the Explanation section into three distinct paragraphs. The first Explanation
paragraph would start with a topic sentence that describes the enclosure anchor according to case law. Then, the paragraph would include specific facts,
holdings, and reasoning from binding cases that explain the enclosure anchor. The second paragraph would explain the anchor relating to openings
in curtilage, and so on. Depending on their complexity, some anchors can be
described in a sentence or two, while others will require a paragraph or more.

The following Explanation section example describes the curtilage anchors. The first paragraph explains the enclosure anchor. The second paragraph combines the explanation of the other two anchors because they are
closely related:

Sam Perry's compound would likely qualify as curtilage because a picket —This Conclusion begins the
fence encloses most of the yard, lending support to Chapman's burglary CREAC and answers the
conviction. Burglary means "entering or remaining in a dwelling, a struc- legal question.
ture, or a conveyance with the intent to commit an offense therein...." —This Rule section takes up two
Fla. Stat. §810.02(b)(1) (2011). A "dwelling" includes a "building or sentences because Florida
has two applicable statutes:
conveyance...which has a roof over it and is designed to be occupied by one that defines burglary
people lodging therein at night, together with the curtilage thereof." *Id.* and another that defines
§810.011(2). dwelling. Not all issues will be
governed by statute(s). Some
Rule sections will include
one or more rules from cases
instead.

---

3. *Morse v. Frederick*, 551 U.S. 393, 396-97 (2007).
4. *See, e.g., Hamilton*, 660 So. 2d at 1038.

Florida courts have established that "some form of an enclosure" is required for the area surrounding a residence to be considered "curtilage," as required by the burglary statute. *State v. Hamilton*, 660 So. 2d 1038, 1040 (Fla. 1995). Curtilage originally referred to the areas surrounding castles that were fenced in with high stone walls, but Florida courts have enlarged the modern definition to include land and structures close enough to a dwelling that they "deserve the dwelling's protection." *Martinez v. State*, 700 So. 2d 142, 143 (Fla. Dist. Ct. App. 1997). The enclosure requirement avoids "unreasonable, harsh, or absurd consequences," such as convicting a person of burglary after he innocently wanders into an open yard "in broad daylight, without the homeowner's consent, with the intent to take a piece of fruit from a tree." *Hamilton*, 660 So. 2d at 1045.

> This paragraph covers anchor no. 1. It starts with a broad topic sentence about the enclosure requirement and then provides specific details to explain the enclosure rule. This topic sentence also provides a strong transition from the statutory rules in the first paragraph by showing that curtilage is defined by case law. The organization of this paragraph looks like an upside-down triangle because it moves from the broad to the specific.

But curtilage does not need not to be completely enclosed. *DeGeorge v. State*, 358 So. 2d 217 (Fla. Dist. Ct. App. 1978). For example, a paved area next to a structure that was partially enclosed by a fence and a brick wall qualified as curtilage. *Id.* Similarly, a fenced yard that had a 10-to-15-foot gap in the fencing to make room for a boat and trailer was deemed curtilage. *Chambers v. State*, 700 So. 2d 441, 442 (Fla. Dist. Ct. App. 1997). Courts have recognized that, as a practical matter, a property owner has an interest in maintaining convenient access to his property. *Id.* But an unfenced area that is bordered only by "several unevenly spaced trees" does not have an enclosure sufficient to support a burglary conviction. *Hamilton*, 660 So. 2d at 1042.

> This topic sentence is broad enough to cover anchor nos. 2 and 3, which are closely related and combined in one paragraph here.

> This sentence provides the specific facts from one case that help show how the court defined curtilage.

> This sentence provides a fact-specific holding from a second applicable case. It also shows how the court defined curtilage.

> This sentence explains the court's reasoning for the holding in the previous sentence.

> This sentence provides an example to contrast with the examples from the *DeGeorge* and *Chambers* cases. Giving examples of what curtilage is and is not helps the reader understand the boundaries of the law.

C. Tailor the Level of Detail to Reflect Each Case's Importance

The amount of detail provided in the Explanation about a particular case should reflect the importance of that case to the outcome of your legal issue. An Explanation section should describe only those case details that are relevant to an anchor. Most anchors can be illustrated through brief case descriptions of one or two sentences per case that include only the details of the cases that are relevant to the anchor.

In the following paragraph, the *Chambers* case is described in two sentences, and the *DeGeorge* and *Hamilton* cases are each described in a single sentence. Every detail about the facts, holding, and reasoning is directly relevant to the anchors being illustrated in the paragraph. This paragraph illustrates two anchors: whether the enclosure has openings for entering and exiting the property and whether the enclosure is irregular or fortifying.

But curtilage does not need to be completely enclosed. *DeGeorge v. State*, — Broad topic sentence
358 So. 2d 217 (Fla. Dist. Ct. App. 1978). For example, a paved area next
to a structure that was partially enclosed by a fence and a brick wall quali- — Single sentence describing
fied as curtilage. *Id.* Similarly, a fenced yard that had a 10- to 15-foot gap relevant facts and holding of
in the fencing to make room for a boat and trailer was deemed curtilage. *DeGeorge v. State*
Chambers v. State, 700 So. 2d 441, 442 (Fla. Dist. Ct. App. 1997). Courts — Two sentences describing
have recognized that, as a practical matter, a property owner has an inter- relevant facts, holding,
est in maintaining convenient access to his property. *Id.* But an unfenced and reasoning of
area that is bordered only by "several unevenly spaced trees" does not *Chambers v. State*
have an enclosure sufficient to support a burglary conviction. *Hamilton*, — Single sentence describing
660 So. 2d at 1042. relevant facts and holding of
State v. Hamilton

A longer case description, where a single case is discussed for an entire paragraph or more, is necessary only when an issue is controlled by a seminal case or when a single authority is particularly important and on point. For instance, if you are analyzing a state law issue, and the state's highest court has issued only one opinion on the matter, a longer case description paragraph may be necessary to help your reader understand the legal issue. To determine whether your issue is controlled by a seminal or particularly important case, ask the following questions:

- Is there a case that dominates the field of this legal issue due to its weight of authority or recency?
- Would the typical legal reader expect an in-depth discussion of this case?
- Would the document be incomplete without an in-depth discussion of this case?

If you answer yes to any of these questions, then you have a seminal or particularly important case that will require a longer case description.

Once you have identified a case that deserves a description of more than a sentence or two, create a short outline before drafting your description paragraph by identifying the fundamental pieces of the case description: the holding, key facts, background, and reasoning. Make sure that each piece is relevant to your legal question.

After you identify and review these relevant pieces, draft a topic sentence that summarizes the main point of the description. Usually, the main point will be the aspect of the case that helps explain the anchor that is relevant to your legal question. A logical organization of a description paragraph would start with a topic sentence that may include the holding. Then, the specific facts, background, and reasoning can help you explain how and why the court reached its holding. Use your judgment to explain the case in the easiest possible terms to your reader. But take care to provide the holding before the relevant facts and reasoning. A fact likely will seem out of context if its relation to the outcome of the case is not clear from the start.

For instance, in the 2007 free speech case *Morse v. Frederick*, Chief Justice Roberts wrote a long case description for the landmark decision in *Tinker v. Des Moines Independent Community School District.* Writing a description of *Tinker* was an obvious choice. The 1969 case helped define students' First Amendment rights and set forth the standard for determining when a school's disciplinary actions are unconstitutional. Any legal question that deals with students' First Amendment rights would likely warrant an explanation of *Tinker.* Chief Justice Roberts wrote two paragraphs for his *Tinker* description, each with a topic sentence.

Here's the first topic sentence: "In *Tinker,* this Court made clear that 'First Amendment rights, applied in light of the special characteristics of the school environment, are available to teachers and students.'"[5] The sentence introduces the case name and provides a broad summary of a major principle from the case. The sentence sets the stage for the more specific information that follows.

And here's the second topic sentence: "*Tinker* held that student expression may not be suppressed unless school officials reasonably conclude that it will 'materially and substantially disrupt the work and discipline of the school.'"[6] This sentence is more specific than the first topic sentence, and it summarizes the case's holding. A holding can be a strong opening sentence for a case description paragraph because it does exactly what a topic sentence should. The holding tells the reader the main point of the paragraph and provides a summary of the case's outcome that sets the stage for the facts and reasoning to come.

Take a look at the various parts of Chief Justice Roberts' complete *Tinker* description:

> In *Tinker,* this Court made clear that "First Amendment rights, applied in — Topic sentence
> light of the special characteristics of the school environment, are avail-
> able to teachers and students." 393 U.S. at 506. *Tinker* involved a group — Key facts, listed chronologically
> of high school students who decided to wear black armbands to protest
> the Vietnam War. School officials learned of the plan and then adopted
> a policy prohibiting students from wearing armbands. When several
> students nonetheless wore armbands to school, they were suspended. *Id.*
> at 504. The students sued, claiming that their First Amendment rights — Key procedural background fact
> had been violated, and this Court agreed.
>
> *Tinker* held that student expression may not be suppressed unless school — Topic sentence, providing the holding
> officials reasonably conclude that it will "materially and substantially
> disrupt the work and discipline of the school." *Id.* at 513. The essential — A more specific topic sentence to introduce the facts of the case
> facts of *Tinker* are quite stark, implicating concerns at the heart of the
> First Amendment. The students sought to engage in political speech, us-
> ing the armbands to express their "disapproval of the Vietnam hostilities — Key facts, with specific quotes for support
> and their advocacy of a truce, to make their views known, and, by their
> example, to influence others to adopt them." *Id.* at 514. Political speech,

---

5. *Morse,* 551 U.S. at 403.
6. *Id.*

of course, is "at the core of what the First Amendment is designed to protect." *Virginia v. Black*, 538 U.S. 343, 365 (2003). The only interest the Court discerned underlying the school's actions was the "mere desire to avoid the discomfort and unpleasantness that always accompany an unpopular viewpoint," or "an urgent wish to avoid the controversy which might result from the expression." *Tinker*, 393 U.S. at 509, 510. That interest was not enough to justify banning "a silent, passive expression of opinion, unaccompanied by any disorder or disturbance." *Id.* at 508.[7]

— Key background from a more recent case that explains an important principle and uses quotations to signify important language

— Reasoning, again quoting key language

Notice how Chief Justice Roberts used a rule from *Virginia v. Black* in the middle of his *Tinker* description. That's because an explanation of only one case usually makes for an incomplete explanation of the law. As a result, description paragraphs should be used for only the most important cases. Most—if not all—of the paragraphs in the Explanation section should use multiple cases to explain the anchors and how they are applied by courts in different contexts.

---

7. *Id.* at 403-04.

chapter 10

Writing an Objective Analysis Section

The Analysis section is the most complex part of any CREAC. The Analysis is also known as the Application or the Argument, but its purpose is always the same—to describe in detail the legal reasoning that supports the Conclusion. The Conclusion is your answer, and the Analysis is the place where you show your work for how you reached that answer.

The Analysis proves that the Conclusion is correct by demonstrating how the relevant law will be applied to the facts of your case. You predict how the rules will be applied by comparing your case to similar cases. This comparison, which is called analogizing and distinguishing, shows the reader that you have legal support for your Conclusion.

In addition, the Analysis section will show the reader that you have legal support for the Conclusion by detailing counterarguments and refuting them. This part of the Analysis section, called the counter-analysis and resolution, shows the reader that the arguments that support the opposite conclusion are weaker than the arguments that support your Conclusion.

Because the Analysis section is objective, providing an impartial examination of the facts and law is crucial. This objective analysis allows you to make sure not only that you reach the correct Conclusion but also that you inform your reader of alternate interpretations of the facts and law.

The following two structures can serve as an outline for most objective Analysis sections:

Analysis

First paragraph:
- Broad thesis sentence stating Conclusion
- Summary of arguments that relate to anchors and support the Conclusion in the order they will be discussed

Second paragraph:
- Topic sentence summarizing how the most important argument supports the Conclusion
- Legal support for the argument, specifying how the argument supports the Conclusion by analogizing and distinguishing relevant cases

Repeat in successive paragraphs for each argument that supports the Conclusion until all supporting arguments have been discussed.

OR

First paragraph:
- Broad thesis sentence stating Conclusion and summarizing arguments that relate to anchors and support the Conclusion
- Legal support for the most important argument, specifying how the argument supports the Conclusion by analogizing and distinguishing relevant cases

Second paragraph:
- Topic sentence summarizing how additional argument(s) supports the Conclusion
- Legal support for the argument, specifying how the argument supports the Conclusion by analogizing and distinguishing relevant cases

Repeat in successive paragraphs for each argument that supports the Conclusion until all supporting arguments have been discussed.

Counter-analysis

- Topic sentence summarizing counterargument(s) regarding anchor that weighs against the Conclusion
- Legal support for first counterargument, specifying how the argument is unfavorable to the Conclusion by analogizing and distinguishing relevant cases

Repeat in successive paragraphs for each argument that weighs against the Conclusion until all counterarguments have been discussed.

Resolution

- Topic sentence refuting counterargument(s)
- Legal support for refutation of counterargument, including summarizing previous arguments, analogizing and distinguishing relevant cases, or both
- Summary of support for Conclusion

Note: When the counter-analysis is brief, the counter-analysis and resolution can be combined in a single paragraph. The resolution may be stated in a single sentence that summarizes why the arguments support the Conclusion.

Writing an Objective Analysis Section

1. Start with a broad thesis
2. Use topic sentences to organize your analysis
3. Analogize and distinguish
4. Detail counterarguments; then refute them

1. STEP ONE: START WITH A BROAD THESIS

The Analysis should start with your thesis. Your thesis is the broad conclusion of your objective document. By making your thesis the first sentence of your Analysis, you will remind the reader exactly what your Analysis is going to prove.

Your thesis should include your answer to the legal question and the reasons that support that answer. Those reasons will summarize the most important facts from your case and how they fit with the anchors that you identified in the relevant law. The anchors are particularly important in the Analysis section because the focus of the Analysis section is to provide specific legal support for your Conclusion. By focusing on the anchors, you will focus on the most relevant parts of the law.

In addition, because the anchors help you focus the Analysis, a strong thesis will summarize all of your arguments, as they relate to the anchors, in the order you are going to discuss them. For instance, the following sentence is the Conclusion in the curtilage example:

> Sam Perry's compound would likely qualify as curtilage because a picket fence encloses most of the yard, lending support to Tom Chapman's burglary conviction.

To begin your Analysis section, you would want to summarize this Conclusion with a similar thesis statement, focusing on your arguments as they relate to the anchors. You could rewrite the Conclusion as a thesis as follows:

> Sam Perry's compound would likely qualify as curtilage because the compound has a picket fence that encloses most of the yard.

This thesis draws the reader's attention to the arguments and the relevant law. It also tells the reader that you are going to discuss the fence first and the enclosure of the yard second. Be sure to describe the arguments in the thesis in the same order that you will discuss them in the Analysis.

The thesis statement above summarizes only two arguments, and they were closely related. But you may write a CREAC with too many relevant arguments to summarize in one sentence. In these situations, you should devote a paragraph to stating the thesis and listing the arguments. For instance, here is a thesis to begin an Analysis section where there are three arguments:

> Sam Perry's compound would probably not qualify as curtilage for three reasons. First, only the front yard is enclosed; the back yard is unbounded. Second, the front yard's enclosure is provided by low, uneven shrubs. Last, three breaks in the shrubs allow for entering and exiting the yard.

Whether your thesis requires one sentence or one paragraph, it sets up the remainder of the Analysis where you will discuss each of your arguments in detail.

2. STEP TWO: USE TOPIC SENTENCES TO ORGANIZE YOUR ARGUMENTS

After the thesis, organize your arguments in order of importance. Start with the strongest argument. Your discussion of each argument (or group of arguments if you combine your discussion of some of the arguments) must begin with a topic sentence. These topic sentences provide the backbone for your Analysis section. Each topic sentence should summarize why that argument and the relevant facts from your case support your Conclusion. Think of these topic sentences as mini-conclusions that add up to the broad thesis that is the first sentence of the Analysis section.

In the previous curtilage example, the Analysis would begin with the following thesis:

> Sam Perry's compound would likely qualify as curtilage because the compound has a picket fence that encloses most of the yard.

The next step is to write a topic sentence for each of the two arguments in the Analysis:

> The compound would probably be considered curtilage because Sam Perry installed a picket fence that is six feet tall, which is a sufficient fortification.

> The compound would likely qualify as curtilage because the picket fence encloses 90 percent of the yard.

These topic sentences tell the reader how the arguments relate to the anchors and the supporting law and why they support the Conclusion in your case. They summarize the major arguments and do not reference any other cases. In the paragraphs that follow each topic sentence, you will discuss in detail the application of each anchor to the facts of your case.

3. STEP THREE: ANALOGIZE AND DISTINGUISH

After a topic sentence summarizing why an argument supports your prediction, you have to provide legal support. This legal support comes from drawing comparisons between your case and similar cases. You can draw two types of comparisons: analogies and distinctions.

Analogies show the reader why your case is similar to relevant cases. Distinctions show the reader how your case differs from relevant cases. Because an analogy is an affirmative, rather than a defensive, argument, analogies are generally considered to be more effective than distinctions. Accordingly, in your Analysis, you usually will want to use analogies first.

A. Analogize to Similar Cases That Support Your Analysis of the Anchor in Your Case

Analogizing requires you to compare the analysis of the anchor in a relevant case to how the anchor should be analyzed in your case. This comparison involves putting the facts, reasoning, or holdings of relevant cases next to the specific facts, reasoning, or predicted holding of your case. This form of analogical reasoning explains how the anchors apply to your case and provides authority for your Conclusion.

Usually, the cases that should be used for analogies are those cases that are binding authority and have an outcome similar to the outcome you have predicted in your Conclusion. To be effective, an analogy must be substantive, parallel, and specific. This means that the analogy should be tied to an anchor, should compare like with like, and should be narrowly drawn.

i. Substantive

An analogy is substantive if it is closely related to one of the anchors that you have identified. Because the anchors are the grounds or bases for the courts' decisions in relevant cases, an analogy that is not tied to an anchor will not be helpful in predicting the court's decision in your case.

Cases may have similarities that are not substantive. For instance, two cases could both involve plaintiffs named John Lee. That similarity, however, would not be tied to an anchor (unless one of the anchors was the name of the plaintiff), so it would not be substantive.

ii. Parallel

An effective analogy must be parallel, meaning it compares apples to apples. An analogy will not succeed if it compares things that are not comparable (i.e., the holding of a case to a specific person). The first step in drawing a parallel analogy is to compare the same types of information from your case and the relevant case.

TYPES OF PARALLEL ANALOGIES

- **Fact to fact:** The yard in the present case is like the yard in *Chambers* because both yards were almost completely enclosed by man-made fences.
- **Reasoning to reasoning:** The court in *Chambers* noted that a small gap in a yard's enclosure does not mean that it is not enclosed because a gap is necessary to enter and exit the property. Similarly here, the court will likely find that the small gap in the fence did not prevent the yard from being enclosed.
- **Holding to predicted holding:** The *Chambers* court held that the yard qualified as curtilage because it satisfied the "some form of enclosure" requirement. Here, the court will likely reach the same holding because the picket fence provided "some form of enclosure" for Sam Perry's property.

The next step is to combine these parallel analogies into an argument that compares the facts, reasoning, and holding of the relevant case to your case. If your case and the relevant case share similar facts, but the comparable case's holding and reasoning are inapplicable, your analogy will not be effective. Similarly, an analogy that compares the holding in a case to the predicted holding in your case will not be useful unless it also establishes that the underlying facts are sufficiently similar to support the same reasoning. Thus, the Analysis for the curtilage example would include all three of the analogies in the previous example.

In *City of Erie v. Pap's A.M.*, Justice Sandra Day O'Connor drew an analogy between the nude dancing case before the Court and an earlier case involving draft card burning. The analogy compares the facts, reasoning, and holdings of the two cases:

> [T]his case is similar to *O'Brien*. O'Brien burned his draft registration card as a public statement of his antiwar views, and he was convicted under a statute making it a crime to knowingly mutilate or destroy such a card. This Court rejected his claim that the statute violated his First Amendment rights, reasoning that the law punished him for the "noncommunicative impact of his conduct, and for nothing else." 391 U.S. at 382. In other words, the Government regulation prohibiting the destruction of draft cards was aimed at maintaining the integrity of the Selective Service System and not at suppressing the message of draft resistance that O'Brien sought to convey by burning his draft card. So too here, the ordinance prohibiting public nudity is aimed at combating crime and other negative secondary effects caused by the presence of adult entertainment establishments like Kandyland and not at suppressing the erotic message conveyed by this type of nude dancing.[1]

— This analogy is based on a fact-to-fact comparison of a law banning public nudity and a law punishing the burning of draft cards.

— This analogy compares the reasoning in *O'Brien* — that the governmental interest behind a law punishing the burning of draft cards was to maintain the integrity of the draft, not suppress expression — to the Court's reasoning in this case — that the governmental interest behind the ban on public nudity was to combat crime, not suppress expression.

— This analogy compares the holding in *O'Brien*, that the draft card law did not violate the First Amendment, to the holding in this case that the ban on public nudity did not violate the First Amendment.

iii. Specific

Even if an analogy is substantive and parallel, it will not be effective if it lacks specificity. Being specific makes an analogy credible because it shows the reader that the comparison is analytically sound. For instance, a writer's comparison of only the holdings of two cases would lack the detail necessary to make it effective:

> In *Barton v. Smith*, the plaintiff prevailed. Similarly, the plaintiff should prevail in this case.

---

1. *City of Erie v. Pap's A.M.*, 529 U.S. 277, 291 (2000).

This analogy fails because it is not specific. It does not tell the reader why the plaintiff prevailed in *Barton v. Smith*, nor does it tell the reader why that same holding is appropriate in the present case. Indeed, it is so general that it asks the reader to assume that all of the underlying specifics are the same. Because it does not show the reader those specifics and how they are similar, it is not credible. It sounds like the writer is asserting the plaintiff should prevail in the present case simply because the writer wants it to be so. Obviously, more legal support and specificity are required.

To make an analogy specific, you must harvest all of the details from your case and the relevant cases that are necessary to flesh out the analogy. For instance, in the example comparing the yard in the present case to the yard in a relevant case, the more details you include about the yard, the more specific and effective the analogy becomes.

- **Lacks specificity:** The yard in the present case is like the yard in *Chambers*.
- **Some improvement:** The yard in the present case is like the yard in *Chambers* because both yards were almost completely enclosed.
- **Very specific:** The yard in the present case is like the yard in *Chambers* because both yards were enclosed by man-made fences, except for small gaps that were necessary to enter and exit the property.

Although these examples are a single sentence, you may need multiple sentences to draw an analogy that is substantive, parallel, and specific. An effective analogy between your case and a relevant case may take an entire paragraph to describe.

For example, in her concurring opinion in *Florida v. Jardines*, Justice Kagan used a paragraph to draw a specific analogy between the facts, reasoning, and holding of the dog-sniffing case before the Court and an earlier case involving thermal-imaging technology:

> The *Kyllo* Court held that police officers conducted a search when they used a thermal-imaging device to detect heat emanating from a private home, even though they committed no trespass. Highlighting our intention to draw both a "firm" and a "bright" line at "the entrance to the house," we announced the following rule:
>
>> "Where, as here, the Government uses a device that is not in general public use, to explore details of the home that would previously have been unknowable without physical intrusion, the surveillance is a 'search' and is presumptively unreasonable without a warrant."
>
> That "firm" and "bright" rule governs this case: The police officers here conducted a search because they used a "device . . . not in general public use" (a trained drug-detection dog) to "explore details of the home" (the presence of certain substances) that they would not otherwise have discovered without entering the premises.[2]

---

2. *Florida v. Jardines*, 133 S. Ct. 1409, 1419 (2013) (Kagan, J., concurring) (citations omitted).

B. Distinguish Negative Cases to Support Your Analysis

After you have written the analogies necessary to provide legal support for each argument, you should consider whether any relevant cases need to be distinguished. Usually, the only candidates for distinction are those cases that are binding authority and have an outcome contrary to your Conclusion. To determine whether you need to distinguish a case in your Analysis, consider the following questions:

- Is the case binding authority or one of the most recent decisions on the issue from a relevant court?
- Would a memo reaching the conclusion opposite to your Conclusion likely use the case as support?
- Would not distinguishing the case hurt the credibility of your objective analysis by making it appear one sided?

If you answer yes to any of these questions, you should distinguish the case.

The guidelines for effective distinctions are the same as those for analogies. Any distinctions should be substantive, parallel, and specific. For example, in his dissent in *Florida v. Jardines*, Justice Alito presented a specific distinction of the same case that Justice Kagan analogized to in her concurrence:

> Contrary to the interpretation propounded by the concurrence, *Kyllo* is best understood as a decision about the use of new technology. The *Kyllo* Court focused on the fact that the thermal imaging device was a form of "sense-enhancing technology" that was "not in general public use," and it expressed concern that citizens would be "at the mercy of advancing technology" if its use was not restricted. 533 U.S. at 34-35. A dog, however, is not a new form of "technology" or a "device." And, as noted, the use of dogs' acute sense of smell in law enforcement dates back many centuries.[3]

C. Repeat for Each Argument

After you have fully supported your analysis of an anchor with the necessary analogies and distinctions, you should move on to the next argument. If necessary, you can write a short conclusion to transition between paragraphs. You should continue to write paragraphs of this kind until you have discussed all of the arguments that support your Conclusion. Each of these paragraphs should have the same structure:

- Topic sentence summarizing how the argument supports the Conclusion
- Legal support through analogy and distinction proving that the analysis of the anchor and its application to your facts is correct

---

3. *Id.* at 1425 (Alito, J., dissenting).

4. STEP FOUR: DETAIL COUNTERARGUMENTS; THEN REFUTE THEM

Typically, at least one anchor, fact, or argument will not support your prediction. Indeed, most memos are assigned because the legal question is a close one—where both sides have viable arguments. An argument that is contrary to your Conclusion provides a counterargument. An Analysis section needs to include a counter-analysis and resolution where counterarguments are explained and refuted.

Because the purpose of your analysis is to objectively analyze a legal question, you cannot ignore counterarguments. Failing to include a counter-analysis and resolution hurts the credibility and usefulness of your analysis. A senior attorney or client cannot rely on your analysis if you have not considered all of the possible arguments that weigh for and against your Conclusion.

Counterarguments should usually be addressed after you have discussed all of the arguments that support your Conclusion. The organization of the counter-analysis and resolution paragraphs should be similar to that of the other paragraphs in the Analysis section. The counter-analysis paragraphs can have the following format:

- Topic sentence summarizing counterargument(s) regarding anchor that weighs against the Conclusion
- Legal support for first counterargument, specifying how the argument is unfavorable to the Conclusion by analogizing and distinguishing relevant cases

Repeat in successive paragraphs for each argument that weighs against the Conclusion until all counterarguments have been discussed.

Because the counter-analysis describes the arguments that weigh against your Conclusion, you need to resolve the discrepancy between the analysis and the counter-analysis before restating your Conclusion. This resolution may be a sentence or longer, and its purpose is to show your reader why the arguments, when considered together, still support the Conclusion. If the resolution requires a paragraph, use the following format as a guide:

- Topic sentence refuting counterargument(s)
- Legal support for refutation of counterargument, including summarizing previous arguments, analogizing and distinguishing relevant cases, or both
- Summary of support for the Conclusion

When the counter-analysis is brief, the counter-analysis and resolution can be combined into a single paragraph. The resolution may be stated in a single sentence that summarizes why the arguments support the Conclusion and that logically flows to the final Conclusion of the CREAC.

In the curtilage example, the counter-analysis and resolution paragraph could be as follows:

> However, the defendant may argue that Sam Perry's compound should not qualify as curtilage because the gap in Perry's fence is larger than the gap in the fence in *Chambers*. *See* 700 So. 2d at 441. In *Chambers*, the gap in the fence was only 10- to 15-feet wide, which is approximately half the size of the gap in this case. *Id.*

— Topic sentence summarizing counterargument and introducing it with a transition

— Legal support, including specific reference to distinguishable facts that set up refutation

> Although the gap in the present case is larger than the gap in the fence in *Chambers*, the reasoning from *Chambers* still applies. *See id.* "Total enclosure" is not required for curtilage, and the gap in Perry's fence, like the gap in *Chambers*, was necessary for "ingress or egress" to the compound. *See id.* at 442. Accordingly, the yard will be considered curtilage because Perry's fence provided some form of enclosure as required.

— Topic sentence refuting counterargument

— Legal support for refutation, including analogizing to relevant case

— Short conclusion summarizing support for Conclusion

Courts often analogize and distinguish cases to support their decisions. For example, Justice Ruth Bader Ginsburg writing for the Court in *Skilling v. United States* focused on the anchors to distinguish numerous relevant cases when an Enron executive challenged his conviction on the basis, among other things, of juror prejudice.

> First, we have emphasized in prior decisions the size and characteristics of the community in which the crime occurred. In *Rideau*, for example, we noted that the murder was committed in a parish of only 150,000 residents. Houston, in contrast, is the fourth most populous city in the Nation: At the time of Skilling's trial, more than 4.5 million individuals eligible for jury duty resided in the Houston area. Given this large, diverse pool of potential jurors, the suggestion that 12 impartial individuals could not be empaneled is hard to sustain.

— Topic sentence summarizing how anchor no. 1 supports the Court's Conclusion that the jurors were not prejudiced

— Legal support for Conclusion describing comparable facts of relevant case related to anchor no. 1

— Support for Conclusion on anchor no. 1 describing distinguishable facts of present case

> Second, although news stories about Skilling were not kind, they contained no confession or other blatantly prejudicial information of the type readers or viewers could not reasonably be expected to shut from sight. Rideau's dramatically staged admission of guilt, for instance, was likely imprinted indelibly in the mind of anyone who watched it. *Cf. Parker v. Randolph*, 442 U.S. 62, 72 (1979) (plurality opinion) ("[T]he defendant's own confession [is] probably the most probative and damaging evidence that can be admitted against him." (internal quotation marks omitted)). Pretrial publicity about Skilling was less memorable and prejudicial. No evidence of the smoking-gun variety invited prejudgment of his culpability.

— Topic sentence summarizing how anchor no. 2 supports the Court's Conclusion that the jurors were not prejudiced

— Legal support for Conclusion describing comparable facts of relevant case tied to anchor no. 2 with parenthetical adding further support

— Support for Conclusion on anchor no. 2 describing distinguishable facts of present case

> Third, unlike cases in which trial swiftly followed a widely reported crime, *e.g.*, *Rideau*, 373 U.S., at 724, over four years elapsed between Enron's bankruptcy and Skilling's trial. Although reporters covered

— Topic sentence summarizing how anchor no. 3 supports the Court's Conclusion that the jurors were not prejudiced

Enron-related news throughout this period, the decibel level of media attention diminished somewhat in the years following Enron's collapse.

Support for Conclusion on anchor no. 3 describing distinguishable facts of present case

Finally, and of prime significance, Skilling's jury acquitted him of nine insider-trading counts. Similarly, earlier instituted Enron-related prosecutions yielded no overwhelming victory for the Government. In *Rideau, Estes,* and *Sheppard,* in marked contrast, the jury's verdict did not undermine in any way the supposition of juror bias. It would be odd for an appellate court to presume prejudice in a case in which jurors' actions run counter to that presumption. *See, e.g., United States v. Arzola-Amaya,* 867 F.2d 1504, 1514 (5th Cir. 1989) ("The jury's ability to discern a failure of proof of guilt of some of the alleged crimes indicates a fair minded consideration of the issues and reinforces our belief and conclusion that the media coverage did not lead to the deprivation of [the] right to an impartial trial.").[4]

Topic sentence summarizing how anchor no. 4 supports the Court's Conclusion that the jurors were not prejudiced

Legal support for Conclusion describing facts and reasoning of relevant cases tied to anchor no. 4

Support for Conclusion on anchor no. 4 describing distinguishable facts of present case

---

4. *Skilling v. United States,* 130 S. Ct. 2896, 2915-16 (2010).

chapter 11

Writing an Objective Conclusion

A Conclusion should start and end each CREAC to keep the reader focused on your answer to the legal question. Although you will write a specific Conclusion at the start of your CREAC, you do not want to repeat the exact same sentence at the end. The reader does not want to encounter the exact same sentence twice in the same document. Instead, rephrase your Conclusion, making sure to provide a specific reason in support and to keep precise legal terminology the same.

For example, the following Conclusions could start and end a CREAC on the curtilage question.

Opening Conclusion:
Sam Perry's compound would likely qualify as curtilage because a picket fence encloses most of the yard, lending support to Tom Chapman's burglary conviction.

Ending Conclusion:
Thus, Tom Chapman will likely be convicted of burglary because a picket fence encloses nearly all of the Perry yard, making the compound part of the curtilage of the home.

Both Conclusions should state your overall answer to the precise legal question and provide one or more specific reasons in support. For complex legal questions, the Conclusion could take up a whole paragraph. The following Conclusions begin and end Justice Anthony M. Kennedy's landmark majority opinion in *United States v. Windsor*, which held that the Defense of Marriage Act was unconstitutional. Note how the Conclusions serve as an effective introduction and closing, respectively, to the case.

Opening Conclusion:
Two women then resident in New York were married in a lawful ceremony in Ontario, Canada, in 2007. Edith Windsor and Thea Spyer returned to their home in New York City. When Spyer died in 2009, she left her entire estate to Windsor. Windsor sought to claim the estate tax exemption for surviving spouses. She was barred from doing so, however, by a federal

law, the Defense of Marriage Act, which excludes a same-sex partner from the definition of "spouse" as that term is used in federal statutes. Windsor paid the taxes but filed suit to challenge the constitutionality of this provision. The United States District Court and the Court of Appeals ruled that this portion of the statute is unconstitutional and ordered the United States to pay Windsor a refund. This Court granted certiorari and now affirms the judgment in Windsor's favor.[1]

Ending Conclusion:

DOMA instructs all federal officials, and indeed all persons with whom same-sex couples interact, including their own children, that their marriage is less worthy than the marriages of others. The federal statute is invalid, for no legitimate purpose overcomes the purpose and effect to disparage and to injure those whom the State, by its marriage laws, sought to protect in personhood and dignity. By seeking to displace this protection and treating those persons as living in marriages less respected than others, the federal statute is in violation of the Fifth Amendment. This opinion and its holding are confined to those lawful marriages. The judgment of the Court of Appeals for the Second Circuit is affirmed.[2]

---

1. *United States v. Windsor*, 133 S. Ct. 2675, 2682 (2013).
2. *Id.* at 2696.

part III

Putting the Legal Memorandum Together

chapter 12

Incorporating Your CREAC into a Cohesive Document

The office memorandum is a common assignment for law students, new lawyers, and judicial clerks. Memoranda answer one or more legal questions about a specific case and make a prediction or recommendation about the outcome of that case. You will typically write a memorandum for your supervisor—whether that person is a supervising attorney, senior judicial clerk, judge, or law professor. But your memo could be shared with a client or with clerks and judges in other chambers. In a law firm where similar legal questions arise in the future, memoranda could be read and adapted for years to come.

This part of the *Handbook* details how to incorporate your CREAC analysis into a formal legal memorandum. You'll start by creating a template for your memo based on how many legal issues you are addressing. Then, you will add a section that describes the facts relating to your legal question. Finally, you will add introductory paragraphs called roadmaps to help your reader follow your analysis, and you will add transitions and headings to make sure your final document is cohesive and clear.

Writing a Legal Memo

1. Create a template for your memo
2. Outline and draft your Facts section
3. Draft a roadmap
4. Create a cohesive document

chapter 13

Create a Template for Your Memo

The format of an office memorandum will depend on the number and complexity of the legal questions you are addressing. The following structure can serve as an outline for most memos that address a single issue:

Single-Issue Memos

1. Heading
2. Question Presented
3. Brief Answer
4. Facts section
5. Discussion section with a CREAC
6. Final Conclusion section (optional)

For memos that address more than one issue, the exact structure will depend on the type of questions you have been asked, but the following structures can serve as a guide:

Multiple-Issue Memos

1. Heading
2. Question Presented addressing all legal issues
3. Brief Answer addressing all legal issues
4. Facts section
5. Discussion section that begins with a roadmap paragraph describing all legal issues and sets up the analysis to come
   A. CREAC discussion section for the first legal issue
   B. CREAC discussion section for the second legal issue
   C. *Repeat for each successive legal issue.*
6. Final Conclusion section summarizing the Conclusions for all legal issues and the predicted outcome for the case as a whole

Or, when your legal questions cannot neatly be summed up in a single Question Presented, write a Question Presented and Brief Answer for each legal issue, using the following structure as a guide:

Multiple-Issue Memos

1. Heading
2. Questions Presented
   A. Addressing first issue
   B. Addressing second issue
   C. *Repeat for each successive legal issue.*
3. Brief Answers
   A. Addressing first issue
   B. Addressing second issue
   C. *Repeat for each successive legal issue.*
4. Facts section
5. Discussion section that begins with a roadmap paragraph describing all legal issues and sets up the analysis to come
   A. CREAC discussion section for the first legal issue
   B. CREAC discussion section for the second legal issue
   C. *Repeat for each successive legal issue.*
6. Final Conclusion section summarizing the Conclusions for all legal issues and the predicted outcome for the case as a whole

1. USE A FORMAL MEMORANDUM HEADING

Once you decide on the basic organizational structure for your memo, create a template for your document, beginning with a formal memorandum heading. The heading should contain four pieces of information: (1) your supervisor's name, (2) your name, (3) the date, and (4) a "re" line that briefly describes the subject of your memo. Here's an example of a formal memo heading. (See Figure 13.1)

MEMORANDUM

To: Supervising Attorney
From: Student
Date: August 1, 2012
Re: Analysis of seller's intent to make binding offer in New York contract dispute for client Sandra Lee

---

QUESTION PRESENTED

Figure 13.1

2. CREATE THE HEADINGS FOR THE ADDITIONAL MEMO PARTS

Next, add headings for each of the additional parts of your memo: (1) Question(s) Presented, (2) Brief Answer(s), (3) Facts, (4) Discussion, and (5) Conclusion. Put into place each of the memo pieces that you have already completed—the Question(s) Presented, the Brief Answer(s), and the CREAC for each legal issue. (See Part II for a review.) Then, you can start to create and fill in the missing pieces.

chapter 14

Outline and Draft Your Facts Section

The Facts section provides the story behind your legal problem. The Facts section should include all facts that are important to the Discussion section and any background facts needed to pull the story together. Because your goal in writing the memo is to be objective, the Facts section should provide an honest account of what happened. As a result, take care to include all the facts that are important to your Discussion, even if they do not support your Conclusion.

1. IDENTIFY THE IMPORTANT FACTS

Any fact connected to an anchor or included in the Analysis portion of your CREAC should be a prominent part of your Facts section. These facts are legally significant because if they changed even slightly, the outcome of the case could change as well. To identify the legally significant facts, review the anchors from your applicable authorities. Then, review the facts for your case, and highlight every fact that is connected to an anchor. Make a list of these legally significant facts; they will form the basis of your Facts section.

2. TIE THE STORY TOGETHER

Providing a list of legally significant facts would not be particularly helpful or interesting. As a result, the Facts section should provide a well-organized story that describes the legally significant facts and how they might be related to each other. This story should use (1) background facts, (2) a logical organization, and (3) transitions and topic sentences to tie the story together.

A. Add Background Facts

The Facts section should use background facts where needed to provide context and describe important details. For example, with a question about whether a yard is curtilage, a fact about the property's entrances and exits is legally significant. The fact that the owner used an entrance to take his boat and trailer out every other Tuesday might not be legally significant, but that detail could help illustrate and explain the legally significant fact about the property's entrance. In contrast, the fact that the owner had three Labrador retrievers is probably not legally significant or helpful to understanding a legally significant fact, so it should be omitted from the Facts section.

B. Use a Logical Organization, Topic Sentences, and Transitions

Once you have a list of the legally significant facts and essential background facts, consider how to logically organize them into a story. Organizing the facts chronologically provides a good starting point. If you have multiple players or issues in a case, organizing the story by topic might work as well.

Then, break the story down into short paragraphs. Each paragraph can cover a particular point in time or a specific issue in the case. To help your reader follow the story, use a topic sentence or a transition at the start of every paragraph. For example, for the memo focusing on curtilage, the following framework would provide a logical organization for the Facts section:

¶1 Paragraph describing the alleged burglary, starting at the beginning of the chronology of events
- **Topic sentence:** In November 2010, Tom Chapman visited Sam Perry's home on a country road in unincorporated Palm Beach County.

¶2 Paragraph describing what happened next, including the arrest
- **Topic sentence:** After receiving a phone call at 8 p.m., sheriff's deputies arrived at the Perry home and arrested Chapman in the yard behind the home.

¶3 Paragraph describing the scene of the alleged crime, including the yard that might be considered curtilage
- **Topic sentence:** The Perry property stretches across nearly two acres, and most of the yard is surrounded by either a white picket fence or shrubs.

¶4 A second paragraph providing more details about the yard
- **Topic sentence:** In addition, the parking area is protected by a six-foot-high automatic gate.

¶5 Final paragraph describing the current state of the case or a transition to the Discussion
- **Topic sentence:** The next day, on November 18, 2010, prosecutors formally charged Chapman with burglary.

Note that paragraphs 1, 2, and 5 have topic sentences that introduce a time element. The third paragraph has a broad topic sentence describing the yard, and the fourth paragraph starts with a transition that shows the reader that the description of the yard is continuing. Paragraph markers like these make your reader's job easier and help keep your reader focused on the distinct parts of your story.

chapter 15

Draft a Roadmap for Complex Memos

At this point, a draft of most of your memo should be complete. The heading, Question(s) Presented, Brief Answer(s), Facts, and Discussion are all in place. The next step is to tie everything together.

Memos that cover more than one issue need one more piece to tie the issues together: an introductory roadmap of the issues. The roadmap can be one or more paragraphs that introduce your reader to the overarching legal issue in your case, the minor issues that are the focus of each CREAC, and how the issues relate to each other. Because it is an introduction, the roadmap will start the Discussion section, preceding the individual CREAC discussions of each issue. The roadmap should summarize the legal issues you have analyzed in the order that you address them in your memo.

The roadmap should start with the overall Conclusion. It also should include any broad rules that govern all of the issues. These broad rules establish the legal context for the more specific rules in the individual CREACs. Therefore, a rule in the roadmap should not be repeated later in the memo. The roadmap also should provide a summary of the analysis that follows. In the example below, the legal question is whether Blackhurst's adverse possession claim will succeed. Adverse possession in Blackhurst's jurisdiction has five elements. This roadmap begins a memo that will address two of the five elements: notice and continuous use.

Discussion

Blackhurst's adverse possession claim is likely to succeed because she continuously used the small parcel for more than five years and her use provided constructive notice to the owner. In California, adverse possession is defined as follows: "Where it appears that there has been an actual continued occupation of land, under a claim of title, exclusive of any other right, but not founded upon a written instrument, judgment or decree, the land so actually occupied, and no other, is deemed to have been held adversely." Cal. Civ. Proc. Code §324 (West 2012). Land is "deemed to have been possessed and occupied" only where "it has been

This Conclusion provides a broad summary of the predicted outcome. The subsections that follow will provide more specific Conclusions for each issue.

The roadmap then provides the broad Rules that govern both issues, beginning with the highest authority. These rules will not be repeated in the individual CREACs.

protected by a substantial enclosure" and "has been usually cultivated or improved." *Id.* §325.

To establish adverse possession, a plaintiff must prove (1) actual occupation that is sufficiently "open and notorious" to give the owner reasonable notice; (2) possession "hostile to the owner's title," which includes possession that occurred through mistake; (3) a claim by the possessor that the property is "his own, either under color of title, or claim or right"; (4) "continuous and uninterrupted" possession for five years; and (5) payment by the possessor of "all taxes levied and assessed upon the property." *West v. Evans*, 175 P.2d 219, 220 (Cal. 1946). This memorandum addresses whether Blackhurst's occupation of the small parcel was "open and notorious" and whether her use was "continuous and uninterrupted." Blackhurst's adverse possession claim will likely succeed because her actions on the parcel, including erecting signs, provided the owner with constructive notice. In addition, her use was continuous because she exerted daily control over the parcel.

The last three sentences summarize the analysis that follows. The first sentence is a transition explaining that only two of the five adverse possession elements will be addressed.

The last two sentences provide a thesis for each of the legal issues, in the order that they will be discussed.

chapter **16**

Create a Cohesive Document

Despite its many parts, a legal memorandum should be a cohesive and consistent document. A reader should be able to easily follow your analysis from beginning to end. Adding transitions, headings, subheadings, and a separate Conclusion section will help your reader understand how each part of your memo ties together.

1. ADD SUBHEADINGS FOR EACH CREAC IN MULTIPLE-ISSUE MEMOS

For memos that address multiple issues, inserting headings for each CREAC you have written will help guide your reader through your memo. The headings should be concise and straightforward, and they should reference the precise legal issue for the CREAC. Here are subheadings that could follow the roadmap in Blackhurst's adverse possession case. Note how they use similar language.

A. Blackhurst can likely establish the open and notorious possession element of her adverse possession claim.

(CREAC on open and notorious element)

B. Blackhurst probably will prove the continuous and uninterrupted element of her adverse possession claim.

(CREAC on continuous and uninterrupted element)

2. ADD A SEPARATE CONCLUSION SECTION IN MULTIPLE-ISSUE MEMOS

For multiple-issue memos, each CREAC will end with a Conclusion on the precise legal issue. Following your discussion of all the issues, you should add a separate Conclusion section that summarizes each Conclusion and includes your prediction for the case as a whole. This section can be a single sentence or it can include a sentence for each issue and a sentence for the overall Conclusion. The following example summarizes the overall Conclusion for the adverse possession case first and then summarizes the individual Conclusions for the two minor issues.

Conclusion

Blackhurst will likely prevail in her adverse possession claim because her use of the small parcel was continuous and open. Blackhurst continuously and consistently used the parcel of land for more than five years. In addition, her installation of the shed and "No Trespassing" signs provided constructive notice of her open use to the owner.

3. REVIEW YOUR MEMO IN ITS ENTIRETY

With the roadmap, headings, and Conclusion in place, the first draft of your memo is nearly complete. Because you might have written the various sections of the memo at different times, review each part and make sure it logically flows to the next section. The goal is to create one cohesive document—not a collection of disjointed parts. Use the checklist below as a guide.

Single-Issue Memos

☑ Read the Question Presented and Brief Answer. Does the Brief Answer reference the question and directly answer it by explaining how the facts from the question fit with the law?

☑ Read the Facts section. Does it logically follow the Brief Answer? The Facts section should introduce the parties and describe all the legally significant facts, even those details that were in the Question Presented.

☑ Does the Facts section end with a statement about the current state of the litigation or a transition that sets up the Discussion section and Conclusion?

Multiple-Issue Memos

☑ Read the Question(s) Presented and Brief Answer(s). Does each Brief Answer reference the question and directly answer it by explaining how the facts from the question fit with the law?

☑ Read the Facts section. Does it logically follow the Brief Answer? The Facts section should introduce the parties and describe all the legally significant facts, even if those details that were in the Question(s) Presented.

☑ Does the Facts section end with a statement about the current state of the litigation or a transition that sets up the Discussion section that follows?

☑ Does the Discussion begin with a roadmap that introduces the issues in the CREACs?

☑ Does each CREAC begin with a concise, straightforward heading?

☑ Does the memo end with a separate Conclusion section that addresses all issues and summarizes the overall Conclusion?

4. REVISE, REVISE, REVISE

With all the pieces in place, the first draft of your memo is complete—but it remains a first draft. Take care to revise and edit your document so it reflects your best work. Review Part IV "Writing Tools for the New Legal Writer" for guidance.

Putting your document aside for a day or even a few hours before you read it again can help you catch errors. Read the document critically and consider whether each section, paragraph, sentence, and word is as strong as you can make it. Reading the document aloud—slowly—is also a good way to catch grammar errors, missed words, and awkward wording. In addition, reviewing a printed copy of your memo will help you catch formatting errors and stranded headings. In a profession where a single mistake can affect your credibility, taking the time to polish your final work product will pay off in the end.

5. REVIEW EXAMPLES

On the following pages, you'll find two office memo examples. The first is a single-issue memo addressing an adverse possession question. The second example incorporates an additional question on the same adverse possession claim to create a multiple-issue memo.

MEMORANDUM

Example
Memo 16.1

To: Supervising Attorney
From: Student
Date: August 1, 2012
Re: Analysis of open and notorious possession element under California adverse possession law for Despina Blackhurst

---

QUESTION PRESENTED

Under California law, does Despina Blackhurst satisfy the open and notorious element for adverse possession when she mistakenly believed that she owned a small parcel of land across an alley from the larger parcel of land where she lives, she stored equipment in a padlocked shed on the parcel, and she erected "No Trespassing" signs on the parcel while the owner was out of the country and unaware of Blackhurst's use?

— The question gives the jurisdiction in the first clause and then provides the precise legal question. It also lists four facts that are parallel grammatically and balanced — the first three facts favor Blackhurst and the fourth hurts her claim.

BRIEF ANSWER

Probably yes. For a use to be open and notorious, the adverse claimant must provide constructive notice of the adverse possession to the owner. Blackhurst's shed and signs provided this constructive notice. Thus, Blackhurst can likely establish that her possession of the small parcel was open and notorious.

*— This section gives a direct answer. It also summarizes the applicable law, and the strongest argument in support of the **Conclusion**.*

STATEMENT OF FACTS

In June 2005, Despina Blackhurst purchased property in North Lake Tahoe from her uncle. As part of the agreement with her uncle, Blackhurst understood that the property included both a large parcel and a smaller parcel across an alley from the larger parcel. The large parcel contained Blackhurst's two-bedroom home.

*— The **Facts** section begins with a topic sentence and an opening clause with a date that sets up the chronological story.*

On the small parcel, Blackhurst installed a shed that contained snow removal equipment. She used a combination lock to secure the shed. In October 2010, Blackhurst discovered that teenagers were hanging out in the shed on the small parcel. She chased them away and changed the lock's combination. Blackhurst then posted "No Trespassing" signs on the parcel.

— Concise descriptions of legally significant facts in short paragraphs tell the story behind the case.

In June 2012, the owner of the property adjacent to the small parcel claimed that, according to county records, he owned the small parcel. He told Blackhurst that he had been living in Norway for the past seven years and had been renting out the property. Now, Blackhurst seeks to quiet title by proving that she acquired the parcel through adverse possession.

— The section ends with a summary of the current state of the litigation.

DISCUSSION

Blackhurst can likely establish the open and notorious possession element for an adverse possession claim because her use of the small parcel provided constructive notice to the owner. In California, adverse possession is

*— The **Conclusion** states the answer to the precise legal question and provides a reason.*

defined as follows: "Where it appears that there has been an actual continued occupation of land, under a claim of title, exclusive of any other right, but not founded upon a written instrument, judgment or decree, the land so actually occupied, and no other, is deemed to have been held adversely." Cal. Civ. Proc. Code § 324 (West 2012). Land is "deemed to have been possessed and occupied" only where "it has been protected by a substantial enclosure" and "has been usually cultivated or improved." *Id.* § 325.

*— The **Rule** starts with the highest authority. The second sentence builds on the first by providing a definition of key terms.*

To establish adverse possession, a plaintiff must prove (1) actual occupation that is sufficiently "open and notorious" to give the owner reasonable notice; (2) possession "hostile to the owner's title"; which includes possession that occurred through mistake; (3) a claim by the possessor that the property is "his own, either under color of title, or claim of right"; (4) "continuous and uninterrupted" possession for five years; and (5) payment by the possessor of "all taxes levied and assessed upon the property." *West v. Evans*, 175 P.2d 219, 220 (Cal. 1946). This memorandum addresses only the open and notorious element for adverse possession.

*— This **Rule** paragraph begins with the broadest rule from the case law that interprets the statutes cited above. The sentence quotes selective language and provides the elements in a parallel list.*

— This transition explains that the memo will address only one element.

The intent behind the open and notorious element is to give the owner actual or reasonable constructive notice of the adverse use. *Nielsen v. Gibson*, 100 Cal. Rptr. 3d 335, 341 (Ct. App. 2009). To be open and notorious, an adverse use must provide reasonable notice by being "visible to the true owner and others." *Id.* The use must be open, visible, and notorious to the extent "that it will raise a presumption of notice" of the adverse claim. *Wood v. Davidson*, 145 P.2d 659, 661-62 (Cal. Dist. Ct. App. 1944). When an adverse use is sufficiently open and notorious to raise the presumption of notice, actual notice by the owner is not required. *Nielsen*, 100 Cal. Rptr. 3d at 341-42. An owner, therefore, cannot avoid the legal consequences of an adverse use by ignoring it. *Id.* at 342. For example, an owner was held to have had constructive notice even though he was out of the country during the period of the open and notorious use. *Id.*

*— This **Explanation** paragraph starts broadly, explaining a crucial anchor for the open and notorious element: notice. It includes a brief description of a case that will be the basis for a comparison in the Analysis section.*

Whether an adverse use is sufficiently open and notorious to constitute notice is a question of fact that "depends on the particular land and its condition, locality, and appropriate use." *Id.* at 341. Courts have considered whether the adverse claimant enclosed, maintained, and improved the property to determine whether the possession was open and notorious. *See, e.g., id.* For example, when adverse claimants fenced, irrigated, improved, and built a go-cart course on the property, the possession was sufficiently open and notorious that it "created a presumption of notice to the world." *Nielsen*, 100 Cal. Rptr. 3d at 342.

*— This **Explanation** paragraph provides more specific details about the notice anchor, giving an example from one case. Because the case's facts are comparable to Blackhurst's case, this Explanation sets up the Analysis to come.*

Similarly, adverse claimants' occupation of a property for twenty-five years, which included improving and making additions, constituted "reasonable notice that they claimed the property as their own." *Lobro v. Watson*, 116 Cal. Rptr. 533, 536, 538 (Ct. App. 1974). The improvements, all made at the claimants' expense, included fencing the lot, replacing the roof, and planting trees and flowers. *Id.*

*— This **Explanation** paragraph includes another example from case law that shows how one court interpreted the "notice" anchor. It also sets up a comparison to Blackhurst's facts in the Analysis section.*

However, a possession of a vacant lot was not sufficiently open and notorious where the land was not improved or regularly cultivated and where evidence was conflicting about the extent that the claimants used the property. *Klein v. Caswell*, 199 P.2d 689, 691-92 (Cal. Dist. Ct. App. 1948). In *Klein*, the claimant testified that she occasionally visited the property over a twenty-two-year period for picnics, and at one time, she asked a neighbor to keep the lot cleaned up. *Id.* at 691. But several neighbors who frequently passed the lot said that it always appeared neglected, the same as other unoccupied, vacant lots in the area. *Id.* This "slight use" was not sufficient to constitute adverse possession. *Id.* at 692.

> This **Explanation** paragraph provides a contrasting example to describe a use that did not provide the required notice. A comparison to these facts will serve as a counterargument.

A court will likely find that Blackhurst's possession was open and notorious because her conduct provided reasonable notice to the owner of her adverse possession. In particular, Blackhurst installed and maintained a shed that she kept locked. Further, Blackhurst hung "No Trespassing" signs on the shed after she discovered that teenagers were using the parcel without her permission. Like a fence or a go-cart course, Blackhurst's shed and signs were sufficiently visible to provide notice to the owner of her adverse claim. *See Nielsen*, 100 Cal. Rptr. 3d at 342.

> The **Analysis** section begins with a broad thesis summarizing the Conclusion.
>
> This Analysis paragraph shows the reader how Blackhurst provided notice by giving the facts that best support the notice argument and by making a fact-to-fact comparison to *Nielsen*.

The shed and signs showed the owner that Blackhurst was occupying, maintaining, and improving the parcel. Her actions are comparable to those of the successful claimants in *Lobro*, where installing a fence and planting flowers created "reasonable notice." *See* 116 Cal. Rptr. at 536-37. Because Blackhurst's use of the property was visible to anyone who walked by the parcel, a court will likely presume that the owner had notice of her adverse claim. *See Nielsen*, 100 Cal. Rptr. 3d at 342.

> This **Analysis** paragraph begins with a topic sentence and gives a specific comparison to provide legal support. The last sentence compares the predicted Conclusion to the *Nielsen* holding.

In addition, Blackhurst's use of the property was active and not occasional. The use goes far beyond the occasional picnic that was found to be an insufficient use in *Klein*. *See* 199 P.2d at 691. Moreover, unlike *Klein*, where the evidence about the claimants' use was conflicting, the evidence that Blackhurst regularly used the shed and attempted to chase trespassers away is undisputed. *See id.*

> A transition shows that more legal support is being offered. This time, the support comes from distinguishing a case that does not support the Conclusion.

The owner may argue that he did not have actual notice of Blackhurst's adverse use because he was in Norway during the five years of her adverse possession. Actual notice, however, is not required, and an owner cannot defeat an open and notorious use by willfully ignoring it. *See Nielsen*, 100 Cal. Rptr. 3d at 341.

> The counter-analysis begins with a topic sentence that summarizes the counterargument. A rule from a key case refutes the counterargument.

The owner cannot refute Blackhurst's open and notorious possession simply by claiming that he was out of the country. The owner here is like the owner in *Nielsen*, who was in Ireland during the period of adverse possession. *See id.* In *Nielsen*, the court rejected the owner's argument that he could not have had notice, holding that "[w]hen an adverse claimant is 'in open possession and the true owner fails to look after his interests and remains in ignorance of the claim, it is his own fault.'" *Id.* Similarly, here, if the owner had conducted an inspection of the parcel at any time, he would have seen the shed and signs and had notice of Blackhurst's open and notorious possession.

> The resolution paragraph begins with a topic sentence refuting the counterargument.
>
> Here, the counterargument is refuted by a comparison to the facts and holding of the *Nielsen* case.

CONCLUSION

Because Blackhurst installed the shed and signs on the small parcel, she can likely prove the open and notorious possession element for adverse possession.

> The **Conclusion** states the answer to the precise legal issue and provides a reason.

MEMORANDUM

To: Supervising Attorney
From: Student
Date: August 15, 2012
Re: Analysis of Despina Blackhurst's adverse possession claim under
         California law

——This multiple-issue memo includes the analysis of a second element under adverse possession law. As a result, this memo includes two Questions Presented, two Brief Answers, a roadmap paragraph to begin the Discussion section, and two separate CREACs—each addressing a precise legal question.

QUESTION PRESENTED

I. Under California law, does Despina Blackhurst satisfy the open and notorious element for adverse possession when she mistakenly believed that she owned a small parcel of land across an alley from the larger parcel of land where she lives, she stored equipment in a padlocked shed on the parcel, and she erected "No Trespassing" signs on the parcel while the owner was out of the country and unaware of Blackhurst's use?

II. Under California law, does Despina Blackhurst satisfy the continuity of possession element for a claim of adverse possession when she used the small parcel to store kayak equipment and to access Lake Tahoe, left the small parcel vacant during part of the summer of 2011, had a tenant during part of the summer of 2011, but only visited the parcel five times per year?

——This memo adds a second Question Presented to address the second element: continuity of possession. The question uses the under-does-when format. The jurisdiction is in the first clause, and the precise legal question is in the second. The third part lists four facts that are parallel and balanced.

BRIEF ANSWERS

I. Probably yes. For a use to be open and notorious, the adverse claimant must provide constructive notice of the adverse possession to the owner. Blackhurst's shed and signs provided this constructive notice. Thus, Blackhurst can likely establish that her possession of the small parcel was open and notorious.

II. Probably yes. For a use to be continuous, the adverse claimant must use the claimed property in the claimant's ordinary fashion in a manner appropriate to the property's character. Blackhurst can likely establish that her possession of the small parcel was continuous because she used the small parcel to store kayak equipment and to access Lake Tahoe, which shows that she took advantage of the parcel's design.

——These Brief Answers respond to the questions in the order they are presented above. The second answer uses a similar organization to the first. It provides a direct answer and then summarizes the applicable law on the continuity of possession element. Then, the answer references the strongest argument in support of the Conclusion.

STATEMENT OF FACTS

In June 2005, Despina Blackhurst purchased property in North Lake Tahoe from her uncle. As part of the agreement with her uncle, Blackhurst understood that the property included both a large parcel and a smaller parcel across an alley from the larger parcel. The large parcel contained Blackhurst's two-bedroom home. The small parcel abutted Lake Tahoe and contained a steeply sloping pathway to the lake's edge.

On the small parcel, Blackhurst installed a shed that contained kayak equipment. She used a combination lock to secure the shed. An avid kayaker, Blackhurst typically visited the shed five times per year between April and October to prepare for her kayak trips. She would begin her kayak trips

——The Facts section uses a chronological organization to tell the story of the case. Note how dates are used throughout the section to keep the order of the story clear to the reader.

by walking down the steep path to Lake Tahoe and launching her kayak at the lake's edge. In October 2010, Blackhurst discovered that teenagers were hanging out in the shed on the small parcel. She chased them away and changed the lock's combination. Blackhurst then posted "No Trespassing" signs on the parcel.

In 2011, Blackhurst enrolled in a summer study abroad program that started on May 1 and ended on August 31. Blackhurst was able to secure a tenant for the months of June and July. She left the tenant the keys to her home, the combination to the shed, and instructions to return the keys on July 31.

In June 2012, the owner of the property adjacent to the small parcel claimed that, according to county records, he owned the small parcel. He told Blackhurst that he had been living in Norway for the past seven years and had been renting out the property. Now, Blackhurst seeks to quiet title by proving that she acquired the parcel through adverse possession.

This paragraph provides most of the legally significant facts for the continuous possession element. Note how the facts are presented objectively—so that they do not favor Blackhurst or the owner.

Each paragraph begins with a topic sentence. This final paragraph ends with a brief summary of the state of the litigation.

DISCUSSION

Blackhurst will likely prevail on her adverse possession claim. First, she can likely establish the open and notorious possession element for an adverse possession claim because her use of the small parcel provided constructive notice to the owner. Additionally, Blackhurst can likely establish the continuity of possession element for an adverse possession claim because her use of the small parcel to store kayak equipment demonstrates continued possession for the ordinary use of the occupant.

*The memo begins with a **Conclusion** on the overall issue. It then provides a Conclusion specific to each CREAC. This framework provides a "roadmap" of the analysis to come, and it's often called the roadmap.*

In California, adverse possession occurs "[w]here it appears that there has been an actual continued occupation of land, under a claim of title, exclusive of any other right, but not founded upon a written instrument, judgment or decree...." Cal. Civ. Proc. Code § 324 (West 2012). Land is "deemed to have been possessed and occupied" only where "it has been protected by a substantial enclosure" and "has been usually cultivated or improved." *Id.* § 325.

*The roadmap should provide the broad **Rules** that apply to all the issues. These broad **Rules** establish the legal context for the specific rules in the individual CREACs. The broad **Rules** are not repeated later in the memo.*

To establish adverse possession, a plaintiff must prove (1) actual occupation that is sufficiently "open and notorious" to give the owner reasonable notice; (2) possession "hostile to the owner's title," which includes possession that occurred through mistake; (3) a claim by the possessor that the property is "his own, either under color of title, or claim of right"; (4) "continuous and uninterrupted" possession for five years; and (5) payment by the possessor of "all taxes levied and assessed upon the property." *West v. Evans*, 175 P.2d 219, 220 (Cal. 1946). This memorandum addresses only the open and notorious possession and continuity of possession elements for adverse possession.

*Note how the **Rule** section begins with the broad rule and then provides more narrow rules that logically follow.*

This transition lists the two elements analyzed in the memo—in the order that they appear below.

I. Blackhurst will likely establish open and notorious possession of the small parcel under California adverse possession law.

*Headings that summarize the **Conclusion** on each legal issue help guide the reader through the multiple-issue memo.*

Blackhurst can likely establish that her possession of the small parcel was open and notorious because she installed a shed and signs. To be open and notorious, an adverse use must provide reasonable notice by being "visible to the true owner and others." *Nielsen v. Gibson*, 100 Cal. Rptr. 3d 335, 341 (Ct. App. 2009). The use must be open, visible, and notorious to the extent "that it will raise a presumption of notice" of the adverse claim. *Wood v. Davidson*, 145 P.2d 659, 661-62 (Cal. Dist. Ct. App. 1944). The intent behind the open and notorious element is to give the owner actual or reasonable constructive notice of the adverse use. *Nielsen*, 100 Cal. Rptr. 3d at 341.

When an adverse use is sufficiently open and notorious to raise the presumption of notice, actual notice by the owner is not required. *Id*. An owner, therefore, cannot avoid the legal consequences of an adverse use by ignoring it. *Id*. at 342. For example, an owner was held to have had constructive notice even though he was out of the country during the period of the open and notorious use. *Id*.

Whether an adverse use is sufficiently open and notorious to constitute notice is a question of fact that "depends on the particular land and its condition, locality, and appropriate use." *Id*. at 341. Courts have considered whether the adverse claimant enclosed, maintained, and improved the property to determine whether the possession was open and notorious. *See, e.g., id*. For example, when adverse claimants fenced, irrigated, improved, and built a go-cart course on the property, the possession was sufficiently open and notorious that it "created a presumption of notice to the world." *Id*. at 342.

Similarly, adverse claimants' occupation of a property for twenty-five years, which included improving and making additions, constituted "reasonable notice that they claimed the property as their own." *Lobro v. Watson*, 116 Cal. Rptr. 533, 538 (Ct. App. 1974). The improvements, all made at the claimants' expense, included fencing the lot, replacing the roof, and planting trees and flowers. *Id*.

However, a possession of a vacant lot was not sufficiently open and notorious where the land was not improved or regularly cultivated and where evidence was conflicting about the extent that the claimants used the property. *Klein v. Caswell*, 199 P.2d 689, 691-92 (Cal. Dist. Ct. App. 1948). In *Klein*, the claimant testified that she occasionally visited the property over a twenty-two-year period for picnics, and at one time, she asked a neighbor to keep the lot cleaned up. *Id*. at 691. But several neighbors who frequently passed the lot said that it always appeared neglected, the same as other unoccupied, vacant lots in the area. *Id*. This "slight use" was not sufficient to constitute adverse possession. *Id*. at 692.

A court will likely find that Blackhurst's possession was open and notorious because her conduct provided reasonable notice to the owner of her adverse possession. In particular, Blackhurst installed and maintained a shed that she kept locked. Further, Blackhurst hung "No Trespassing" signs on the shed after she discovered that teenagers were using the parcel without her permission. Like a fence or a go-cart course, Blackhurst's shed and signs were sufficiently visible to provide notice to the owner of her adverse claim. *See Nielsen*, 100 Cal. Rptr. 3d at 342.

The shed and signs showed the owner that Blackhurst was occupying, maintaining, and improving the parcel. Her actions are comparable to those of the successful claimants in *Lobro*, where installing a fence and planting

— Note the differences between this memo and the single-issue memo on pages 80-82. The **Conclusion** is worded differently to avoid repetition, and the rule statement addresses the **Rule** for the precise legal issue, rather than the broad **Rule** for adverse possession, which appears in the roadmap.

— This **Explanation** section explains what open and notorious means under California law. The section uses specific facts from case law to first explain what is open and notorious. Then, in the third paragraph, the **Explanation** illustrates what is not open and notorious.

— The **Analysis** for this issue is identical in the single- and multiple-issue memos.

Both begin with a strong thesis statement that summarizes the analysis to come, and they both use topic sentences at the start of each paragraph to summarize each major point.

The **Analysis** section provides the analysis first, then the counter-analysis, and then a resolution to resolve the discrepancies between the two.

flowers created "reasonable notice." *See* 116 Cal. Rptr. at 536-37. Because Blackhurst's use of the property was visible to anyone who walked by the parcel, a court will likely presume that the owner had notice of her adverse claim. *See Nielsen*, 100 Cal. Rptr. 3d at 342.

In addition, Blackhurst's use of the property was active and not occasional. The use goes far beyond the occasional picnic that was found to be an insufficient use in *Klein*. *See* 199 P.2d at 691. Moreover, unlike *Klein* where the evidence about the claimants' use was conflicting, the evidence that Blackhurst regularly used the shed and attempted to chase trespassers away is undisputed. *See id.*

The owner may argue that he did not have actual notice of Blackhurst's adverse use because he was in Norway during the five years of her adverse possession. Actual notice, however, is not required, and an owner cannot defeat an open and notorious use by willfully ignoring it. *See Nielsen*, 100 Cal. Rptr. 3d at 341.

The owner cannot refute Blackhurst's open and notorious possession simply by claiming that he was out of the country. The owner here is like the owner in *Nielsen*, who was in Ireland during the period of adverse possession. *See id.* In *Nielsen*, the court rejected the owner's argument that he could not have had notice, holding that "[w]hen an adverse claimant is 'in open possession and the true owner fails to look after his interests and remains in ignorance of the claim, it is his own fault.'" *Id.* at 342. Similarly, here, if the owner had conducted an inspection of the parcel at any time, he would have seen the shed and signs and had notice of Blackhurst's open and notorious possession. Thus, because she installed the shed and signs on the small parcel, Blackhurst will likely establish the open and notorious element.

— The **Conclusion** provides an answer to the precise legal question and a specific reason in support

II. Blackhurst will likely establish continuous possession of the small parcel under California adverse possession law.

Because Blackhurst regularly used the small parcel to prepare for her regular kayak outings, she likely will establish continuous possession. To establish adverse possession, an individual must demonstrate continuous and uninterrupted possession for five years. *Cal. Md. Funding, Inc. v. Lowe*, 44 Cal. Rptr. 2d 784, 787 (Ct. App. 1995).

— The **Conclusion** here states the answer for the continuity element and provides a reason.

— This **Rule** statement summarizes the rule for the continuity element.

Courts will examine a claimant's intent to determine whether the claimant's use amounts to continuous possession. *See Montgomery & Mullen Lumber Co. v. Quimby*, 128 P. 402, 404 (Cal. 1912); *Merrill v. Hooper*, 13 P.2d 786, 787 (Cal. Dist. Ct. App. 1932). When a claimant demonstrates an intent to abandon the property, continuous occupation cannot be found. *Merrill*, 13 P.2d at 787. The claimant's actions in *Merrill*, for example, did not evince "any intention of abandonment" over a period of six years. *Id.* During that time, the claimant rented the property first as a store, then as a cigar factory, and later to tenants whom she was forced to evict. *Id.* Despite the property's vacancy, the court found that because the claimant kept the property locked and advertised for a new tenant, she demonstrated continuous possession. *Id.*; *see also Quimby*, 128 P.2d at 404 (holding that temporary periods of vacancy between tenancies will not destroy the claimant's continuous possession).

— This **Explanation** section illustrates what continuous possession means under California law. The first paragraph explains the anchor of intent, and it uses three cases to provide a comprehensive explanation of the law.

In addition, courts will find continuous use when a claimant uses a property for its "ordinary" use, which "means a use appropriate to the location and character of the property." *Posey v. Bay Point Realty Co.*, 7 P.2d 1020, 1022 (Cal. 1932). If adversely claimed land is suitable only for particular or slight use, a claimant satisfies the requirement for continuous use if he uses the land accordingly. *Id.* In *Posey*, the court found continuous use even though the claimants pastured their cows on the claimed swampland during only part of the year. *Id.* Because high water often made the swampland inaccessible and high salinity made it of poor quality, the use was "ordinary" and sufficiently continuous. *Id.*

Conversely, possession of two residential lots was not sufficiently ordinary or continuous when the claimant made infrequent visits and only three improvements to the property. *Madson v. Cohn*, 10 P.2d 531, 532 (Cal. Dist. Ct. App. 1932). The claimant in *Madson* visited the property four to six times a year and never fenced or leased the property. *Id.* He planted a few bushes and trees, but the plants were later killed by boys who used the lots for a ball ground. *Id.* The court found that the evidence did not establish continuity of possession sufficient to constitute adverse possession. *Id.*

A court will likely find that Blackhurst's possession of the small parcel was continuous for two reasons. First, Blackhurst made ordinary use of the shed to store her kayak equipment and that use was appropriate for the property's character. Second, she demonstrated her intent to continuously use the property by renting the large and small parcels when she was out of the country for a brief time.

First, Blackhurst used the small parcel in an ordinary manner consistent with its character. In particular, Blackhurst stored kayak equipment in a shed that she installed and used the sloping pathway to bring her equipment to the lake's edge. Blackhurst did not use the land during the winter months, when the frozen lake would prevent kayaking. Like the claimant in *Posey*, who entered the land to pasture cows only when it was accessible, Blackhurst took advantage of the parcel's ordinary use by using it to access the lake during the summer months. *See* 7 P.2d at 1022. Her use was sufficiently suited to the land's character to constitute continuous possession. *See id.*

In addition, Blackhurst's lease of the property during one summer when she was out of the country establishes her intent to continuously occupy the property. More specifically, when Blackhurst left the small parcel vacant in May and August 2011, she provided instructions to her tenant to return the keys to her. *See Quimby*, 128 P. at 404 (holding that continuity of possession does not require "a continuous personal presence on the lot"). Similar to the claimant in *Merrill*, where temporary periods of vacancy did not show an intent to abandon possession, Blackhurst's temporary absence fails to show that she intended to abandon the small parcel. *See* 13 P.2d at 787. Moreover, Blackhurst's instructions to return the keys to the property demonstrate her intent to resume occupancy of the small parcel.

However, the neighboring owner may argue that Blackhurst failed to establish continuous possession because she visited the property only five times per year. The owner could argue that the property can and should be

---

— While the first **Explanation** paragraph begins with a topic sentence about the intent anchor, this paragraph introduces the anchor of ordinary use. Then, the specific facts from the *Posey* case explain what equals ordinary use.

— The third **Explanation** paragraph adds to the description of the ordinary use anchor by providing a case that explains what does not equal ordinary use. By using cases with opposite holdings, the writer illustrates the parameters of the law.

— The **Analysis** section begins with a thesis paragraph that summarizes the two major arguments—based on the anchors of intent and ordinary use—and it provides specific factual reasons in support of both.

— This paragraph begins with a topic sentence and then details specific facts that support the ordinary use argument. The writer then connects the facts to supporting case law with a substantive, parallel, and specific analogy.

— This **Analysis** paragraph follows the same format as the preceding paragraph: it starts with a topic sentence and then provides more specific details in support.

— A clear transition marks the start of the counteranalysis. The counteranalysis includes a detailed counterargument with a citation to case law as support.

used during the winter months for winter sports, such as skiing. *See Madson*, 10 P.2d at 532 (finding that infrequent visits to two residential lots were not sufficiently ordinary or continuous).

But an adverse claimant does not have to continuously occupy a prop- —— This paragraph resolves
erty to satisfy the continuous possession element. The sloping nature of the   the discrepancy created by
property could make the property dangerous in snowy or icy weather, which   the counteranalysis and
is comparable to the regularly inaccessible swampland in *Posey*. *See* 7 P.2d at   summarizes the best points in
1022. Thus, Blackhurst's use of the small parcel in the summer for kayaking   support of the Conclusion.
is "usual and ordinary…according to its particular location and character."
See id. Blackhurst, therefore, will likely establish continuous possession of —— The **Conclusion** here focuses
the property, despite a brief period of vacancy, due to her ordinary use of the   specifically on the continuous
land to store her kayak equipment and to access Lake Tahoe.   possession element.

CONCLUSION

Blackhurst can likely prove the open and notorious possession element —— The **Conclusion** section pro-
for adverse possession because she installed the shed and signs on the small   vides a separate conclusion
parcel. In addition, because her regular kayaking was an ordinary use of the   for each element in dispute.
property, she will likely establish the continuous possession element. Thus,   It then provides an answer to
Blackhurst will likely establish that she acquired the small parcel through   the overall question.
adverse possession and prevail in her quiet title claim.

part IV

Writing Tools for the New Legal Writer

chapter 17

Introduction to Grammar, Punctuation, and Style

Good lawyers know how to put a sentence together. Their collective reputation as poor writers comes from a simple truth: Too many lawyers too often try to cram too much law, information, and legalese into an otherwise proper sentence. The rules of good writing don't vanish because a writer needs to explain a complex set of facts or legal rules. On the contrary, complicated legal doctrine is best explained and understood when presented in plain language. And so, this part of the *Handbook* includes a review of eight basic grammar rules. It also details grammar principles that are particularly important for the new legal writer. In addition, this part includes tips on revising and editing your document—so that you can transform a wordy, legalese-riddled document into one that's concise, direct, and thus, more effective.

chapter 18

Grammar Basics

Grammar Basics for the New Legal Writer	
1. Sentences	5. Modifiers
2. Commas	6. Pronouns
3. Semicolons	7. Apostrophes
4. Colons	8. Hyphens

1. SENTENCES

Sentences—A Brief Review
1. Make the subject match the verb
2. Avoid run-ons
3. Fix fragments

A. Rule 1: Make the Subject Match the Verb

A proper sentence has a subject and a verb that match. Singular subjects, including "each," "neither," "everyone," "corporation," and "defendant," take a singular verb. Plural subjects take a plural verb. That matchup remains true even if many words separate the subject and the verb. In the two examples below, the singular subjects of "opinion" and "court" take singular verbs, despite intervening phrases that contain plural nouns.

> The majority opinion—written by Justice Scalia and joined by Justices Thomas, Ginsburg, Sotomayor, and Kagan—holds that using a drug-sniffing dog on a porch to investigate the contents of a home is a search for Fourth Amendment purposes.

> The court interpreting the statutes is hearing oral arguments today.

While you want to ensure that subjects and verbs match in complex sentences, keep in mind that one principle of good writing is to keep subjects and verbs close together. In the example below, from Justice Kagan's concurrence in *Florida v. Jardines*, note how the main subjects are next to the main verbs.

> For me, a simple analogy clinches this case. . . . A stranger comes to the front door of your home carrying super-high-powered binoculars. He doesn't knock or say hello. Instead, he stands on the porch and uses the binoculars to peer through your windows, into your home's furthest corners.[1]

B. Rule 2: Avoid Run-Ons

In addition, a proper sentence should contain commas and semicolons as needed to avoid creating a run-on. Fusing two sentences into one without punctuation or with only a comma connecting them creates a run-on. The following examples provide five ways to fix run-ons.

Incorrect

A public figure in a defamation action must prove that a false statement was published by an individual with reckless disregard for the truth, he also must prove that the statement is defamatory. — This run-on fuses two independent clauses together with a comma.

Correct: Semicolon

A public figure in a defamation action must prove that a false statement was published by an individual with reckless disregard for the truth; he also must prove that the statement is defamatory. — 1. A semicolon can combine two closely related independent clauses.

Correct: Coordinating conjunction

A public figure in a defamation action must prove that a false statement was published by an individual with reckless disregard for the truth, and he must prove that the statement is defamatory. — 2. A coordinating conjunction (and, or, but, so, for, yet) plus a comma can combine the clauses.

Correct: Conjunctive adverb,[2] semicolon, comma

A public figure in a defamation action must prove that a false statement was published by an individual with reckless disregard for the truth; furthermore, he must prove that the statement is defamatory. — 3. A semicolon, conjunctive adverb, and a comma can combine the independent clauses.

Correct: Two sentences

A public figure in a defamation action must prove that a false statement was published by an individual with reckless disregard for the truth. He also must prove that the statement is defamatory. — 4. Making the two independent clauses into two sentences corrects the run-on.

Correct: One subordinate clause

After a public figure in a defamation action proves that a false statement was published by an individual with reckless disregard for the truth, he also must prove that the statement is defamatory. — 5. Make one of the independent clauses into a subordinate clause.

---

1. *Florida v. Jardines*, 133 S. Ct. 1409, 1418 (2013) (Kagan, J., concurring).
2. You may use conjunctive adverbs to combine clauses and show their relation. See the chart on page 98 for a list of common conjunctive adverbs.

The previous examples have slightly different meanings, depending on how the writer combines the clauses. Varying sentence structure allows the writer to emphasize different words and different parts of the sentence. For instance, the writer emphasizes the end of the sentence in the last example and the beginning of the sentence in the first example. Varying sentence length also can make your writing more interesting and less monotonous. Consider using different sentence forms in your writing to emphasize your best points and liven up your prose.

C. Rule 3: Fix Fragments

Finally, a proper sentence should contain a subject and main verb so that it is not a fragment. In the last example, the subordinate clause could not stand alone as a sentence. Similarly, a sentence that incorrectly uses a verb ending in "—ing" (a participle or gerund) or a verb used with "to" (an infinitive) cannot stand alone as a sentence. To fix fragments, make sure that each sentence expresses a complete thought.

Incorrect: Fragment with subordinate clause
After a public figure in a defamation action proved that a false statement was published by an individual with reckless disregard for the truth

Incorrect: Fragment with "—ing" verb
A public figure in a defamation action proving that a false statement was published by an individual with reckless disregard for the truth

Incorrect: Fragment with infinitive
A public figure in a defamation action to prove that a false statement was published by an individual with reckless disregard for the truth

Correct: Main verb
The public figure in a defamation action proved that a false statement was published by an individual with reckless disregard for the truth.

Some writers use fragments purposefully for emphasis. If you choose to copy this technique, make sure your reader will recognize your writing as artful prose, as Chief Justice Roberts does in this dissent from *Pennsylvania v. Dunlap*:

North Philly, May 4, 2001. Officer Sean Devlin, Narcotics Strike Force, was working the morning shift. Undercover surveillance. The neighborhood? Tough as a three-dollar steak. Devlin knew. Five years on the beat, nine months with the Strike Force. He'd made fifteen, twenty drug busts in the neighborhood. Devlin spotted him: a lone man on the corner. Another approached. Quick exchange of words. Cash handed over; small objects handed back. Each man then quickly on his own way. Devlin knew the guy wasn't buying bus tokens. He radioed a description and Officer Stein picked up the buyer. Sure enough: three bags of crack in the guy's pocket. Head downtown and book him. Just another day at the office.[3]

---

3. 555 U.S. 964, 964-65 (2008) (Roberts, C.J., dissenting from denial of cert.).

2. COMMAS—FIVE RULES THAT COULD SAVE YOU MILLIONS

Commas create frustration among legal writers. A misplaced comma can change the meaning of a sentence and thus, the meaning of a written agreement or opinion. In one contract dispute, a company initially lost $2.13 million dollars[4] because of the second comma in the following statement:

> This agreement shall be effective from the date it is made and shall continue in force for a period of five (5) years from the date it is made, and thereafter for successive five (5) year terms, unless and until terminated by one year prior notice in writing by either party.

Because commas surround the phrase, "and thereafter for successive five (5) year terms," the phrase is nonrestrictive, meaning the clause does not restrict the meaning of the sentence. The sentence can operate without the clause, which means that the initial five-year agreement can be terminated by one year's notice. But without the second comma, the clause about termination would apply only to the successive contracts, creating an initial, firm, five-year deal. This $2 million lesson leads us to the first of five comma rules that will help ensure your prose conveys the intended meaning.

Commas—A Brief Review

1. Use commas to set off nonrestrictive clauses
2. Use the serial comma
3. Use commas after the day and year in dates
4. Use commas to separate elements in locations
5. Use commas around clauses, phrases, and conjunctive adverbs for clarity

---

A. Rule 1: Use Commas to Set Off Nonrestrictive Clauses

Nonrestrictive clauses add nonessential information to a sentence. They typically begin with "which," "when," "who," or "where" and provide information that does not restrict the meaning of the sentence. These phrases or clauses always require commas.

> Police took a drug-sniffing dog to Jardines' front porch, where the dog gave a positive alert for narcotics.[5]

> Here, police officers came to Joelis Jardines' door with a supersensitive instrument, which they deployed to detect things inside that they could not perceive unassisted.[6]

These clauses add important information, but their removal would not cause the sentences to lose their basic meaning.

---

4. *Rogers Cable Commc'ns Inc. v. Bell Aliant*, Telecom Decision CRTC 2006-45, *rev'd*, Telecom Decision CRTC 2007-75.

5. *Jardines*, 133 S. Ct. at 1411.

6. *Id.* at 1418 (Kagan, J., concurring).

In addition, I know that odors coming from my building, when they reach — These clauses add important
these locations, may be strong enough to be detected by a dog.[7] information, but their
removal would not cause
the sentences to lose their
basic meaning.

Restrictive clauses, however, restrict the meaning of the sentence. The sentence would lose its meaning if you took a restrictive clause out of it; therefore, no commas should be used. Restrictive clauses often begin with "that" or "who."

Police received an anonymous tip that the defendant was growing marijuana in his home.

These sentences would
lose their meaning if
you took out the words
following "that" and
"who."

Mail carriers and persons delivering packages and flyers are examples of
individuals who may lawfully approach a front door without intending to
converse.[8]

Determining whether a phrase is restrictive or nonrestrictive can be tricky in some cases. For example, both of the following statements are grammatically correct, but their meanings differ because of the commas.

The team's chocolate Labrador, Franky, alerted its handler to the scent — The name provides additional,
of narcotics. nonessential information.

The team's chocolate Labrador Franky alerted its handler to the scent of — Here, "Franky" identifies the
narcotics. specific dog, which would be
necessary if the team has more
than one chocolate Labrador.

B. Rule 2: Use the Serial Comma

Lawyers like to make lists: lists of elements in a rule, lists of witnesses, lists of reasons for a particular outcome. The serial comma—also known as the Oxford comma—will clearly identify each item in your list and help you avoid a potential misreading. In the following examples, Weaver and Walsh are trained police canine handlers, but their status is clear only when the serial comma is used.

The scent of narcotics was apparent to the drug-sniffing dogs, Weaver — Without the serial comma,
and Walsh. Weaver and Walsh are
identified as dogs.

The scent of narcotics was apparent to the drug-sniffing dogs, Weaver, — With the serial comma,
and Walsh. Weaver and Walsh are correctly
identified as police officers.

C. Rule 3: Use Commas After the Day and Year in Dates

When listing a specific date in a sentence, always use a comma after the day and the year.

---

7. *Id.* at 1425 (Alito, J., dissenting).
8. *Id.*

On January 9, 2013, the Court decided *Missouri v. McNeely*.

The attorneys met on April 8, 2012, to discuss the proposed settlement. — Commas belong after the day and year, even when the date is in the middle of a sentence.

The attorneys met in April 2012 to discuss the proposed settlement. —— But use no commas when using only the month and year.

D. Rule 4: Use Commas to Separate Elements in Locations

Additionally, commas should follow both elements in a location, including a city and state or a city and country. When listing a full address in a sentence, add a comma where you would separate the mailing address with a line.

The pro bono attorney flew to Guantanamo Bay, Cuba, to meet his client. — Commas separate the elements in geographic locations, and they set off locations within a sentence.

The Commission issued its decision from Ottawa, Canada, and found that the French version of the contract controlled.

The Oregon Supreme Court heard arguments on March 14, 2013, at — When listing a mailing address, use commas after the street address, after the city, and after the zip code. 1515 Agate Street, Eugene, Oregon 97403, at the University of Oregon School of Law.

E. Rule 5: Use Commas Around Clauses, Phrases, and Conjunctive Adverbs for Clarity

Clauses, phrases, and conjunctive adverbs at the beginning, middle, and end of sentences require commas for clarity. First, always use a comma to offset an introductory word or words in your sentence. Second, use commas around conjunctive adverbs and other interrupting phrases and clauses in the middle of your sentence. Finally, use a comma to set off a dependent clause at the end of your sentence.

In a decision that drew criticism from veterans groups, Chief Justice — A comma follows the introductory clause at the start of the sentence. Roberts wrote that the First Amendment protects "even hurtful speech on public issues to ensure that we do not stifle public debate."[9]

However, Justice Alito included an emotional appeal in the dissent in — A comma follows "however," and sets off the dependent clause at the **end** of the sentence. *Snyder v. Phelps*, arguing that the church's protest brutalized the family.[10]

Justice Alito, arguing that the church's protest brutalized the family, — Commas surround a dependent clause in the **middle** of the sentence. included an emotional appeal in the dissent.[11]

Justice Alito, however, included an emotional appeal in the dissent in — Commas also surround "however" when the conjunctive adverb is in the **middle** of the sentence and the dependent clause is at the **end** of the sentence. *Snyder v. Phelps*, arguing that the church's protest brutalized the family.[12]

---

9. *See Snyder v. Phelps*, 131 S. Ct. 1207, 1220 (2011).
10. *See id.* at 1222-28 (Alito, J., dissenting).
11. *See id.*
12. *See id.* at 1222.

CONJUNCTIVE ADVERBS		
• Accordingly	• Instead	• Still
• Consequently	• Moreover	• Then
• Furthermore	• Nevertheless	• Therefore
• Hence	• Nonetheless	• Thus
• However	• Similarly	

3. SEMICOLONS

Semicolons are a useful tool when combining independent clauses and drafting complex sentences.[13] They also are helpful when listing complex items in a series. For instance, if you list more than two items and at least one of the items requires a comma, use a semicolon for clarity.

> An adverse possession claim requires the plaintiff to prove that the possession is (1) continuous; (2) hostile or adverse to the interests of the true owner; (3) open and notorious, which provides the true owner with notice of a trespasser; (4) actual, so that the true owner has a cause of action for trespass; and (5) exclusive.

— The third and fourth items in the series contain commas; using semicolons to separate all the items in the list creates clarity.

4. COLONS

In addition, colons are useful for setting off lists, quotations, and explanations in legal writing. A colon should not be used before a list that follows an incomplete clause, like the one above. But colons are required when an independent clause precedes a list or explanation. A colon or a comma may introduce a quotation.

> Chief Justice Roberts wrote the following in conclusion: "Speech is powerful. It can stir people to action, move them to tears of both joy and sorrow, and—as it did here—inflict great pain. On the facts before us, we cannot react to that pain by punishing the speaker. As a Nation we have chosen a different course—to protect even hurtful speech on public issues to ensure that we do not stifle public debate."[14]

— This colon follows an independent clause that sets up a quote. A comma may also be used.

> The court held that only two of the required five adverse possession elements were met: Possession was continuous, and possession was exclusive.

— A colon is required after an independent clause before an explanation. When what follows the colon is an independent clause, you may capitalize the first letter.

---

13. See section 1.B. at the start of this chapter for a refresher on using a semicolon and a conjunctive adverb, such as "however," to combine independent clauses into a more complex sentence.

14. *Snyder*, 131 S. Ct. at 1220.

The court held that only two of the required five adverse possession elements were met: continuous possession and exclusive possession.

— Do not capitalize what follows the colon if it is an incomplete clause.

To establish adverse possession, a plaintiff must prove the following five elements: (1) continuous possession; (2) hostile possession or possession that is adverse to the interests of the true owner; (3) open and notorious possession, which provides the true owner with notice of a trespasser; (4) actual possession, so that the true owner has a cause of action for trespass; and (5) exclusive possession.

— A colon is required after an independent clause before a list.

5. MODIFIERS

Modifying the wrong word or phrase will change the meaning of your sentence. Just like subjects and verbs should be placed close together, modifiers should be placed next to the word or clause they modify. Note how the meaning changes in the following sentences, depending on where the modifier "only" is placed.

Correct
The defendant wanted only to talk to the police.

— This sentence means that the defendant wanted to talk; he did not want to provide a written statement or provide any other type of evidence.

Correct
The defendant wanted to talk only to the police.

— This sentence means that the defendant would talk to the police and no one else.

Incorrect
The defendant only wanted to talk to the police.

— The meaning here is unclear.

In addition, modifiers should modify an existing noun to avoid "dangling."

Incorrect
Finding the evidence flawed, the conviction was reversed.

— The actor in the sentence — the court — is missing, leaving the modifier dangling.

Correct
Finding the evidence flawed, the court reversed the conviction.

— The introductory clause modifies the actor, "court."

Incorrect
The jury weighed the evidence about the defendant and the car containing a large bag of marijuana, which was registered to the defendant's girlfriend.

— This sentence states that the marijuana, not the car, was registered to the defendant's girlfriend.

Correct
The jury weighed the evidence about the defendant and the car, which was registered to the defendant's girlfriend and contained a large bag of marijuana.

— This sentence conveys the facts correctly.

Incorrect

The witness, who testified that she heard Terri McMahon laughing on — It's unclear whether the
the other side of the apartment wall around 11 p.m., said that she was   witness or McMahon was
regularly drunk at night.   drunk.

Correct

The witness, who testified that she heard Terri McMahon laughing on the — This sentence conveys the
other side of the apartment wall around 11 p.m., said that McMahon   correct information.
was regularly drunk at night.

6. PRONOUNS

Pronoun errors create ambiguity and imprecision in your writing. The following four rules will keep the pronouns in your prose clear.

Pronouns—A Brief Review

1. Make pronouns and antecedents match
2. "It's" is a contraction, not a possessive
3. Pronouns should refer to an existing antecedent
4. Who is for subjects; whom is for objects

A. Rule 1: Make Pronouns and Antecedents Match

When a pronoun represents a singular noun or a collective noun, use a
singular pronoun. Common collective nouns that should be represented by
"it" include court, jury, board, company, majority, committee, family, or team.
Similarly, pair plural nouns with a plural pronoun; jurors or corporations
pair with "they." And use "who"—not "that"—when clauses refer to people.

Incorrect

The appellate panel erred when they affirmed the defendant's conviction. — An appellate panel is a
                                                                            collective noun; therefore,
Correct   the correct pronoun is "it."

The appellate panel erred when it affirmed the defendant's conviction.

Correct

The appellate judges erred when they affirmed the defendant's convic- — If using "it" to refer to a
tion.   panel of three judges
                                                                       seems awkward, rewrite
Incorrect   the sentence.

The appellate judges that affirmed the defendant's conviction agreed to — Use "who," not "that" when
rehear the case en banc.   a clause refers to people.

Correct

The appellate judges who affirmed the defendant's conviction agreed to
rehear the case en banc.

B. Rule 2: "It's" Is a Contraction, Not a Possessive

The word "it's" means "it is" and should be used only when you want to use an informal contraction. The word "its" is the possessive of "it" and may be used when paired with a singular or collective noun.

Incorrect
The Supreme Court issued it's decision.

Correct
The Supreme Court issued its decision.

— "Its" denotes the possessive correctly here.

C. Rule 3: Pronouns Should Refer to an Existing Antecedent

Avoid using a pronoun when it refers to an ambiguous idea or a nonexisting noun. Pronouns that often are ambiguous when used in legal writing include "it," "this," "that," "such," and "which." A pronoun should always refer clearly to its antecedent. In the previous sentence, the antecedent for "its" is "pronoun."

Incorrect
Judges become frustrated when attorneys make pronoun errors, so carefully proofread your document to eliminate them.

— It's unclear whether "them" refers to errors or judges.

Correct
Judges become frustrated when attorneys make pronoun errors, so carefully proofread your document to eliminate all errors.

Incorrect
This means that the Court should vacate the conviction.

Correct
This lack of evidence means that the Court should vacate the defendant's conviction.

— Even if the writer thinks that the reasons for vacating the conviction were clearly spelled out within the document, "this" is unclear here. "This" and other ambiguous pronouns should always be followed with an explicit noun.

D. Rule 4: Who Is for Subjects; Whom Is for Objects

Use the pronoun "who" when referring to the subject of a sentence or the subject of a clause, just as you would use "she" or "he." When referring to the object of a sentence, use "whom," "her," or "him."

Here's a tip to figure out whether to use "who" or "whom": Rework the clause to use either "he" or "him." If the clause would use "he," the pronoun is a subject and "who" is the correct pronoun. If the clause would use "him," the pronoun is an object and "whom" is the correct choice. See how this trick works in the examples below.

Incorrect
The judge sealed the records relating to the juvenile, whom was identified only as "TM" in publicly released documents.

Correct

The judge sealed the records relating to the juvenile, who was identified only as "TM" in publicly released documents. — If you rework the clause to use "he" or "him," it reads: He was identified as TM in court documents. Therefore, you can conclude that "who" is the correct pronoun because "he" refers back to a subject, not an object.

Incorrect

The newspaper contained allegedly defamatory statements about Terri J. Spencer, who the union hopes to elect to the vacant County Commission seat.

Correct

The newspaper contained allegedly defamatory statements about Terri J. Spencer, whom the union hopes to elect to the vacant County Commission seat. — Use the tip and rework the clause to use "he" or "him" (even though Terri is female). It reads: The union hopes to elect "him." Thus, you can tell that "whom" is required because it refers to the object of the union's efforts.

7. APOSTROPHES

Apostrophes form possessives. Add an apostrophe and an "s" to singular nouns to form the possessive. For plural nouns, add just the apostrophe. When a singular noun ends in "s," you may follow either option: Add an apostrophe or add an apostrophe and an "s" to form the possessive. For example, both Congress' and Congress's are grammatically correct—U.S. Supreme Court Justices write the possessive both ways. Just make sure that you are consistent in applying one rule throughout your document.

Incorrect

The defendants testimony led to the court's decision to dismiss the contract dispute case. — This sentence is missing the apostrophe to form the possessive.

Correct

The defendant's testimony led to the court's decision to dismiss the contract dispute case. — In this sentence, only one defendant testified.

Correct

The defendants' testimony led to the court's decision to dismiss the contract dispute case. — Here, two defendants testified.

8. HYPHENS

A hyphen combines compound adjectives when they precede a noun. When hyphenated adjectives or nouns can be written as a single word, you should use the nonhyphenated version. For instance, "re-written" should be "rewritten," "semi-colon" should be "semicolon," "by-laws" become "bylaws," and so on. For compound adjectives, where an adjective is composed of more than one word, use a hyphen to combine most words when they collectively modify a noun and come before it. The exception is that words ending in "–ly" should not be hyphenated.

Incorrect

The civil rights scholar filed an amicus brief.

Correct

The civil-rights scholar filed an amicus brief. — The hyphenated adjective collectively modifies scholar.

Correct

The scholar of civil rights filed the amicus brief. — When the adjectives follow the noun they modify, use no hyphen.

Incorrect

The thoroughly-researched brief outlined three arguments to refute the — Do not hyphenate adjectives that end in "-ly." petitioner's rational basis claim.

Correct

The thoroughly researched brief outlined three arguments to refute the — Note the hyphen for the compound modifier, "rational-basis." petitioner's rational-basis claim.

Correct

The sixty-year-old tenant won a three-hundred-dollar judgment in small- — Use multiple hyphens when more than two words modify a noun. claims court.

Correct

The talented, hard-working student accepted the writing award at the — Here, "talented" and "hard-working" describe "student." national conference. As coordinate adjectives, they are separated by a comma.

chapter 19

Grammar Principles for the New Legal Writer

Legal writers face challenges that many other writers do not. Their words are regularly met by doubt, criticism, dissection, and even hostility by judges, supervising attorneys, clients, and opposing counsel. The following four sections provide a review of advanced grammar techniques that the new legal writer should master to write credibly and effectively.

> **Grammar Principles for the New Legal Writer**
>
> 1. Prefer the active voice
> 2. Use parallel construction
> 3. Quote with care
> 4. Use em-dashes and parentheses to shift emphasis

1. PREFER THE ACTIVE VOICE

The active voice is more direct and therefore preferable to the passive voice. In rare instances, however, a writer may use passive voice to alter the emphasis in a sentence or to deflect attention away from the actor.

Active voice
The jury announced its verdict.   — This statement is more direct.

Passive voice
The verdict was announced by the jury.   — Passive voice puts the actor—the jury—in a wordy prepositional phrase.

Passive voice
The verdict was announced.   — This construction is vague because the actor is unknown.

Although writers should prefer the active voice, some writers may choose to use the passive voice when they need to shift the emphasis in a sentence.

For instance, consider why the defense team for JK Corp. would prefer the third example below, where the actor is unnamed.

Active voice
JK Corp. allegedly spilled billions of gallons of oil into the Gulf of Mexico. — This sentence emphasizes the actor, JK Corp.

Passive voice
Billions of gallons of oil were spilled into the Gulf of Mexico allegedly by JK Corp. — This construction emphasizes the oil and identifies the actor.

Passive voice
Billions of gallons of oil were spilled into the Gulf of Mexico. — This construction avoids referencing the actor.

2. USE PARALLEL CONSTRUCTION

Parallel phrasing will add elegance and clarity to your writing. Parallelism means using a similar grammatical form for elements in a pair or series. Use parallel phrasing each time you list two or more elements, which are typically joined by a conjunction, including "and," "but," "not," "or," "yet," "either," or "neither."

After you identify a pair, list, or series that should be parallel, make sure that the elements match. When the elements begin with a verb, each element must begin with a verb in the same tense. When the elements begin with a noun, each element must begin with a noun, although the nouns can be singular or plural or include an adjective.

Create Parallel Phrasing

1. Identify a list, series, or pair of elements, which are typically joined by a conjunction, such as "and," "nor," or "either"
2. Make sure all elements match—all nouns, all adjectives, all independent clauses, all verbs, etc.
3. Verb tenses must match exactly

Correct: Parallel list of nouns
The Lucky Dog Food Corp. sued Baxter Brands for misappropriation of the following trade secrets: (1) cheesy dog chow, (2) cheesy dog treats, and (3) Organix Vegetable Mix. — This phrasing is parallel because it lists three nouns, even though the first element is singular, the second is plural, and the third is a proper noun.

Incorrect
Baxter Brands denied the allegations, arguing that it has no products that are either cheese-flavored or mixed with organic vegetables. — The elements following "either" do not match.

Correct: Parallel pair of verbs

Baxter Brands denied the allegations, arguing that it has no products that —The elements beginning
are either flavored with cheese or mixed with organic vegetables. with "flavored" and "mixed"
match because they are both
past-tense verbs.

Incorrect

Under the Illinois burglary statute, is a vacant lot curtilage when it —The elements following
surrounds an abandoned shed, the former owner had abandoned the "when" do not match.
shed, enclosed by a few bushes, and has been used by neighborhood kids
for Chicago-style softball games?

Correct: Parallel list of independent clauses with matching verbs

Under the Illinois burglary statute, is a vacant lot curtilage when the lot —The elements match because
surrounds an abandoned shed, a few bushes enclose the lot, and neigh- each is an independent clause
borhood kids use the lot for Chicago-style softball games? with a present-tense verb. The
second element in the incorrect
example was removed because
it was repetitive.

3. QUOTE WITH CARE

Careful legal writers ensure that each quotation they use is exact. When legal
writers modify a quote, they use brackets, an ellipsis, or both to mark the
change. A legal writer's credibility depends on quoting sources accurately; the
reader may be misled if a writer alters a quote without proper punctuation.
The following three rules illustrate how to use quotations and punctuate
them correctly.

Quote with Care

1. Use double quotation marks for quotes and single quotation marks for quotes within quotes
2. Commas and periods always go inside quotation marks
3. Use brackets, an ellipsis, or both to show a change in a
   quote
4. For essential, longer quotes, indent the quote as a text
   block

A. Use Double Quotation Marks for Quotes

Quotations should be surrounded by double quotation marks. Single quotation marks denote a quote within a quote.

Incorrect

Chief Justice Roberts wrote, 'Our cases make clear that students do not —All three quote marks are
"shed their constitutional rights to freedom of speech or expression at the incorrect here.
schoolhouse gate."[1]

---

1. *Morse v. Frederick*, 551 U.S. 393, 396 (2007) (quoting *Tinker v. Des Moines Indep. Cmty. Sch.
Dist.*, 393 U.S. 503 (1969)).

Correct

Chief Justice Roberts wrote, "Our cases make clear that students do not 'shed their constitutional rights to freedom of speech or expression at the schoolhouse gate.'" — The quote is surrounded by double quotation marks. Roberts' quote of *Tinker* is surrounded by single quotation marks; hence, the closing quote includes the single and double quotation marks.

B. Commas and Periods Always Go Inside Quotation Marks

Commas and periods always belong inside quotations, regardless of their placement in the original quote. Place larger punctuation marks—colons, semicolons, exclamation points, and question marks—inside quotation marks only when they are part of the original quote.

Incorrect

The court noted that "[t]he *way* Frederick was going to fulfill his ambition of appearing on television was by unfurling a pro-drug banner at a school event;" however, Frederick's motive was unclear.[2] — The semicolon is not part of the original text and belongs after the quotation mark.

Correct

"But that is a description of Frederick's *motive* for displaying the banner;" however, Frederick did not provide any interpretation of the text.[3] — The semicolon is in the original quote, so it is placed inside the quotation marks.

C. Use Brackets, an Ellipsis, or Both to Show a Change to a Quote

Legal writers denote any alteration of a quote with brackets, an ellipsis, or both. The following examples show how to alter the beginning, middle, and end of a quote.

Original quote

"Our cases make clear that students do not 'shed their constitutional rights to freedom of speech or expression at the schoolhouse gate.'"

Brackets mark a change at the quote's beginning

Chief Justice Roberts wrote, "[o]ur cases make clear that students do not 'shed their constitutional rights to freedom of speech or expression at the schoolhouse gate.'" — A bracket—not an ellipsis—marks the change in capitalization at the beginning of a quote.

Brackets mark a change to a word

Chief Justice Roberts wrote that previous cases "ma[de] clear that students do not 'shed their constitutional rights to freedom of speech or expression at the schoolhouse gate.'" — A bracket shows that the writer changed the verb tense to "made."

An ellipsis marks an omission in the middle

Chief Justice Roberts wrote, "[o]ur cases make clear that students do not 'shed their constitutional rights . . . at the schoolhouse gate.'" — An ellipsis—consisting of three spaced periods—marks an omission in the middle of a quote.

---

2. *Id.* at 402.
3. *Id.*

An ellipsis marks an omission at the end

Chief Justice Roberts wrote, "[o]ur cases make clear that students do not 'shed their constitutional rights to freedom of speech or expression....'" — Here, the ellipsis consists of three spaced periods plus the period to end the sentence. It marks an omission of the end of a quote.

D. For Essential, Longer Quotes, Indent the Quote as a Text Block

Legal writers should use quotes sparingly. Quotes with multiple brackets and ellipses may appear unreadable. Pages that use more quotes than original text appear uninspired. When a page is full of quotes, consider paraphrasing to make your point more directly. On the rare occasion that you need to use a quote of 50 or more words, set it off without quotation marks, indents on the right and left, and single-spacing.[4]

4. USE EM-DASHES AND PARENTHESES TO SHIFT EMPHASIS

Legal writers may set off information within a sentence using three tools: em-dashes, commas, and parentheses. Em-dashes provide the most emphasis to the information contained within, while parentheses provide the least. Use them in moderation and for variation in your writing.

Two em-dashes

The couple provided extensive evidence—photos, letters, and testimony— to successfully establish the validity of their marriage at the immigration hearing. — Two em-dashes call attention to the information in the middle of the sentence.

One em-dash

At the immigration hearing, the couple successfully established the validity of their marriage by providing extensive evidence—photos, letters, and testimony. — One em-dash may set off information at the beginning or end of the sentence. As a matter of style, the em-dash has no spaces around it.

Parentheses

At the immigration hearing, the couple successfully established the validity of their marriage by providing extensive evidence (photos, letters, and testimony). — Parentheses show the information contained within is of secondary importance.

Parentheses

Despite the property's vacancy, the court found that because the claimant kept the property locked and advertised for a new tenant, she demonstrated continuous possession. *Merrill v. Hooper*, 13 P.2d 786, 787-88 (Cal. Ct. App. 1932); *see also Montgomery & Mullen Lumber Co. v. Quimby*, 128 P. 402, 404 (Cal. 1912) (holding that temporary periods of vacancy between tenancies will not destroy the claimant's continuous possession). — Legal writers often use parentheses to provide additional information about a case.

---

4. *Bluebook* Rules B12.2 and 5.1.

Despite the property's vacancy, the court found that because the claimant kept the property locked and advertised for a new tenant, she demonstrated continuous possession. *Montgomery & Mullen Lumber Co. v. Quimby*, 128 P. 402, 404 (Cal. 1912) ("Constant occupancy and use is not always required.").

— A parenthetical about a case may include a clause or a full sentence. Here, the quoted full sentence also has a period within the parentheses.

chapter 20

Plain Language

Good writing is good writing. Whether writing appears in a legal brief, a novel, or a newspaper, the same principles of good writing apply. Legal writers frequently confront complex subjects, and they should strive to describe and analyze those subjects in plain, simple prose to convey their message most effectively. The following principles should be your guide as you write, rewrite, and revise your documents.

> **The Handbook's Guiding Principles of Plain Language**
>
> 1. Make every word count
>   - Cut out the unnecessary, the redundant, and the unhelpful
> 2. Use vigorous English
>   - Use forceful, direct, and concise language, avoiding weak and negative wording
> 3. Use short words, short sentences, and short paragraphs

1. MAKE EVERY WORD COUNT

Legal writers often don't think through an issue fully until they complete a first draft. The writing process helps them organize their thoughts and analysis, so a first draft might not get to the point as quickly as it should. Thus, legal writers should rewrite and revise until every word in the document counts.

Every word in your document should advance your reader's understanding of your case. If a word, phrase, or sentence fails to add to your reader's understanding, cut it. If a word, phrase, or sentence repeats an idea that you have already conveyed, cut it. And if a word, phrase, or sentence fails to help your reader better understand your cause, cut it. By creating a lean document, your writing will be more direct and effective.

A. Cut Out the Unnecessary

First, cut out unnecessary words by focusing on using strong nouns and active verbs. Avoid using too many adjectives and adverbs, which are crutches for a weak writer. Avoid intensifiers, including "clearly," "certainly," and "obviously," unless you have the rare case where the issues are clear, certain, or obvious. And avoid qualifiers, such as "really," "very," and "rather," which undermine your point.

Weak wording

Clearly, Jones was rather enthusiastic about the news that a settlement was reached in the lawsuit.

Strong wording

Jones was enthused because the lawsuit settled.

The revision cuts out the intensifier "clearly" and the qualifier "rather." It also transforms the adjective "enthusiastic" and the noun "settlement" into strong verbs.

Second, cut out phrases that detract from your point because they are timid or serve as mere warm-ups to your main point. These wordy warm-ups often begin with "there is" or the undefined pronoun "it." The following list provides only a sample of the many wordy warm-ups that you should avoid using in legal writing. In most cases, the writer can eliminate the wordy warm-up to create a more direct sentence.

Weak wording

It is significant to note that the ruling below is inconsistent with this Court's decision in *Stanton*.

Strong wording

The ruling below is inconsistent with this Court's decision in *Stanton*.

Weak wording

There is no evidence showing that Kern Corp. breached the contract.

Strong wording

No evidence shows that Kern Corp. breached the contract.

WORDY WARM-UPS	
• Arguably	• It is to be noted
• As noted above	• It might be said that
• In light of the fact that	• It must be recognized that
• In order to	• It seems
• It could be argued that	• It seems likely that
• It is	• It should also be noted
• It is clear	• It would appear that
• It is crucial to consider	• It would be helpful to consider
• It is important to note that	• The fact that
• It is worth considering	• There are/is/was/were
• It is generally recognized that	• There is little doubt that
• It is interesting to consider	• With regard/respect to

B. Cut Out the Redundant

Because legal writers often use the first draft to think through their analysis, repetition of words, phrases, and ideas is common. As you revise your document, read it aloud to identify needless repetition. Do you have two consecutive paragraphs that explain the same anchor or detail the same argument? If yes, revise your document to make each point only once. In addition, look out for repetitious phrases. Writers sometimes repeat themselves in a single phrase: "First and foremost," "never before," and "past history" use two or three words when one will do. Cutting out unnecessary repetition will make your writing more concise, direct, and effective.

A writer should repeat key legal terms, however, when the repetition is necessary for clarity and consistency. For instance, if a letter to a client details a proposed settlement, a lawyer could confuse the client if she described the settlement in other terms, such as "agreement," "understanding," or "resolution," throughout the letter. Similarly, a writer should describe key aspects of the case in consistent terms. If referring to a party as "Plaintiff," the writer should use "Plaintiff" for each reference. And when describing an anchor or key fact, the writer should use the same terms to make sure that the reader can easily identify connections throughout the document. Using different words to describe the same term is called "elegant variation"—a tactic that is impractical in legal writing.

In addition, some repetition may enhance a writer's style. The repetition of sounds through alliteration (repeated consonants) or assonance (repeated vowels) can lend elegance. Parallel phrasing also can lend sophistication. But legal writers should use these techniques sparingly. Forcing style can make a writer's prose awkward and ostentatious. Good legal writers focus on conveying their points directly using a style that comes naturally.

> Respondents and other members of their church have strong opinions on certain moral, religious, and political issues, and the First Amendment ensures that they have almost limitless opportunities to express their views. They may write and distribute books, articles, and other texts; they may create and disseminate video and audio recordings; they may circulate petitions; they may speak to individuals and groups in public forums and in any private venue that wishes to accommodate them; they may picket peacefully in countless locations; they may appear on television and speak on the radio; they may post messages on the Internet and send out e-mails. And they may express their views in terms that are "uninhibited," "vehement," and "caustic." *N.Y. Times Co. v. Sullivan*, 376 U.S. 254, 270 (1964).[1]

— Justice Alito's repetition of parallel phrases lends sophistication to this paragraph from a dissent.

C. Cut Out the Unhelpful

Early drafts of a legal document might also be weak because they use placeholders that do not add to a reader's understanding of a case. Placeholders

---

1. *Snyder v. Phelps*, 131 S. Ct. 1207, 1222 (2011) (Alito, J., dissenting).

detract from an otherwise effective document because they take up space and do not advance the writer's cause. For instance, the following topic sentences for Explanation paragraphs fail to advance the reader's understanding of the relevant law. Writers should delete unhelpful sentences and replace them with sentences that add to the reader's understanding of the relevant law and analysis.

Weak wording

Michigan courts have decided many adverse possession cases.

— Instead of providing an unhelpful introduction to case law, the writer should summarize an anchor or rule that advances a reader's understanding of the relevant law.

Weak wording

Whether the claimant's possession is open and notorious is a major factor in determining adverse possession.

— This sentence summarizes a relevant anchor without any context.

Strong wording

An individual's possession must be open and notorious to provide notice to the true owner, or the adverse possession claim fails.

— This sentence provides the holding relative to the "open and notorious" anchor to provide context.

2. USE VIGOROUS ENGLISH

Legal writing should be forceful, direct, and concise. Legal writers should avoid weak, negative, and passive wording. They should choose strong nouns and active verbs and keep subjects and verbs close together. Legal writers should also write with authority, avoiding qualifying language. Note the authoritative language that Justice Ginsburg employs in a brief for the ACLU, written 17 years before she joined the Court:

> The Oklahoma legislation in question is a curiosity, apparently the only law of its kind left in the nation. Similarly, the ruling below is an anomaly. It is inconsistent with this Court's decision in *Stanton v. Stanton*, 421 U.S. 7 (1975), and out of step with an array of authority in lower courts, federal and state, decisions that have made museum pieces of male/female age of majority differentials.

— Ginsburg demonstrates her authority on the subject through knowledge of case law.

* * *

> The decision below apart, the sole authority for differential treatment of the sexes in relation to alcoholic beverage association is *Goesaert v. Cleary*, 335 U.S. 464 (1948). Widely criticized in commentary, in square conflict with decisions of this Court in the current decade and with national equal employment opportunity policy, and politely discarded by the nation's lower courts, *Goesaert* is a decision overdue for formal burial.

— Ginsburg uses strong language to urge the court to overturn *Goesaert*.

* * *

Just as drinking preferences and proclivities associated with a particular —Ginsburg continues her
ethnic group or social class would be perceived as an unfair and insub- constitutional attack on the
stantial basis for a beverage sale or service prohibition directed to that Oklahoma statute.
group or class, so a gender-based classification should be recognized
as an inappropriate, invidious means to the legislative end of rational
regulation in the public interest.[2]

You can start to energize your prose by choosing positive wording and
by avoiding grouping multiple negative words together. Any time you use
the word "not" with an adjective, consider that the English language probably provides one word for you to use instead—and that word might be more
precise.

Negative Wording	→	Positive Wording
Not current	→	Outdated or Obsolete
Not correct	→	Incorrect
Not on time	→	Late
Not precise	→	Imprecise
Not significant	→	Insignificant

In addition, using more than one negative in a sentence confuses meaning. Consider the following revision from a negative to a positive statement:

Negative statement
The contract stated, however, that the provision would not become null
and void, unless one party provides notice that the other party has not
acted reasonably.

Positive statement
The contract stated that the provision is void when one party provides notice that the other party acted unreasonably.

Finally, legal writers can energize their prose by making sure they do not
turn active verbs into nouns called "nominalizations." Nominalizations not
only add unnecessary words to your document, but they also make your writing less direct by burying the action in a sentence. The following list shows
how to transform some common nominalizations into active verbs. Note that
nominalizations often end in "—ing," "—ion," or "—ment."

Nominalization	→	Active Verb
Advancement	→	Advance
Agreement	→	Agree
Assumption	→	Assumed
Commencement	→	Commence (or begin, start)
Consideration	→	Consider

---

2. Brief for ACLU as Amici Curiae Supporting Appellants, *Craig v. Boren*, 429 U.S. 190
(1976) (No. 75-628), 1976 WL 181333 at *10-11, 24.

Nominalization	→	Active Verb
Decision	→	Decide
Dependence	→	Depend
Determination	→	Determine
Emphasis	→	Emphasize
Emphasizing	→	Emphasize
Failure	→	Fail
Filed a motion	→	Moved
Improvement	→	Improve
Investigation	→	Investigate
Modification	→	Modify
Settlement	→	Settle
Violation	→	Violate

Statement with nominalizations

The parties' contract contained provisions requiring good-faith dealings and allowing the wronged party to effect a termination upon the violation of the good-faith provision.

Revised statement

The parties' contract provided that the parties must deal in good faith or the wronged party may terminate the agreement.

3. USE SHORT WORDS, SHORT SENTENCES, AND SHORT PARAGRAPHS

No matter how complicated the topic or dense the issue, lawyers convey their point best when they write in plain, simple prose. Start by using simple words. Consider this timeless advice from *The Elements of Style* to be a guiding principle: "Avoid fancy words. Avoid the elaborate, the pretentious, the coy, and the cute. Do not be tempted by a twenty-dollar word when there is a ten-center handy, ready and able."[3] The ten-centers will endear you to busy readers more than the vague, obscure, and foreign.

Big words abound in the law, and using them may be required on occasion. But make sure that each word you choose is the best word to convey your meaning—not the most impressive choice out of a thesaurus search. A "good test," according to Justice Scalia, is "if you used the word at a cocktail party, would people look at you funny? You talk about *the instant case* or *the instant problem*. That's ridiculous. It's legalese. *This case* would do very well."[4]

---

3. William Strunk, Jr., & E.B. White, *The Elements of Style*, 76-77 (3d ed. 1979).

4. Bryan A. Garner, ed., *The Scribes Journal of Legal Writing*, "Interviews with Supreme Court Justices," 58 (2010), available at http://legaltimes.typepad.com/files/garner-transcripts-1.pdf.

The same principle holds true for foreign words. Translate Latin phrases for clarity—so *inter alia* becomes "among others," *sui generis* becomes "one of a kind" or "unique," and so on. Reserve Latin and legal jargon for the rare legal term of art, including *de novo* and *mens rea*. Additionally, choose precise replacements for clichés, which, by definition, have lost their original meaning. Instead of "slippery slope" or "tip of the iceberg," write what you mean.

Judges have become increasingly impatient with wordy, legalese-ridden filings. U.S. District Judge Steven D. Merryday, for example, denied one party's request to increase the page limit for a motion and instead edited the opening paragraph from 168 words to a lean 42 words.[5] Judge Merryday chastised the party's lawyer in an exaggeratingly wordy rebuke: "A review of the proposed twenty-nine-page motion's commencement confirms that a modicum of informed editorial revision easily reduces the motion to twenty-five pages without a reduction in substance."[6] Judge Merryday, no doubt, knew he could trim more than half the words from his own sentence without a loss of meaning: Informed editing easily reduces the 29-page motion to 25 without reducing its substance.

Lawyers do not safeguard an exalted profession by using words that only other lawyers can understand; instead, they isolate themselves from clients, juries, and the public. Chief Justice Roberts, who writes in an approachable style, says that he admires Justice Robert H. Jackson's writing for its plain style:

> You read one of his opinions, and it makes an impression on you—not just the law, but the felicity of expression and the breadth of analogy and reference. And at the same time, it has a very plainspoken approach to it. You don't have to be a lawyer to read one of Justice Jackson's opinions and understand exactly what he's saying. And that's very valuable.[7]

In addition to short words, good legal writers know the value of a short sentence. Concise, punchy sentences add interest to your prose. They emphasize your point. Although compound sentences are common in legal writing, declarative statements express meaning most directly. Varying sentence length is a hallmark of good legal writing.

Good legal writers also know the value of short paragraphs. No reader wants to encounter a wall of text upon turning the page. Help maintain your reader's interest by breaking long blocks of text into shorter paragraphs. Keep in mind that every paragraph should have a clear focus, preferably identified

---

5. Joseph Kimble, *Michigan Bar Journal*, "A Federal Judge Takes On Legalese," 1 (Jan. 2013), available at http://www.michbar.org/journal/pdf/pdf4article2139.pdf.

6. *Belli v. Hedden Enters.*, No. 8:12-cv-01001 (M.D. Fla., filed Aug. 7, 2012).

7. Bryan A. Garner, ed., *The Scribes Journal of Legal Writing*, "Interviews with Supreme Court Justices," 9 (2010), available at http://legaltimes.typepad.com/files/garner-transcripts-1.pdf.

in a topic sentence. In addition, help your reader understand the connection between paragraphs by using transitions, such as "first," "second," and "third" or "additionally," "moreover," and "however." Consider Justice Clarence Thomas' advice: "the genius is having a ten-dollar idea in a five-cent sentence, not having a five-cent idea in a ten-dollar sentence."[8]

> Although the elements of the IIED tort are difficult to meet, respondents long ago abandoned any effort to show that those tough standards were not satisfied here. On appeal, they chose not to contest the sufficiency of the evidence. They did not dispute that Mr. Snyder suffered "'wounds that are truly severe and incapable of healing themselves.'" Nor did they dispute that their speech was "'so outrageous in character, and so extreme in degree, as to go beyond all possible bounds of decency, and to be regarded as atrocious, and utterly intolerable in a civilized community.'" Instead, they maintained that the First Amendment gave them a license to engage in such conduct. They are wrong.[9]

— Justice Alito ends the paragraph with a zinger.

---

8. Bryan A. Garner, ed., *The Scribes Journal of Legal Writing*, "Interviews with Supreme Court Justices," 100 (2010), available at http://legaltimes.typepad.com/files/garner-transcripts-1.pdf.

9. *Snyder*, 131 S. Ct. at 1222 (Alito, J., dissenting) (citations omitted).

chapter 21

Confused, Misused, and Misspelled Words

Legal writers strive to convey their meaning with precision. For that reason, the following list of commonly confused, misused, and misspelled words may be helpful in guiding you to choose the precise word you need. Additionally, consider consulting a standard dictionary, a legal dictionary, a legal style manual—or all three—to ensure that the word you choose has the precise meaning you intend. The sources may vary in their definitions. For instance, "since" is defined as referring to a temporal relationship. For that reason, some writers always choose "because" to denote a causal relationship. However, some authorities[1] state that "since" may express a causal relationship but one that is milder than a relationship described with "because." Because nuance is critical in legal writing, referring to dictionaries and related authorities when choosing the precise word you want will be helpful.

---

1. *See, e.g., Garner's Usage Tip of the Day: since,* http://www.lawprose.org/blog/?p=602.

Commonly Confused, Misused, and Misspelled Words	
Adverse / Averse Unfavorable / Opposed	**Council / Counsel** An assembly / To advise
Affect / Effect Verb / Noun	**Fewer / Less** Use with multiple items / Use with single item
Allude / Elude Refer indirectly / Escape	**Imply / Infer** Suggest / Deduce
Among / Between Use with three things / Use with two	**Its / It's** Possessive / Contraction
Assure / Ensure / Insure Make promises / Make certain / Indemnify	**Prescribe / Proscribe** Dictate / Prohibit
Because / Since Generally denotes a causal relationship / denotes a temporal relationship	**Principal / Principle** Primary (adj.) / A truth (noun)
Can / May Expresses ability / Expresses permission	**Their / There / They're** Possessive / Used to show existence / Contraction
Complement / Compliment Something that completes / To praise	**Tortious / Tortuous / Torturous** Relating to a tort / Relating to torture / Twisting and turning
Compose / Comprise The parts compose the whole / The whole comprises the parts	**Trail / Trial** A common misspelling / A court proceeding
Continual / Continuous Intermittent / Unceasing	**Your / You're** Possessive / Contraction

chapter 22

Writing Style

Before finishing your legal document, make sure that you use a consistent style throughout. Review your use of capitalization, first person, fonts, numbers, and references to parties and people.

Capitalization

- ☑ Capitalize "court" only when referring to the U.S. Supreme Court and the court where you file your document. If you file a brief in the U.S. Court of Appeals for the First Circuit, refer to "this Court" for opinions issued by the First Circuit.
- ☑ Capitalize "Plaintiff" and "Defendant" only when referring to the parties in your case. Refer to the parties using the article "the" if your prose seems stilted.
- ☑ Capitalize proper nouns; omit needless capitalization of other terms.

First Person

- ☑ Avoid using the first person ("I," "we," "our,") in any formal legal document (e.g., appellate briefs and motions to dismiss, not letters and emails).
- ☑ Judges may use the first person; appellate courts often use "we" in their opinions.
- ☑ When speaking, avoid using first person. Instead of "I believe the evidence shows," state "the evidence shows," which is more direct.

Fonts

- ☑ Be consistent in using bold, italicized, and underlined fonts for headings and citations.
- ☑ Avoid using bold, italicized, or underlined fonts for emphasis—use strong words instead.

Numbers

- ☑ Spell out numbers zero to ten or when the number begins a sentence.
- ☑ Use numerals for money, percentages, and measurements (e.g., $7 million, 6 percent, and 10 feet).

☑ Do not waste space by repeating numbers—"$2 million" should not be written as $2 million ($2,000,000).

☑ Write times as 9 p.m. or 10:30 a.m.

References to Parties and People

☑ If using courtesy titles to refer to a party or person, use the full name on first reference and the courtesy title with the surname for the second. So, for example, list "Marjory Callahan" on the first reference and "Ms. Callahan" for every subsequent reference. Using only surnames for the second and subsequent references is also proper.

☑ Use parentheses to indicate an abbreviation or acronym only when shortening a name to an abbreviation or acronym that is not obvious. *James Binkler ("Binkler")* wastes space. But *Maryland Center for Strategic Planning ("MCSP")* would be helpful for readers unfamiliar with the acronym.

As with any skill, writing takes practice. Drafting an effective legal document requires sound analytical thinking, organization, rewriting, and revision. To continue to improve your writing skills, practice writing a variety of documents and practice editing your writing and the writing of others. Also, read examples of good writing—from law or literature. And read about good writing. The following list includes our favorite books on good writing.

- Bryan A. Garner, *The Elements of Legal Style* (2d ed., Oxford Univ. Press 2002).
- Anne Lamott, *Bird by Bird* (Anchor 1995).
- William Strunk, Jr., & E.B. White, *The Elements of Style* (3d ed., MacMillan 1979).
- John R. Trimble, *Writing with Style* (Prentice Hall 1975).
- Richard C. Wydick, *Plain English for Lawyers* (5th ed., Carolina Acad. Press 2005).

part V

Persuasive Writing

chapter 23

Constructing CREAC in Persuasive Documents

A lawyer's job is to persuade. When a client comes to a lawyer with a problem, the first step is to analyze the problem and predict the most likely outcome. Then, the fun part begins. A lawyer needs to plan a winning strategy for solving the client's problem. That strategy often includes drafting persuasive documents and arguing in court. The lawyer hopes that these written and oral arguments will convince the court that the client should prevail.

Parts V and VI of the *Handbook* introduce you to the types of persuasive documents that lawyers write, explaining step-by-step how to write a trial motion and an appellate brief. In addition, Chapter 37 in Part VII guides you as you prepare for your first oral argument—and the many arguments that come after it.

In your legal career, you may regularly draft various types of persuasive documents. To initiate a lawsuit, a lawyer files a complaint, which is called a petition in some state courts. Opposing counsel may file an answer or motion in response to the complaint, including a motion to dismiss. During discovery, either party may file a motion to compel or motion for protective order. Before trial, one or both of the parties may file a motion for summary judgment. During and after trial, a party may file a motion for a directed verdict or a new trial. Any time a party files a motion, the party opposing the motion may file a response, and the party filing the motion typically gets the final word by filing a reply to the response.

The party that loses in the trial court may appeal and file an appellate brief, and the opposing party files a brief in response. A party that loses in a federal appellate court or state supreme court and wants to appeal to the U.S. Supreme Court will file a Petition for Writ of Certiorari, and the opposing party will file a Brief in Opposition. If the Court grants certiorari, both the petitioner and respondent will file extensive briefs on the merits of the case.

This far-from-exhaustive list of persuasive documents might seem overwhelming. But rest assured that for each of these documents, you will use many of the techniques, including the CREAC organization, that you already know. You will also use new persuasive techniques to make the best case you can for your client.

Persuasive documents will follow the same general CREAC framework as objective documents, even though you will write them with a different purpose in mind. The major difference is that for each CREAC part, the writer attempts to advance the client's case and achieve a particular outcome, rather than predict the most likely result.

chapter 24

Writing a Persuasive Conclusion

Every persuasive document will contain an Argument section that is logically organized according to the CREAC framework. The Argument section, thus, always begins with a Conclusion, which gives you an early opportunity to persuade the court that it should grant the relief that you seek. The Conclusion should ask the court for a particular outcome and provide a reason. Many writers incorporate references to legally significant facts and the controlling law when giving the reason in the Conclusion.

> **Writing a Persuasive Conclusion**
> 1. Identify the requested relief and the issue
> 2. State your Conclusion and give a reason
> 3. Develop a theme
> 4. Draft your point headings

1. STEP ONE: IDENTIFY THE REQUESTED RELIEF AND THE ISSUE

When tackling a new persuasive writing assignment, identify the relief you are seeking as a preliminary step. For trial court documents, such as a motion to dismiss or motion for summary judgment, the writer will ask the court to grant or deny the motion. For appellate filings, the writer will ask the court to reverse or affirm the lower court's decision. A typical Conclusion in a persuasive trial court document could start like this: "The Court should grant the Motion to Dismiss because _____." Similarly, the Argument section of an appellate brief could begin: "The Court should affirm the decision below because _____."

Next, identify the legal issue or issues. Each major legal issue should have its own CREAC, so try to determine whether your document should be organized around one issue or multiple issues. A simple motion to dismiss might turn on a single issue, while a more complicated motion for summary judgment or appellate brief would likely address multiple distinct issues.

Take care to frame your issue in specific legal terms, which will require an understanding of the relevant facts and underlying law. For instance, suppose your client asks you whether he has to honor an agreement to sell his classic Volkswagen Beetle to a neighbor. Your client put a "For Sale" sign on the car with a very low price to play a practical joke on the neighbor, but the neighbor said he accepted the offer and has sued for specific performance of the contract.

Once you gather facts about the case and research the law, you may determine that the precise legal issue is whether the client made a binding offer to sell the car. Because the case turns on whether an offer was made, you should frame your Conclusion around this specific issue—rather than the larger issue of the contract's validity. If the neighbor's acceptance of the offer is also in dispute, that could be an issue for a second CREAC. An introductory roadmap paragraph addressing the validity of the contract could introduce the two issues.

2. STEP TWO: STATE YOUR CONCLUSION AND GIVE A REASON

Every Argument section should begin with a Conclusion. Simple issues can be summarized within a single Conclusion sentence, while more complicated issues might deserve a full paragraph or more. The first step in developing your Conclusion is to identify your issue. A persuasive Conclusion should do more than summarize what the case is about. It should also frame the issue in a way that favors the writer's position and provide a convincing reason in support.

For a simple issue, the persuasive Conclusion can summarize the issue, the requested relief, and a reason in support in a single sentence. The reason in support should typically reference key facts, the anchor or rule that justifies the relief that you seek, or both.

Suppose your supervising attorney suggests filing a motion to dismiss in the example above regarding the VW Beetle. You could draft your Conclusion using the following steps:

- **Relief Sought:** Grant the Motion to Dismiss the complaint for specific performance
- **Issue:** Whether the client made a valid offer to sell his car
- **Conclusion:** The Court should grant Defendant's Motion to Dismiss because Defendant never made a binding offer to sell his car and the contract is therefore unenforceable.

In addition to stating the relief sought, Conclusions often reference the controlling law, legally significant facts, or both when providing a reason. Consider the following examples:

Jackson's Motion to Dismiss should be granted because the Complaint does not contain sufficient factual allegations to state a claim that is plausible on its face for any of the asserted causes of action.

> —This Conclusion references the relief sought and a rule in support.

Tom Chapman's burglary conviction should be upheld because the picket fence enclosing most of the victim's compound qualifies the yard as curtilage.

> —This Conclusion references the relief sought and specific facts relating to an applicable anchor in support.

The Court should grant the Tribune's Motion for More Definite Statement because the Complaint fails to state the defamation claim with the required specificity and makes no reference to any false statements allegedly made by the Tribune.

> —This Conclusion references the relief sought as well as a rule and facts in support.

More complicated issues merit a more extensive Conclusion. Some Conclusions use a paragraph or more to introduce the reader to the issues, the legally significant facts, the underlying law, and the arguments to come. Chief Justice Roberts' brief, filed in 2002 before he joined the Court, in *Godfrey v. John Doe I* includes an Introduction that begins with this type of Conclusion paragraph.

The Alaska Sex Offender Registration Act ("ASORA") was enacted to protect the public and to assist law enforcement in investigating future crimes. It requires state law enforcement entities to gather truthful information about sex offenders and to make certain of that information available to the public. The State has chosen to make such information available on the Internet. Like all other courts to have considered sex offender registration laws, the Ninth Circuit concluded that the legislature acted with non-punitive intent when it passed the ASORA. The court of appeals erroneously departed from the overwhelming majority of courts, however, in holding that the ASORA was nonetheless so punitive in effect that it violated the Ex Post Facto Clause.[1]

> —First, this Conclusion introduces the relevant law.
>
> —Then, it summarizes the arguments to come using the significant facts and underlying law.
>
> —Last, it refers to the relief sought.

3. STEP THREE: DEVELOP A THEME

A theme in a persuasive document allows you to connect your most persuasive arguments to each other and to the outcome that you seek. The following example starts the Argument section of the Respondent's brief in *Florida v. Jardines*. The U.S. Supreme Court case concerns whether police violated the Fourth Amendment when they took a trained drug-detection dog to the door

---

1. Brief for Petitioners at 2, *Godfrey v. John Doe I*, 536 U.S. 92 (2002) (No. 01-729), 2002 WL 1275055.

of a suspected marijuana grow house. The Argument section starts by introducing the reader to the theme developed throughout the brief by presenting
the party's strongest points and a roadmap of the arguments to come.

> The issue in this case goes to the very heart of the rights secured to an
> individual by the Fourth Amendment. A dog sniff at the front door of
> a home by a narcotics detection dog is a Fourth Amendment search
> requiring a warrant based upon probable cause for two reasons. First, a
> homeowner's reasonable expectation of privacy is violated where a police
> officer uses a narcotics detection dog to reveal any details within the
> interior of a home that could not be discovered by the officer's ordinary
> powers of perception without a physical intrusion into the home. Second,
> and aside from the officer's use of a narcotics detection dog to reveal
> details inside the home, the actions of a police officer in taking a narcot-
> ics dog to the front door of a home also constitute a Fourth Amendment
> search. This is so because the officer's entry into the curtilage of the home
> with a narcotics detection dog is a common law trespass upon a consti-
> tutionally protected area in order to conduct a search for evidence, and
> also because that entry violates the homeowner's reasonable expectation
> of privacy.[2]

— The Respondent's brief establishes the theme that a dog sniff is a threat to privacy and should require a warrant.

As you begin drafting your Conclusion and the rest of the CREAC,
consider how you can develop and incorporate a compelling theme. A well-
developed theme will keep your writing consistent and focused, and it will
make your arguments more persuasive.

4. STEP FOUR: DRAFT YOUR POINT HEADINGS

Most persuasive documents also highlight a version of your Conclusion in
headings and subheadings. These statements—called point headings—are often bolded, underlined, or capitalized to stand out on the page. A simple motion might have a single point heading at the start, while a more complicated
motion or appellate brief might have multiple point headings and subheadings, for each CREAC or major argument in the document.

Like a Conclusion, each point heading typically identifies the relief you
seek, the anchor or rule that justifies that relief, and key facts. Point headings should serve as an outline of the arguments in your document. Appellate briefs list each point heading and subheading in a table of contents, so a
reader can easily scan the major points.

One tricky part is that your point headings must be readable. In general,
they should not take up more than three or four lines on the page. You might
not be able to fit in a reference to the relief you seek, the anchor or rule that

---

2. Brief for Respondent at 14-15, *Florida v. Jardines*, 133 S. Ct. 1409 (2013) (No. 11-564),
2012 WL 2486026.

justifies that relief, *and* key facts. Instead, try to maintain a balance between providing a comprehensive summary of your argument and presenting a statement that is readable.

Keeping your point headings at a readable length will also make them more persuasive. Short, punchy sentences are powerful. Readers who encounter overly complex point headings tend to skip over them. For persuasive documents, you want to take advantage of every opportunity you have to make your best case, and point headings provide an excellent platform to do so.

The example below includes the point headings and subheadings in the State's brief in *Florida v. Jardines*, the Fourth Amendment case regarding the dog sniff. Note that each heading is authoritative, direct, and concise.

Argument

I. A Dog Sniff at the Base of a House's Front Door Is Not a Fourth Amendment Search Requiring Probable Cause. — This point heading emphasizes the controlling law and key facts.

II. A Dog Sniff Does Not Become an Unlawful Fourth Amendment Search Just Because It Occurs Outside a House. — This point heading reinforces the theme—the noninvasive nature of a dog sniff.

   A. The Sniff of a Detector Dog Outside Along the Ordinary Path to the Front Door Did Not Violate the Sanctity of Jardines' Grow House. — This subheading emphasizes key, compelling facts.

   B. *Kyllo*'s Prohibition on the Use of Imaging Devices Does Not Apply to Dog Sniffs. — This subheading distinguishes a crucial case.

   C. This Case Involves a Century-Old Law Enforcement Technique that Will Not Lead to Dragnet-Style Sweeps.[3] — This subheading refutes one of the Respondent's arguments and offers an alternate view of the searches.

---

3. Brief for Petitioner at 13-16, *Florida v. Jardines*, 133 S. Ct. 1409 (2013) (No. 11-564), 2012 WL 1594294.

chapter 25

Writing a Persuasive Rule Section

As with objective documents, the Rule section in persuasive documents provides the controlling law, beginning with the broadest and most important rule. But because your document is persuasive, consider how you can frame the rule in a favorable way. Consider the best way to frame the rule, but take care not to overreach—any misstatement of the law will hurt your credibility and your case.

Writing a Persuasive Rule Section

1. Organize rules from general to specific
2. Include quotations of key language
3. Check your citations

---

1. STEP ONE: ORGANIZE RULES FROM GENERAL TO SPECIFIC

The Rule section should start with the broadest applicable rule. Consider the hierarchy of authority: Constitutions carry more weight than statutes, which carry more weight than case law, and so on. Make sure to use only primary authorities that are binding in your jurisdiction. If you have the rare case of first impression, where there is no binding authority in your jurisdiction, choose persuasive authority from other jurisdictions that favors your position.

A. Start with Constitutions and Statutes

When the legal question is governed by a constitutional provision, the language of the provision would be the broadest rule and should appear first in the Rule section, followed by rules from case law that interpret it. Legal questions governed by statutes should use a similar approach—providing the broadest statute first, then more specific, definitional statute(s) if applicable, and then rules from case law interpreting the statutory language. If you have a constitutional or statutory provision as your main rule, you can use additional, narrower rules from case law in your Rule section to focus your reader's attention on the specific issues in your case. Consider that you want to present the rules in a logical way so that a reader unfamiliar with the area of law would easily understand the legal context.

In *Florida v. Jardines*, the case about the dog sniff outside a home, the starting point is easy to identify: The Fourth Amendment applies and is the broadest applicable rule. The brief for the Respondent begins with this rule and then uses two cases to demonstrate a favorable interpretation of the rule and focus the reader's attention on the theme of protecting individuals' privacy inside their homes.

> The Fourth Amendment to the United States Constitution guarantees that "[t]he right of the people to be secure in their persons, houses, papers, and effects, against unreasonable searches and seizures, shall not be violated, and no Warrants shall issue, but upon probable cause, . . . and particularly describing the place to be searched, and the persons or things to be seized." U.S. Const. amend. IV. "'At the very core' of the Fourth Amendment 'stands the right of a man to retreat into his own home and there be free from unreasonable governmental intrusion.'" *Kyllo v. United States*, 33 U.S. 27, 31 (2001) (quoting *Silverman v. United States*, 365 U.S. 505, 511 (1961)). The Fourth Amendment draws "a firm line at the entrance to the house." *Payton v. New York*, 445 U.S. 573, 589 (1980). The line drawn at the entrance to the house "must be not only firm but also bright—which requires clear specification of those methods of surveillance that require a warrant." *Kyllo*, 533 U.S. at 40. "With few exceptions, the question whether a warrantless search of a home is reasonable and hence constitutional must be answered no." *Id.* at 31.[1]

Margin annotations:
— For the rule, the writer quotes key language from the amendment.
— This favorable language from a controlling case references the major theme of the case.
— *Payton* introduces a convincing rule.
— The Rule section ends with a statement of the rule that the Respondent wants the Court to adopt.

Keep in mind that attorneys have an obligation of candor to the court, and they cannot omit an unfavorable case simply because it does not help their client's position. Although you must present the holdings and facts of unfavorable cases accurately, you can—and should—try to describe unfavorable cases in a way that will allow you to distinguish them later in your argument.

B. Outline Your Case Law

If no constitutional or statutory provision applies, your Rule section will begin with case law. To identify the broadest, most general rule, review your cases to see how the courts present the rules relevant to your issue. Courts usually start with the broadest rule, so your Rule section could use the same starting point.

---

1. Brief for Respondent at 16, *Florida v. Jardines*, 133 S. Ct. 1409 (2013) (No. 11-564), 2012 WL 2486026.

The organization from broad to narrow rules is logical. You may recall from Chapter 8 that rules fit into at least five categories:

1. Rule with key terms that need to be defined
2. Legal test with elements
3. Factors test
4. Balancing test
5. Rule with exceptions

For each type of rule, the reader needs to understand the broad legal context to understand the law surrounding your narrow issue. The rule with key terms that need to be defined, for instance, should start with a rule statement that includes key terms and then define those key terms.

Similarly, suppose you are defending an intentional infliction of emotional distress claim. The rule for intentional infliction of emotional distress is a legal test with elements, and only one element is in dispute in your case. The reader might be confused if you start by providing a rule relating to only one element. Instead, you should start with the broad rule, and then provide the more specific rule that relates to your issue. This organization allows the reader to understand and identify the broad legal context for your issue.

In addition, try to frame the rule in a favorable way. If one of your binding cases uses language that favors your position, you may want to quote that language in your Rule section. Consider that every word and every sentence in your document gives you an opportunity to persuade your reader that your Conclusion is correct.

The following example could start the Argument section of a motion to dismiss the intentional infliction of emotional distress claim.

> The Court should dismiss Plaintiff's claim for intentional infliction of emotional distress because Prudence Jones did not act outrageously when she asked Plaintiff to leave the store after he removed all of his clothes. —Conclusion
>
> The tort of intentional infliction of emotional distress requires a plaintiff to prove (1) extreme and outrageous conduct; (2) intent to cause, or disregard of a substantial probability of causing, severe emotional distress; (3) a causal connection between the conduct and the injury; and (4) severe emotional distress. *Howell v. N.Y. Post Co.*, 612 N.E.2d 699, 702 (N.Y. 1993). —The first rule lists the four elements for the tort in a way that emphasizes the Plaintiff's burden of proof.
>
> Outrageous conduct is "conduct exceeding all bounds usually tolerated by decent society." *Id.* —The second rule statement defines the narrower rule for the element at issue.
>
> Proof of this element "serves the dual function of filtering out petty and trivial complaints that do not belong in court, and assuring that plaintiff's claim of severe emotional distress is genuine." *Id.* (noting that "of the intentional infliction of emotional distress claims considered by this Court, every one has failed because the alleged conduct was not sufficiently outrageous"). —The writer then chooses favorable language from the case to introduce a plaintiff's high burden of proof, which allows the writer to begin to develop the theme.

While the above example from the Defendant's Motion to Dismiss presents language that is favorable to the Defendant's position from controlling case law, the Plaintiff will do the opposite in the Response to the Motion to Dismiss:

> The Court should not grant Defendant's Motion to Dismiss because the —Conclusion
> Complaint states a plausible claim that the Defendant acted outrageously
> when she publicly humiliated the 92-year-old Plaintiff who was suffering
> from dementia. The tort of intentional infliction of emotional distress has —The first rule lists the four
> four elements: (1) extreme and outrageous conduct; (2) intent to cause, elements in a straightforward
> or disregard of a substantial probability of causing, severe emotional dis- way.
> tress; (3) a causal connection between the conduct and the injury; and
> (4) severe emotional distress. *Howell v. N.Y. Post Co.*, 612 N.E.2d 699, 702
> (N.Y. 1993). The tort "imposes liability based on after-the-fact judgments —The second rule emphasizes
> about the actor's behavior" and "is as limitless as the human capacity for language that is favorable for
> cruelty." *Id.* the Plaintiff.

2. STEP TWO: INCLUDE QUOTATIONS OF KEY LANGUAGE

Choosing your words carefully is particularly important when writing persuasive documents, because every word gives you an opportunity to advance your client's case. In the previous examples, each writer chose to quote key phrases from controlling case law that favor the client's position. Each writer also chose to paraphrase statements that were not particularly eloquent or helpful. In the same way, you should try to make a conscious decision to quote—or not to quote—direct language from court opinions.

In many cases, you can choose to paraphrase the wording in a court opinion to make it more persuasive. You can change some rules from positive statements to negative statements, for instance, to favor your client's position.

Consider the examples below. Note how the first statement favors the plaintiff by emphasizing when the manufacturer is liable. The second statement also states the rule accurately, but the writer emphasizes when the manufacturer is not liable by changing the rule statement from a positive to a negative one.

> Plaintiff's rule statement: Positive statement
> A manufacturer will be held strictly liable for failure to warn when the danger involved is foreseeable. *Zaza v. Marquess & Nell, Inc.*, 675 A.2d 620, 632 (N.J. 1996).

> Defendant's rule statement: Negative statement
> A manufacturer of a component part cannot be held strictly liable for failure to warn unless the danger involved is foreseeable. *Zaza v. Marquess & Nell, Inc.*, 675 A.2d 620, 632 (N.J. 1996).

The key to paraphrasing case law is to maintain accuracy while thinking about how to make every word and statement more persuasive for your client.

Although paraphrasing language from case law can help your case, the same practice does not apply when using constitutions and statutes. In general, you should quote the precise language from constitutions and statutes. Unlike rules, holdings, and facts from case law, which are often paraphrased by one court to the next, the precise wording in constitutions and statutes is important. Many legal issues you will analyze in law school and your legal career will relate to interpreting this precise wording.

3. STEP THREE: CHECK YOUR CITATIONS

Finally, make sure that you have provided a citation for each rule in your Rule section. In general, every sentence in the Rule and Explanation sections of your CREAC will have a citation. Next, make sure that every citation is in proper *Bluebook* citation form and that you follow local citation rules when they apply.[2] Use the index in *The Bluebook* to make sure that each part of the citation is correct.

For instance, if you are citing a case, check Rule 10 on case citations; check Table 1 for formats for your jurisdiction; check Table 6 to make sure you have abbreviated the case name properly; and make sure to include a pinpoint citation, or "pincite." Incomplete or incorrect citations could prevent the reader from finding the authorities cited in your Rule section, and they weaken the credibility of your persuasive document.

---

2. Refer to Chapter 42 for detailed instructions on following proper *Bluebook* form.

chapter 26

Writing a Persuasive Explanation Section

A persuasive Explanation has a similar structure to an objective Explanation, but a persuasive Explanation has a different purpose and audience. Unlike an objective Explanation, which is a balanced demonstration of how a rule has been interpreted to justify your prediction, a persuasive Explanation advocates for an interpretation of the law that will result in the court granting your requested relief. Your task is to explain the law so the court interprets it to support your position, rather than your opponent's. If you are writing a motion asking the court to dismiss your opponent's claim, for example, you need to convince the court that the law favors your request.

Writing a Persuasive Explanation Section

1. Categorize the cases
2. Identify the anchors and synthesize multiple cases
3. Use cases to emphasize the persuasive anchors

---

1. STEP ONE: CATEGORIZE THE CASES

To write a persuasive Explanation, you first need to master the universe of relevant cases that interpret and apply your rule. Once you have researched and identified the relevant cases,[1] you need to separate those cases that have a favorable outcome for your case from those that do not. A case with a favorable outcome is one where the court (1) interpreted the rule in the way that you are asking the court to interpret the rule in your case and (2) held for the party that was in the same position as your client. You want to use these favorable cases to write your persuasive Explanation.

For instance, if you were writing a motion to dismiss in a contract dispute on the basis that your client never made a valid offer, you would want to use

---

1. Refer to Chapters 38-41 for detailed instructions on finding relevant authorities.

cases in the Explanation where the courts held that an offer was not valid—because that is the holding you want the court to reach in your case. Cases that describe in detail why an offer is not valid would be the most helpful because they would offer facts and reasoning that you could use for analogizing in your Analysis section.

Cases that have an unfavorable outcome are those that support your opponent's interpretation of the rule and hold for the party in your opponent's position. In a persuasive Explanation, writers rarely discuss in depth a case that has an unfavorable outcome, unless the case is easily distinguishable. Unfavorable cases undermine your persuasive interpretation of the rule and your request for relief. But because you have an obligation of candor to the court, you cannot just ignore unfavorable authority that is binding in your jurisdiction. Thus, you may need to use unfavorable cases sparingly, although they will rarely be the foundation of your persuasive Explanation.[2]

2. STEP TWO: IDENTIFY THE ANCHORS AND SYNTHESIZE MULTIPLE CASES

A persuasive Explanation should be organized around anchors that are drawn from multiple cases and that explain how the rule has been interpreted and applied. The anchors are the grounds or bases for a court's decision, whether those reasons are stated explicitly or implicitly. To identify the anchors in multiple cases, you must read each case closely, identify the anchors in each case, and then synthesize those issues that were the bases for the courts' decisions.

A single case will rarely be sufficient to identify the anchors that explain a rule because different courts often consider different anchors based on the facts of the cases before them. You will need multiple cases to find and describe all of the relevant anchors that courts have used to understand and apply the rule. Your Explanation should be a combination or synthesis of the anchors from all of the relevant cases.

Although your presentation of the anchors should be persuasive, your selection of the anchors cannot be misleading. If you do not acknowledge all of the relevant anchors, your persuasive document will lack credibility with the court because you will be misrepresenting the applicable law. You do not want to ignore or omit relevant anchors just because they do not serve your persuasive arguments.

For instance, in a motion to dismiss a burglary charge because the defendant was not within the curtilage of the home, the cases establish the following anchors to define curtilage: (1) whether the area has an enclosure; (2) whether the enclosure has openings for entering and exiting the property; and (3) whether the enclosure is irregular, like sparse shrubs, or fortifying, like

---

2. You will likely need to distinguish negative cases in your Analysis section.

a privacy fence. If the facts of your case involve a yard that was completely surrounded by low, uneven shrubs, anchor no. 1 would not be persuasive, anchor no. 2 would be neutral, and anchor no. 3 would support your argument that the charge should be dismissed.

To write your persuasive Explanation, you might be inclined to only discuss anchor no. 3 because it is the only anchor that will help you argue that the yard was not curtilage. But doing so would provide the court with an incomplete explanation of the rule, which could hurt the credibility of your document. Your persuasive Explanation must balance your ethical obligations of candor to the court with zealous advocacy of your client's position.

To fully explain the law, you need to describe all relevant anchors. In the burglary example, anchor no. 1 is relevant because the yard in your case is enclosed. Thus, you need to mention anchor no. 1 in your Explanation. In contrast, anchor no. 2 does not apply to your case because there was no opening for entry or exit. It is appropriate to either omit anchor no. 2 or mention it only briefly. Last, you would obviously want to discuss and emphasize anchor no. 3 in your Explanation because it is the anchor that supports your request for relief.

3. STEP THREE: USE CASES TO EMPHASIZE THE PERSUASIVE ANCHORS

Once you have identified the anchors that you will use to explain the rule, you have to organize your anchor paragraphs to emphasize the anchors and cases that are persuasive for your side. An anchor or case is persuasive when it supports your interpretation of the rule and has a favorable outcome that is analogous to your case or an unfavorable outcome that is distinguishable from your case. Although you are not going to analogize or distinguish your case in this section,[3] your persuasive Explanation should set up and support the arguments that you will make later in your document.

A. Start with Persuasive Topic Sentences

Like in an objective Explanation, each persuasive Explanation paragraph must begin with a topic sentence. In a persuasive Explanation, the topic sentences should introduce or summarize the anchors in the most persuasive way for your client. The topic sentences should persuasively guide the court through your Explanation.

The topic sentences should be broad, persuasive statements about the anchors. The sentences that follow should provide more specific details and reasoning to explain the broad statements. The organization is comparable to an upside-down triangle—the broad statements are at the top giving the big picture and the more specific details follow.

---

3. Analogizing and distinguishing your case occurs in the Analysis section.

For instance, in the motion to dismiss a burglary charge because the defendant was not within the curtilage, your topic sentence on anchor no. 3 regarding whether the enclosure is irregular, like sparse shrubs, or fortifying, like a privacy fence, would persuasively summarize the anchor. Then, the paragraph would provide specific details to explain the anchor, including any facts, holdings, reasoning, or language from relevant cases. Although your Explanation should not mention any of the facts of your case, you would want to keep in mind that in your case, the yard was completely surrounded by low, uneven shrubs, so that you can set up the arguments to come.

The following is a persuasive Explanation paragraph for anchor no. 3:

> For an area to be curtilage, it must have a fortifying enclosure that erects a barrier to entry. *Martinez v. State*, 700 So. 2d 142, 144 (Fla. Dist. Ct. App. 1997). An irregular enclosure will not support a burglary charge. *Hamilton v. State*, 660 So. 2d 1038, 1046 (Fla. 1995). For example, an unfenced area that was bordered only by "several unevenly spaced trees" did not have a sufficient enclosure to support a burglary conviction. *Id.*

— This topic sentence persuasively summarizes anchor no. 3.

— This sentence provides a more specific description of the anchor by describing what curtilage does not include. This detail comes from an additional case.

This sentence includes the facts, holding, and language of a relevant case to further explain the anchor.

This Explanation paragraph is effective because it starts with a broad topic sentence and narrows to describe the favorable outcome of a relevant case using quoted language. It also combines details from multiple cases to persuasively explain anchor no. 3.

B. Organize to Account for the Primacy and Recency Effects

For a persuasive Explanation to be an accurate description of a rule, you may need to discuss anchors that are not persuasive for your side. You can minimize the unfavorable impact of these anchors by burying them between the anchors that are most helpful. Readers best remember and pay the most attention to information that they encounter first (primacy effect) and last (recency effect). Thus, your Explanation section and each of the paragraphs in that section should begin and end with persuasive information with less persuasive information sandwiched in the middle.

Here is an example of a persuasive Explanation that is organized to emphasize favorable anchor no. 3 (whether the enclosure is irregular or fortifying). The example de-emphasizes anchor no. 1 (whether the area has an enclosure) by describing it after a persuasive topic sentence broad enough to cover anchor nos. 1 and 3 and before the persuasive details about anchor no. 3.

> Chapman's burglary charge should be dismissed because he was not within the curtilage of the Perry compound. A burglary charge requires

— This Conclusion begins the CREAC and states that the burglary charge should be dismissed.

"entering or remaining in a dwelling, a structure, or a conveyance with the intent to commit an offense therein . . . ." Fla. Stat. §810.02(b)(1) (2011). A "dwelling" includes only "a building or conveyance . . . which has a roof over it and is designed to be occupied by people lodging therein at night, together with the curtilage thereof." Fla. Stat. §810.011(2) (2011).

This Rule section persuasively describes the two relevant Florida burglary statutes to set up the argument that the burglary charge should be dismissed.

For an area surrounding a residence to be curtilage, it must have a fortifying enclosure that erects a barrier to entry. *Martinez v. State*, 700 So. 2d 142, 144 (Fla. Dist. Ct. App. 1997). The requirement that curtilage involve "some form of an enclosure" avoids "unreasonable, harsh, or absurd consequences," such as convicting a person of burglary after he innocently wanders into an open yard "in broad daylight, without the homeowner's consent, with the intent to take a piece of fruit from a tree." *Hamilton v. State*, 660 So. 2d 1038, 1045 (Fla. 1995). An irregular enclosure will not support a burglary charge. *Id.* at 1046. For example, an unfenced area that was bordered only by "several unevenly spaced trees" did not have a sufficient enclosure to support a burglary conviction. *Id.*

This topic sentence acknowledges anchor no. 1 and persuasively summarizes anchor no. 3.

This sentence describes anchor no. 1 and hides it in the middle of a paragraph that is in the middle of the Explanation. The sentence ends with a persuasive detail.

This sentence provides a more specific, persuasive explanation of anchor no. 3 by describing what does not satisfy the anchor.

This sentence describes persuasive details, including the facts, holding, and language of a case that explain anchor no. 3.

The Explanation paragraphs from the Petitioners' brief in the 2007 U.S. Supreme Court case *Morse v. Frederick* demonstrate how to write an effective persuasive Explanation by emphasizing the persuasive anchors from multiple cases. The Petitioners successfully argued that a public school had the right to prohibit students at a school-sponsored, off-campus event from displaying a banner that read "Bong Hits 4 Jesus":

Throughout the fifty States (and the District of Columbia), public education serves what this Court long ago described as "a principal instrument in awakening the child to cultural values." *Brown v. Bd. of Educ.*, 347 U.S. 483, 493 (1954). Through government-operated educational institutions, large and small, the vast majority of young Americans are prepared "for later professional training" and for "adjust[ing] normally to [their] environment." *Kuhlmeier*, 484 U.S. at 272 (quoting *Brown*, 347 U.S. at 493). Those who serve as teachers and administrators in this challenging environment are tasked with a weighty and delicate responsibility. In prescribing and controlling student conduct, public educators are inexorably required to balance students' constitutionally-guaranteed liberties with the bedrock duty to educate young minds, including fashioning "the boundaries of socially appropriate behavior." *Bethel Sch. Dist. No. 403 v. Fraser*, 478 U.S. 675, 681 (1986). Pursuit of these goals inevitably requires authorities to regulate speech, symbolic and otherwise, in a manner impermissible outside the school setting. *Id.* at 682; *accord Bd. of Educ. v. Earls*,

This topic sentence broadly and persuasively describes anchor no. 1—the important role of public education in America, which sets up the more specific explanation that follows relating to the permissibility of regulating the rights of public school students.

These sentences are a detailed explanation of why public schools need to regulate students' rights that quote favorable language from relevant cases.

This sentence is a detailed explanation of why public schools must specifically regulate students' free speech rights.

536 U.S. 822 (2002) (upholding high school's random suspicionless drug- —These parentheticals briefly summarize the favorable outcomes of cases that support anchor no. 1.
testing policy); *Vernonia Sch. Dist. 47J v. Acton*, 515 U.S. 646 (1995) (permitting random drug testing of high school student athletes).

In the First Amendment context, this Court has long emphasized that the —This topic sentence introduces anchor no. 2—students' free speech rights in public schools are limited, which prepares the reader for an explanation of what justifies such limits.
rights of students in the public schools "are not automatically coextensive with the rights of adults in other settings." *Fraser*, 478 U.S. at 682 (citing *New Jersey v. T.L.O.*, 469 U.S. 325, 340-42 (1985)). Thus, while students do not "shed their constitutional rights to freedom of speech or expression at the schoolhouse gate," students' rights must be "applied in light —These sentences describe unpersuasive anchor no. 3, which has been sandwiched in the middle of the Explanation and between details regarding persuasive anchor no. 2—that limits on students' free speech rights are permissible.
of the *special characteristics* of the school environment." *Tinker v. Des Moines Indep. Cmty. Sch. Dist.*, 393 U.S. 503, 506 (1969). The "uninhibited, robust, and wide-open" free speech in adult discourse, as ordained in *New York Times Co. v. Sullivan*, 376 U.S. 254, 270 (1964), is manifestly different from the latitude accorded to schoolchildren in a "custodial and tutelary" environment. *Vernonia*, 515 U.S. at 655.

As this Court has acknowledged on numerous occasions, the resolution —This topic sentence introduces and summarizes anchor no. 4—students' free speech rights should be decided by schools, not federal judges.
of conflicts arising in the daily operation of school systems "is primarily the responsibility of parents, teachers, and state and local school officials, and not of federal judges." *Kuhlmeier*, 484 U.S. at 273. Only when a decision to censor student expression has no valid educational purpose is the First Amendment so "directly and sharply implicate[d]" —The sentences in this paragraph quote favorable language from relevant cases to include specific details about public schools' broad authority to regulate students' free speech rights.
as to require judicial intervention to protect students' constitutional rights. *Id.* (quoting *Epperson v. Arkansas*, 393 U.S. 97, 104 (1968)). Thus, in discerning the proper doctrinal limitations upon the baseline liberty guaranteed by the Free Speech Clause, a guiding principle unifying this Court's teachings is that "[a] school need not tolerate student speech that is inconsistent with its 'basic educational mission.'" *Id.* at 266 (citing *Fraser*, 478 U.S. at 685).[4]

C. Use Signals and Parentheticals to Add Support

Because a persuasive Explanation needs to convince the court that your interpretation of the rule is correct, it should demonstrate that there is extensive support in the case law for your interpretation. You show this support through citations to multiple cases. You can easily add case support to your persuasive Explanation by using signals and parentheticals.

Signals are shorthand to tell the court how the cited cases relate to your proposition.[5] By using signals, you can efficiently include favorable cases and

---

4. Brief for Petitioner at 17-19, *Morse v. Frederick*, 551 U.S. 393, 396 (2007) (No. 06-278), 2007 WL 118979.

5. Refer to sections 3.E. and 3.G. in Chapter 42 for detailed instructions on how to incorporate signals and parentheticals into your document. Additionally, signals are described in Rules B3 and 1.2 of *The Bluebook*.

quietly acknowledge unfavorable cases. The most commonly used persuasive signals are *see*, *see also*, and *see, e.g.*

Explanatory parentheticals are an efficient way to include the facts, holdings, reasoning, or language of cases that explain your anchors.[6] By adding citations with explanatory parentheticals, you show the court that your interpretation of the rule is credible and well supported.

The following is an Explanation paragraph for the motion to dismiss the burglary charge that is similar to the one on page 141, but with signals and parentheticals added for support:

> For an area surrounding a residence to be curtilage, it must have a fortifying enclosure that erects a barrier to entry. *Martinez v. State*, 700 So. 2d 142, 144 (Fla. Dist. Ct. App. 1997) ("Under the common law, merely identifying the boundaries of a property, as opposed to erecting a barrier to entry to the extended residence of the curtilage, falls short of bringing unattached structures within the curtilage of the home."). The requirement that curtilage involve "some form of an enclosure" avoids "unreasonable, harsh, or absurd consequences," such as convicting a person of burglary after he innocently wanders into an open yard "in broad daylight, without the homeowner's consent, with the intent to take a piece of fruit from a tree." *Hamilton v. State*, 660 So. 2d 1038, 1045 (Fla. 1995); *see also J.L. v. State*, 57 So. 3d 924, 926 (Fla. Dist. Ct. App. 2011) (holding that stealing a go-cart, a four-wheeler, and a skateboard from an unenclosed yard was similar to removing a piece of fruit). An irregular enclosure will not support a burglary charge. *Hamilton*, 660 So. 2d at 1046; *cf. Baker v. State*, 636 So. 2d 1342, 1343-44 (Fla. Dist. Ct. App. 1994) (holding that a yard separated from the neighbor's house by a six-foot privacy fence and secluded by shrubs was curtilage). For example, an unfenced area that was bordered only by "several unevenly spaced trees" did not have a sufficient enclosure to support a burglary conviction. *Id.*

[Margin annotations:]
— This parenthetical includes quoted language that supports the persuasive anchor introduced in the topic sentence.

— This citation with a signal and parenthetical describes a favorable outcome to add support to the detailed explanation of the anchor.

— This citation with a signal and parenthetical describes a distinguishable unfavorable outcome to further explain the anchor.

D. Illustrate Seminal or Unavoidable Cases

i. Determine Whether a Single-Case Illustration Is Appropriate

An Explanation section is usually made up of paragraphs that are organized around anchors and synthesize multiple cases to persuasively explain the rule. In some persuasive documents, however, you will need to include an illustration in your Explanation that focuses on a single case and isolates the anchors, holding, facts, background, and reasoning of that case that are relevant to your argument.

Not every persuasive Explanation section will need a single-case illustration. A single-case illustration is only necessary when there is a seminal or unavoidable case that governs your rule. For example, when the highest court in your jurisdiction or the court that will decide your case has issued a single

---

6. Explanatory parentheticals are described in Rules B11 and 1.5 of *The Bluebook*.

decision on your issue or issued a decision very recently, that case is likely seminal or unavoidable. You should include an illustration of a seminal or unavoidable case in your persuasive Explanation, even if that case has an unfavorable outcome, keeping in mind that you will need to distinguish the case in your Analysis. To determine whether your issue is controlled by a seminal or unavoidable case, ask the following questions:

- Does the case dominate the field of this legal issue due to its weight of authority or recency?
- Would the typical legal reader expect an in-depth discussion of this case?
- Would the absence of a case illustration give your opponent a strong argument that you are ignoring negative authority?
- Would the absence of a case illustration hurt the credibility of your document?

If you answer yes to any of these questions, you have a seminal or unavoidable case that will require an illustration, even if it has an unfavorable outcome.

ii. Present the Seminal or Unavoidable Case Persuasively

When your rule is governed by a seminal or unavoidable case, you need to write a persuasive case illustration in your Explanation. Because a seminal or unavoidable case is sure to be familiar to both the court and your opponent, you should be scrupulously accurate. If the seminal or unavoidable case has a negative outcome, you should acknowledge it, rather than ignore it.

Then, the illustration should describe the relevant facts, holding, background, reasoning, and language of the case in the best possible light for your side. In particular, you should identify persuasive anchors in the seminal or unavoidable case. These anchors can be facts that make the case analogous or distinguishable from your case, bases for the court's decision that apply in your case, or language that is persuasive for your side. Your illustration should focus on these persuasive anchors.

In *Morse v. Frederick*, the Petitioners had to illustrate the seminal case *Tinker v. Des Moines Independent Community School District*,[7] which defined students' First Amendment rights and set forth the standard for determining when a school's disciplinary actions are unconstitutional. In *Tinker*, the Supreme Court held that the school had violated the students' right to free speech. Thus, for the *Morse* Petitioners, who were the principal and school district, *Tinker* was a seminal case with an unfavorable outcome. The Petitioners' brief includes an illustration that acknowledges the unfavorable outcome in *Tinker* but also establishes the bases on which the Petitioners persuasively argued that the case was distinguishable.

Here is the illustration of *Tinker* from the Petitioners' brief:

The framework for student speech doctrine begins with *Tinker*. 393 U.S. 503 (1969). In that landmark case, the Court upheld the free speech

— The illustration begins by acknowledging that Tinker is a seminal case with an unfavorable outcome. It then describes key facts that impacted the Court's holding.

---

7. 393 U.S. 503 (1969).

rights of three students to wear anti-war armbands during the school day as a silent, passive political protest. 393 U.S. at 514. The Court reasoned that wearing black armbands, a traditional sign of mourning, was expressive conduct akin to pure speech, which is entitled to comprehensive protection. *Id.* at 505-06. At the same time, the *Tinker* majority recognized the unique characteristics of a public school and the unavoidable reality that administrators and teachers may suppress student speech, whether in class or out of it, that "intrudes upon the work of the schools or the rights of other students." *Id.* at 508. In the record before it, however, the Court could discern no evidence that the passive wearing of two-inch armbands disrupted school operations. *Id.*

— Many of these facts distinguish *Tinker* from *Morse.*

— This sentence describes an aspect of the *Tinker* opinion that is persuasive for Petitioners.

— This sentence describes the Court's holding. Again, this sentence focuses on a fact that distinguishes *Tinker* from *Morse.*

The *Tinker* Court had no occasion to spell out in detail the extent or nature of "disruption" necessary to trigger a school's authority to curtail student speech. *Id.* The Court described the requisite disruption as "interference, actual or nascent, with the schools' work," which is something more than "undifferentiated fear or apprehension of disturbance." *Id.* Under this standard, if a school administrator reasonably perceives (or forecasts) that a student's expressive conduct is presently interfering (or would eventually interfere) with the school's work, then the administrator is warranted in suppressing the particular expression (or expressive conduct). *Id.* Student speech rising to this level of disruption may occur "in class or out of it" and may "stem[] from time, place, or type of behavior." *Id.* at 513. The Court provided further guidance by distinguishing John Tinker's silent, passive conduct from the disciplinary problems posed by "aggressive, disruptive action or even group demonstrations." *Id.* at 507-08. The *Tinker* Court thus foreshadowed its willingness to approve school intervention when speech is accompanied by antisocial conduct. *See id.*

— This paragraph persuasively describes anchors in *Tinker* that favor Petitioners. Petitioners use this illustration paragraph to show the Court that *Tinker* supports their position in *Morse.* Petitioners quote the Court's language and use details from *Tinker* to establish the same persuasive anchors that Petitioners explained in their anchor paragraphs.

Justice Black dissented. *Id.* at 517 (Black, J., dissenting). He lamented that the broad sweep of the majority decision invited students to "use the schools at their whim as a platform" and that courts, rather than schools, "will allocate to themselves the function of deciding how the pupils' school day will be spent." *Id.* Although his opinion failed to carry the day, Justice Black's plain-spoken words continue to echo through the body of student speech law.[8]

— This paragraph describes a dissent in *Tinker* that supports Petitioners' argument.

iii. Avoid Serial Case Briefing

If you do not have a seminal or unavoidable case, you should probably not include single-case illustration paragraphs in your Explanation. Many students try to write an Explanation that is a series of case illustrations or case briefs. But a series of case briefs deprives you of the opportunity to use the Explanation to convince the court to interpret the rule favorably for your side based on your anchors.

---

8. Brief for Petitioner at 20-21, *Morse v. Frederick*, 551 U.S. 393, 396 (2007) (No. 06-278), 2007 WL 118979 at *20-21.

If there are three relevant cases and you simply write a paragraph sum-marizing each case, you have not synthesized the persuasive anchors that will convince the court that you should prevail. Serial case briefs just report the facts, holdings, and outcomes of the cases without persuading the court that your interpretation of the rule is correct. Even when the cases do have positive outcomes, writing case illustrations, rather than synthesizing the persuasive anchors that the cases share, will make your Explanation less persuasive and effective.

chapter 27

Writing a Persuasive Analysis Section

The Analysis section in a persuasive CREAC details the legal arguments that support your Conclusion. In this section, you will apply the law to your facts and draw case analogies and distinctions to show your reader why your arguments are sound and why the court should grant the relief you seek. The key to a strong Analysis section is to detail arguments based on the anchors you identified for the Explanation section. Because the anchors are the bases for the holdings in the applicable case law, you need to show your reader how your facts fit with the anchors to support your Conclusion.

Unlike the Analysis section in objective documents, a persuasive Analysis section has no counter-analysis. That's your opposing counsel's job. Instead, you will provide the strongest arguments that support your Conclusion, refute any arguments that opposing counsel has made, and preemptively refute any potential counterarguments or weaknesses in your position.

In addition, a persuasive Analysis should be written in an authoritative style. An objective Analysis might begin with a thesis statement that states: "A court will likely find that _____." But a persuasive Analysis section should use more convincing language—without any hedging. For instance, the following thesis statement could begin the Analysis section of an argument relating to the contract dispute:

> The Defendant did not make a binding offer to sell his car because he had no intent to sell his revered Volkswagen Beetle when he jokingly placed a "For Sale" sign on it.

Make sure that each sentence you write in the Analysis section shows that you have no doubts about your position. After all, if your writing style is less than convincing, the court likely won't be convinced of your arguments.

Writing a Persuasive Analysis Section

1. Start off strong: Organize and outline your Analysis
2. Start with a broad thesis that incorporates your theme

> 3. Use topic sentences to organize your Analysis, and start with your best argument
> 4. Provide legal support for your Conclusion by analogizing and distinguishing relevant cases
> 5. Refute counterarguments

1. STEP ONE: START OFF STRONG: ORGANIZE AND OUTLINE YOUR ANALYSIS

The purpose of the Analysis section is to advocate for your client's position in the most compelling and credible way you can. Authoritative language and specific arguments based on the anchors are essential. In addition, the arguments within a persuasive Analysis section should be organized and presented in a persuasive way.

The arguments should be logically organized to help the court follow the substance of your Analysis. Thus, if you have a threshold argument, that will need to come first. When organizing your arguments, remember the primacy and recent effects—that readers pay the most attention to information that they encounter first and last. For this reason, you should begin your Analysis with your best point. You may want to bury weaker points in the middle of the Analysis or organize your Analysis with the arguments in descending order, from strongest to weakest.

To identify your best point and rank your other arguments, you will need to create a clear outline. Review the anchors you identified for the Explanation section and review your facts. Make a list of each anchor you want to analyze in the Analysis section and the essential facts that you will use. Then, rank your arguments according to their strength. Think critically about your arguments and evaluate them as a judge or opposing counsel might. The first point should be virtually unassailable, allowing you to capture the reader's attention and build up momentum before you deliver your other points.

Suppose you want to detail three arguments, each based on a relevant anchor, in your Analysis section. One persuasive organization would put the strongest argument first and the weakest argument sandwiched before the third. The following two structures could work well for an Analysis section that addresses three arguments, and the templates can serve as a guide to creating an outline for your persuasive Analysis section.

Analysis Organization—Template No. 1

First paragraph:
- Broad thesis stating Conclusion
- Summary of three arguments supporting Conclusion in the order they will be discussed

Second paragraph:
* Topic sentence summarizing the strongest argument and how it supports Conclusion
* Legal support for argument, including analogizing and distinguishing relevant cases and applying the law to your facts

Third paragraph:
* Topic sentence summarizing the weakest argument and how it supports Conclusion
* Legal support for argument, including analogizing and distinguishing relevant cases and applying the law to your facts

Fourth paragraph:
* Topic sentence summarizing how the third argument supports Conclusion
* Legal support for argument, including analogizing and distinguishing relevant cases and applying the law to your facts

If this organization makes your Analysis section seem repetitious, consider that repetition can be an effective persuasive technique. Still, you might want to use this more concise organization:

Analysis Organization—Template No. 2

First paragraph:
* Broad thesis stating Conclusion and concisely summarizing three arguments in the order they will be discussed
* Legal support for strongest argument, including analogizing and distinguishing relevant cases and showing how the argument supports Conclusion

Second paragraph:
* Topic sentence summarizing the weakest argument and how it supports Conclusion
* Legal support for argument, including analogizing and distinguishing relevant cases and applying the law to your facts

Third paragraph:
* Topic sentence summarizing how the third argument supports Conclusion
* Legal support for argument, including analogizing and distinguishing relevant cases and applying the law to your facts

2. STEP TWO: START WITH A BROAD THESIS THAT INCORPORATES YOUR THEME

A thesis statement at the start of the Analysis section provides the reader with an overview of your best arguments. A thesis also reminds the reader of the relief you seek, and hopefully, begins to sway the reader to agree with your position. For shorter Analysis sections that analyze only one or two anchors, a single thesis sentence could suffice as an introduction. But for more complex Analysis sections, a thesis paragraph will keep your reader focused on your major points.

Including each argument in the order it will be discussed in the thesis sentence or paragraph serves as a helpful roadmap for the reader. The following examples relating to curtilage demonstrate a short and long version of a thesis. The first thesis example summarizes arguments relating to two anchors: the type of enclosure and the extent of the enclosure. The second example analyzes a third anchor: gaps in the enclosure.

> Defendant's burglary conviction should be affirmed because the picket fence and hedgerow enclosing most of the victim's yard are more than adequate to qualify the area around the home as curtilage.

> Mr. Chapman's conviction should be reversed because the Perry compound does not qualify as curtilage for three reasons. First, only the front area is enclosed; the back is unbounded. Second, the front is bordered only by a short, decorative fence and a line of low, uneven shrubs. Last, the area has three extensive gaps allowing any person or vehicle to easily enter or exit the area.

In these examples, the State and defense counsel emphasize the arguments most helpful to their respective positions. By doing so, they also present the major themes of their arguments. In the first example, the State emphasizes the sufficiency of the enclosure around an individual's home. The State's choice of words, such as burglary, picket fence, hedgerow, victim, yard, and home, help illustrate the crime for the reader. The language focuses the reader on the theme that the defendant encroached upon the clear border to an individual's home.

In the second example, the thesis statement supporting the defendant presents an entirely different theme—that the large compound at issue has an inadequate and ineffective enclosure. The second thesis also humanizes the defendant by using his name, and the paragraph avoids mentioning the term victim. Additionally, instead of referencing a home with a picket fence, the writer uses impersonal references to the "Perry compound" and "area," which paint a different picture than that of a home with a picket fence and neat row of hedges. Finally, the thesis paragraph emphasizes the gaps in the enclosure and the difference between the enclosures in the front and back yards, analyzing an anchor that the State chose to leave out. All of these details help illustrate the theme that the enclosure around an impersonal compound is inadequate.

Your theme will likely emerge as you outline your Analysis section. To identify a theme or themes for your argument, review the outline of your anchors and the facts you want to emphasize in your arguments. Consider how your arguments interconnect and how they might relate to policy considerations. For instance, the State's thesis in the curtilage example touches upon the policy concern that individuals have certain privacy guarantees inside their homes' borders.

Your theme is the thread that connects the anchors and your arguments to your Conclusion, and that thread should be a constant throughout your document. Incorporating a theme—not just in the thesis for the Analysis section but in your Argument section as a whole—will make your document cohesive, logical, and more compelling. A strong theme will guide your reader throughout your document and give the reader a reason to be on your side.

To check whether you have successfully incorporated your theme throughout your document, try this self-editing test after completing your first draft: Read every paragraph independently and ask yourself, "Does this paragraph incorporate my theme and support my Conclusion?" If the answer is "no," revise or delete it, and try again.

3. STEP THREE: USE TOPIC SENTENCES TO ORGANIZE YOUR ANALYSIS, AND START WITH YOUR BEST ARGUMENT

Now that you have an outline of your arguments, a thesis to begin your Analysis section, and a convincing theme, you can begin drafting the individual arguments within the Analysis. Consider the paragraph structure of your Analysis section. Devoting one paragraph to the analysis of each anchor is a logical organization. Or, if one anchor deserves extensive analysis, you might devote two or more paragraphs to the analysis. If two or three anchors are related, you could combine the analysis of them in a single paragraph.

Whether you have one argument or multiple arguments in a paragraph, each paragraph should have a topic sentence that persuasively introduces the reader to the topic of the paragraph or summarizes the paragraph's main point. Topic sentences help your document maintain a logical and compelling structure. They also serve as mini-conclusions that combine to provide convincing support for your thesis and Conclusion.

The following thesis from the curtilage example introduces arguments analyzing three relevant anchors:

> Mr. Chapman's conviction should be reversed because the Perry compound does not qualify as curtilage for three reasons. First, only the front area is enclosed; the back is unbounded. Second, the front is bordered only by a short, decorative fence and a line of low, uneven shrubs. Last, the area has three extensive gaps allowing any person or vehicle to easily enter or exit the area.

As a next step, you would write a topic sentence for each argument:

First, the area surrounding the compound cannot be considered curtilage because the enclosure is intermittent in the front and nonexistent in the back.

Second, the compound is rimmed by only sporadic hedges and a short piece of ornamental fencing, which fail to provide the type of enclosure that would allow the yard to be designated curtilage.

Finally, multiple wide-open gaps in the compound's perimeter allow any person or vehicle to access the property at any point, further indicating the lack of definition in the property's border.

These topic sentences are a first step in showing your reader how the analysis of the anchors supports your Conclusion. Note that the topic sentences do not reference or depend on one specific case. Instead, the topic sentences broadly summarize how the analysis of the anchor according to the facts supports the Conclusion.

4. STEP FOUR: PROVIDE LEGAL SUPPORT FOR YOUR CONCLUSION BY ANALOGIZING AND DISTINGUISHING RELEVANT CASES

To provide legal support for your Conclusion, you need to show the reader how the analysis of an anchor in relevant cases supports your analysis of the anchor with your facts. Start by drawing analogies to cases with a favorable outcome—those cases that interpreted the rule in the way that you want the rule interpreted. Analogies create affirmative arguments, which are more persuasive than defensive arguments.

A. Draw Analogies to Make Affirmative Arguments

For each anchor you plan to analyze, determine which cases you can use to draw analogies to support your argument. The comparisons to your case might strike you as obvious. As a result, beginning legal writers often are tempted to write conclusory or poorly constructed analogies, such as the following:

Like *Jones v. Bradwick*, the offer here is not valid.

This statement is ineffective because it does nothing to advance the writer's argument. Opposing counsel could easily refute this statement with the following:

Unlike *Jones v. Bradwick*, the offer here is valid.

The strongest analogies show the reader how and why the cases are comparable. They are not conclusory like the poorly written examples above. Instead, effective analogies are substantive, parallel, and specific. This means that each analogy should be connected to an anchor, compare like with like, and use detailed comparisons.

i. Substantive Analogies

Analogies are substantive when they connect your facts with the relevant law. The topic sentences for your Analysis section should identify one of your major arguments and a relevant anchor. When drawing analogies to provide legal support for your argument, make sure that each analogy is connected to the relevant anchor. Keep in mind that cases may address multiple issues or include interesting but irrelevant details. A good outline and a focused topic sentence will help you keep your argument on track.

ii. Parallel Analogies

Analogies are parallel when they compare like with like. The conclusory analogies on the previous page make a strategic mistake because they require the reader to figure out how the two cases are related. In addition, the statements make a grammatical error by comparing a case to the offer, which is not a parallel construction. A parallel analogy will compare the same types of information from your case and the cases you are using for analogies. Drawing a parallel analogy means you will compare facts to facts, reasoning to reasoning, and holdings to holdings.

TYPES OF PARALLEL ANALOGIES

- **Fact to fact:** The irregular border around the Perry compound is less continuous than the fence in *Martinez*, which the court found was inadequate because it only traced the north and east edges of the property.
- **Reasoning to reasoning:** The court in *J.L.* stated that the Legislature did not intend to apply the burglary statute to an individual who entered an open yard intending to pick a piece of fruit from a tree. Mr. Chapman innocently wandered into the Perry compound because it was open and unbounded, and therefore, the burglary statute should not apply to him.
- **Holding to holding:** The *Hamilton* court held that "several unevenly spaced trees" were not an enclosure. Similarly here, sporadic fencing and landscaping do not create a sufficient enclosure to support a burglary conviction.

Some cases could be so helpful to your position that you can compare the facts, reasoning, and specific holdings to your case. Those cases will provide the strongest support for your Conclusion. But keep in mind that you can and should use multiple cases to support each argument. Thus, in a single Analysis paragraph, you might have comparisons to the facts, reasoning, and holding of one case, a comparison to the facts of a second case, and a comparison to the holding of a third case. More legal support means a more solid and credible argument.

iii. Specific Analogies

The third step in making sure your analogy is not conclusory is to make it specific. To find specific, relevant details to use in your analogies, read and reread your cases. Pull out any detail that you can use to show your reader how and why a case is comparable to yours. More specific analogies produce more effective arguments.

- **Lacks specificity:** Like the claimant's possession in *Klein*, Karr's possession of the property was not sufficiently open and notorious.
- **Some improvement:** Like the claimant in *Klein*, who only occasionally visited the vacant lot, Karr rarely paid visits to the cabin.
- **Very specific:** Karr camped on the property only seven times in six years and left the cabin in disrepair—much like the claimant in *Klein*, who never occupied the lot except for the occasional picnic and left the landscaping unkempt.

The last example is effective because it uses a comparison of specific details to show the reader how and why the *Klein* case is like Karr's. Some cases will be so helpful to your position that you will want to devote an entire paragraph or more to developing a detailed comparison.

iv. Parenthetical Support

In addition, you can use signals and parentheticals to add specific legal support to your arguments. The most common signals in a persuasive Analysis section are *see*, *see also*, and *see, e.g.*[1] Signals with parentheticals can effectively and concisely show your reader that relevant cases have comparable facts, reasoning, and holdings. When constructing a parenthetical, keep in mind that it should also be substantive, parallel, and specific.

ANALOGIES WITH PARENTHETICAL SUPPORT

- Karr's possession of the property was not open and notorious because he camped on the property only seven times in six years and left the cabin in disrepair. *See Klein*, 199 P.2d at 691-92 (holding that possession was not open and notorious where the claimant occasionally picnicked on a vacant lot and left the landscaping unkempt).
- Blackhurst installed a shed and "No Trespassing" signs on her land, which shows she was occupying, maintaining, and improving the land enough to provide notice to the owner. *See Nielsen*, 100 Cal. Rptr. 3d at 341; *see also Lobro*, 116 Cal. Rptr. at 536-38 (finding that that the adverse claimants' occupation of the property for twenty-five years, which included improving and making additions, constituted "reasonable notice that they claimed the property as their own").

---

1. Refer to sections 3.E. and 3.G. in Chapter 42 for detailed instructions on how to incorporate signals and parentheticals into your document.

- Mr. Chapman innocently wandered into the Perry compound because it was open and unbounded, and he had no intent to enter a private yard. *See, e.g., J.L.,* 57 So. 3d at 926 ("[T]he Legislature did not intend the burglary statute to be applied to an individual who, without the homeowner's consent, enters an open yard with the intent to take a piece of fruit from a tree located in the yard.").

These parentheticals provide specific and substantive information to support the writer's argument. In addition, the information in each parenthetical is relevant to the anchor referenced in the statement preceding it. The first two examples address whether the property was properly maintained; the third addresses legislative intent.

B. Distinguish Unfavorable Cases

If you identified binding cases that have an unfavorable outcome in your Explanation, then you should consider whether you need to distinguish those cases in your Analysis. You should draw case distinctions in your persuasive Analysis only if (1) the distinction is obvious and strengthens your argument or (2) the case is recent, mandatory authority and your opponent will likely use the case as support. To make case distinctions effective, they also should be substantive, parallel, and specific. The following example provides an effective distinction with a parenthetical for added legal support.

DISTINCTION THAT IS SUBSTANTIVE, PARALLEL, AND SPECIFIC

- The hedgerow and fencing that enclose most of the *Perry* compound are far more extensive than the unevenly spaced trees that were found to be inadequate in *Hamilton*. *See* 660 So. 2d at 1046 (noting that the evidence was undisputed that the victim's yard was not enclosed in any other manner).

C. Draw Analogies and Distinctions for Each Anchor

Once you have drafted the relevant analogies and distinctions for your analysis of the first anchor, repeat the process for each anchor you plan to analyze. Consider using a transition to guide your reader to the next point. Transitions like "similarly," "in addition," "furthermore," and "moreover," build momentum from one argument to the next and make your analysis more confident and persuasive.

Also, make sure you use topic sentences to keep your reader focused on the specific anchor you are analyzing. This method of providing specific and substantive case analogies and distinctions—without hyperbole or inflation—will reveal the merits of your case and allow you to present a compelling and credible argument that the relief you seek is warranted.

5. STEP FIVE: REFUTE COUNTERARGUMENTS

Within your Analysis section, you will need to decide how to strategically confront and rebut counterarguments. If your argument is unassailable and every case on point supports your position, you probably would not be litigating the matter. Every case has certain weak points. And every good lawyer has to be aware of those weak points and determine how and when to refute them.

First, try to identify the major weaknesses in your position. Consider what your opponent is likely to argue based on the facts and applicable case law. In addition, consider what arguments a judge will likely find relevant upon reviewing the legal documents and applicable law. Your job is to identify the obvious weaknesses in your position so you can confront them and move the argument along to your stronger points.

Second, consider that your rebuttal does not need to be comprehensive and address every potential counterargument that your opponent may raise. If your analysis reveals a counterargument that is obscure, addressing it might disclose an otherwise unknown argument. Lawyers have to strike a careful balance when preemptively refuting an opponent's argument.

After you identify which counterarguments you need to refute, think about how you can present your rebuttal in a way that is not defensive. Also, make sure you do not make your opponent's argument by restating it, especially at the start of the paragraph.

For example, suppose you represent the defendant in a lawsuit for intentional infliction of emotional distress and plan to file a motion to dismiss. The only element at issue is whether your client's conduct was outrageous when she asked the plaintiff to leave her store after he took off all of his clothes. From the plaintiff's complaint, you are aware that the plaintiff is 92 years old and suffers from dementia. And from your research, you are aware of a major weakness in your position—that the law in this area generally favors vulnerable plaintiffs, including the elderly and those with mental illness.

As a result, you need to preemptively refute the argument that the plaintiff is vulnerable. Consider how you can affirmatively address the vulnerable plaintiff counterargument with the facts, applicable law, or both. Start your rebuttal by focusing your topic sentence on your argument, rather than your opponent's argument.

- **Weak rebuttal:** Opposing counsel may argue that the plaintiff is vulnerable because he is 92 years old and suffers from dementia, but the plaintiff regularly takes cycling trips.
- **Strong rebuttal with factual support:** The plaintiff is an active, independent 92-year-old, who traveled alone to Texas six days before the incident and completed a 50-kilometer bicycling race.
- **Strong rebuttal with legal support:** Intentional infliction of emotional distress claims have failed in New York courts even where the plaintiff is a patient at a psychiatric facility. *See Howell v. N.Y. Post Co.*, 612 N.E.2d 699,

702 (N.Y. 1993) (noting that "of the intentional infliction of emotional distress claims considered by this Court, every one has failed because the alleged conduct was not sufficiently outrageous").

The first example is weak because it restates the opponent's argument, which puts the writer on the defensive. To refute an argument effectively, you need to use the facts or law in a way to gain the advantage. Also, consider how you can strategically place your rebuttal within your Analysis section. Taking into account the primacy and recency effects, the best location for a rebuttal is often buried in the middle of the stronger arguments within your Analysis section.

6. CONSULT EXPERT EXAMPLES

The excerpt below of a persuasive Explanation and Analysis comes from the Respondents' brief in the immigration and human rights case, *Hui v. Castaneda*. Mr. Castaneda, represented by California attorney Conal Doyle, sued California and the United States for negligent medical treatment while he was held by immigration authorities.

A. This Case Is Functionally Equivalent to *Carlson*, but with a More Compelling Factual and Legal Basis

— A heading introduces the Explanation and Analysis relating to a key, binding case.

Carlson upheld the availability of a *Bivens* remedy against BOP and PHS medical personnel who were deliberately indifferent to a federal prisoner's serious medical needs. 446 U.S. at 16-17. As in this case, the federal employees' deliberate indifference caused a man to die, and this Court found the FTCA inadequate to remedy the constitutional violation at issue: cruel and unusual punishment resulting in the deprivation of life. *See id*.

— This Explanation section begins by continuing the description of *Carlson* (introduced in an earlier section) and by focusing on one anchor from the case.

In *Carlson*, the Court held that it was "crystal clear" that "Congress views FTCA and *Bivens* as parallel, complementary causes of action." 446 U.S. at 20. In so holding, the Court concluded that Congress did not view the FTCA as providing "an alternative remedy which it explicitly declared to be a *substitute* for recovery directly under the Constitution and viewed as equally effective." *Id*. at 18-19 (emphasis in original). *Carlson* further found that the FTCA did not preclude *Bivens* actions because "no special factors counsell[ed] hesitation" against permitting a deliberate indifference claim against officials that included a PHS employee. *Id*. at 19.

— This Explanation paragraph persuasively describes how *Carlson* interpreted a statute and an earlier case.

This case provides an even more powerful basis than *Carlson* for rejecting Petitioners' bid for immunity from *Bivens*. Like *Carlson*, this is a wrongful death and survival action based on the deliberate indifference of prison medical personnel and officials. But this case is more factually compelling than *Carlson*. There, the decedent's treatment for an asthma attack was

— This Analysis section begins with a specific fact comparison to *Carlson*. The analogy is especially persuasive because *Carlson* had a favorable outcome and because Doyle, the attorney, shows how the facts are more compelling here.

delayed for eight hours, then he was given contra-indicated medication and died soon afterwards. 446 U.S. at 16 n.1. Castaneda, in contrast, was denied treatment for *eleven months* . . . .

This case also has a much stronger legal basis than *Carlson* because, eight years after *Carlson*, Congress passed the Westfall Act, clarifying that the FTCA's "exclusive remedy" extends only to common-law torts and does not preclude *Bivens* actions. 28 U.S.C. §2679(b). This express *Bivens* exception demonstrates that Congress does not view the FTCA as an adequate substitute for *Bivens*. So here, unlike in *Carlson*, this Court need not strive to infer whether Congress intended to preserve *Bivens* claims— the Westfall Act answers the question with resounding certainty.

— After making a fact-based argument, Doyle makes an argument based on the underlying law. He again shows how this case is more compelling than *Carlson*.

Petitioners attempt to distinguish *Carlson* by arguing that Respondents' *Bivens* claims are against a new category of defendants, and that *Carlson* did not involve §233(a) immunity. In so arguing, Petitioners fail to recognize that one of the *Carlson* defendants was a PHS officer: the Assistant Surgeon General of the United States. Moreover, when evaluating immunity, "this Court has long favored a 'functional' inquiry— immunity attaches to particular official functions, not to particular offices." *Westfall*, 484 U.S. at 296 n.3. *Carlson* and this case involve claims against officials performing the same function: providing medical care to detainees. There is no principled basis for distinguishing among medical personnel employed by the BOP, PHS, DIHS, or any other federal agency. As for Petitioners' claim that *Carlson* is irrelevant because it did not involve §233(a) immunity, §233(a) does not apply to *Bivens* actions and is, therefore, no more relevant here than it was in *Carlson*.

— Doyle then rebuts an argument in the Petitioners' brief.

— Doyle uses authoritative language throughout the Analysis to make his case.

In short, Petitioners' attempts to distinguish *Carlson* are unavailing. *Carlson* is on all fours with this case, but this case provides an even more compelling basis on which to conclude that §233(a) does not immunize petitioners from *Bivens* liability.[2]

— The section ends with a powerful Conclusion that summarizes the reasoning above.

---

2. Brief for Respondents at 51-52, *Hui v. Castaneda*, 559 U.S. 799 (2010) (No. 08-1529), 2010 WL 197357.

Writing a Persuasive Conclusion

A Conclusion in a persuasive document gives you an opportunity to make your client's case and to put forth your strongest reason or reasons. To keep your reader focused on the outcome you seek, start and end each CREAC with a Conclusion.

The ending Conclusion in your CREAC should not be exactly the same as the opening Conclusion. Restating the exact same sentence could make your document seem monotonous, and obvious cutting and pasting of the same language may irritate the reader. Even a small variation in wording can help maintain your reader's interest.

When you rephrase your Conclusion, try to incorporate the theme you have developed throughout your document. Also, make sure to provide a specific reason in support—whether the reason is factually based, legally based, or both. The following Conclusions could begin and end an Argument section on the contract dispute case.

Opening Conclusion

The Court should grant the Defendant's Motion to Dismiss because he never made a binding offer to sell his car and the contract is therefore unenforceable.

Ending Conclusion

The Defendant did not make a binding offer to sell his revered Volkswagen Beetle when he jokingly put a sign on it that read: "The World Ends Tomorrow. Must Sell Today. $150 obo." Therefore, the Court should grant the Defendant's Motion to Dismiss.

Both Conclusions persuade the reader to find for the Defendant and provide specific reasons in support. Keep in mind that the Conclusion statement gives you the first—and last—opportunity to convince the court to grant the relief you seek. Take advantage of this opportunity by putting forth your best reason.

part VI

Putting Persuasive Documents Together

chapter 29

Introduction to Persuasive Documents

Lawyers write persuasive documents to advocate for their clients. Throughout your law school and legal career, you may write persuasive documents, including trial court motions and appellate briefs, that ask a court to resolve an issue in your client's favor. These persuasive documents are read by the judge or judges presiding over your case, opposing counsel, and possibly the clients on both sides. This part of the *Handbook* will provide directions for how to incorporate a persuasive CREAC into formal documents that could be filed with a court.

An effective persuasive document presents a cohesive and zealous argument supporting the relief it requests, while also satisfying the lawyer's ethical obligation to be candid and truthful about the facts and law. It also establishes the author's credibility through scrupulous proofreading and adherence to the rules governing format, substance, and timeliness.

chapter 30

Trial Court Documents

Trial court documents are one form of persuasive legal writing. The most common form of trial court document is a motion, which is a written request to the court. During the trial court phase of a case, lawyers may prepare and respond to several motions. Motions can be narrow, for example, asking the court to enter an order requiring a party to make a witness available for deposition, or broad, asking the court to decide the issues in the case as a matter of law.

Motion formats vary widely from jurisdiction to jurisdiction. Filings often consist of two parts. First, the "notice of motion" contains legally operative language describing the requested relief and information regarding when the court will hear the motion. Second, the "memorandum of law" or "memorandum of points and authorities" includes the legal argument for why the motion should be granted. In some courts, these documents are combined into a single document, while in other courts they are filed separately. Either way, together they compose the "motion."

Once a motion has been filed, the opposing party must prepare a response (also called an opposition), and then the moving party may be allowed to file a reply. The response and reply usually use a format that is similar to the format for the memorandum of law in support of the motion.

This chapter provides general instructions for preparing a trial court memorandum of law, but you should always follow any jurisdiction-specific rules that govern the document you are preparing.

Writing a Trial Court Memorandum of Law

1. Create a template for your document
2. Prepare a persuasive Facts section
3. Prepare a Legal Standard section if necessary
4. Add persuasive roadmaps and subheadings to guide the court
5. Write a compelling Introduction
6. Scrutinize and revise

---

1. STEP ONE: CREATE A TEMPLATE FOR YOUR DOCUMENT

The format of a trial court memorandum of law is determined by the rules of civil procedure and local rules of the court where the document will be filed. The court can reject any document that does not comply with the rules, so you must follow them closely. Most trial court memoranda of law have some variation of the following format:

Trial Court Memorandum of Law

1. Caption
2. Introduction
3. Facts section
4. Legal Standard
5. Argument with CREAC and point headings
6. Conclusion section
7. Signature block

Put your trial court memorandum of law together by creating a template for your document, beginning with the caption. Follow the rules regarding the required font type, size, and spacing and take note of any page or word limits. In addition, check the rules for deadlines to ensure that your document is timely filed.

A. Create the Caption

The caption appears at the beginning of a trial court memorandum of law and usually contains the following pieces of information: (1) the court, (2) the name of the case, (3) the case number, and (4) the title of the document. In some courts, the caption will also include the name and contact information for the lawyers representing the party filing the document.

Court rules differ regarding the spacing, orientation, and organization of the information in the caption. Court websites often provide a template for a properly formatted caption. Figure 30.1 shows an example of a caption for a memorandum of law filed in the federal District Court for the Southern District of Florida.

B. Add Headings for Each Section

Next, add headings for each additional section of your memorandum of law: (1) Introduction, (2) Facts, (3) Legal Standard, (4) Argument, and (5) Conclusion. Put into place the Argument section with the persuasive CREAC(s) and point headings that you have already prepared. (See Part V for a review.) Now, you can create and fill in the missing pieces. You don't have to prepare the sections of the document in order. You may want to start with the Conclusion section, which is easy and formulaic, and end with the Introduction, which is challenging because it needs to summarize the cohesive document.

> UNITED STATES DISTRICT COURT
> FOR THE SOUTHERN DISTRICT OF FLORIDA
> MIAMI DIVISION
> CASE NO. 06-21265-CIV-JORDAN
>
> LEAGUE OF WOMEN VOTERS OF FLORIDA, PEOPLE
> ACTING FOR COMMUNITY TOGETHER (PACT), *et al.*
>
>   Plaintiffs,
>
>   v.
>
> SUE M. COBB, individually and in her official capacity as
> Secretary of State for the State of Florida, and DAWN
> ROBERTS, individually and in her official capacity as
> Director of the Division of Elections,
>
>   Defendants.
> _____/
>
> **DEFENDANTS' MOTION TO DISMISS**
> **AND MEMORANDUM OF LAW IN SUPPORT THEREOF**

Figure 30.1

C. Insert the Conclusion Section and Signature Block

A trial court memorandum of law usually ends with a Conclusion section and signature block. The Conclusion section states in a single sentence, using customary language, what the document has asked the court to do, and the signature block provides a place for the attorney submitting the document to sign her name. The typical language for a Conclusion is as follows:

> "For the foregoing reasons, _____[party]_____ requests that the Court _____[relief]_____."

By signing the filing, the attorney represents to the court that the document has legal and evidentiary support and that it is filed for a proper purpose.[1] Many documents are now filed electronically and have an electronic signature, rather than a handwritten signature. An electronic signature is the author's name, preceded by "/s/." Check the local rules and then insert a properly formatted signature block.

Figure 30.2 shows an example of a Conclusion section with the Conclusion section heading and signature block for a memorandum of law for the federal District Court for the Southern District of Florida.

2. STEP TWO: PREPARE A PERSUASIVE FACTS SECTION

In a trial court memorandum of law, the Facts section must tell a story from your client's point of view that supports the relief you request. This story

---

1. *See* Fed. R. Civ. P. 11(b).

CONCLUSION

For the foregoing reasons, the Court should deny Defendant's Motion to Dismiss Plaintiff's Complaint.

Dated: November 11, 2012

Respectfully submitted,

/s/ Levon I. Cavin

Levon I. Cavin (Fla. Bar No. 11111)
1400 Prudence Blvd.
Suite 13
Miami, FL 33133
(305) 288-1111
(305) 288-2222 (fax)
levonicavin@cavinlaw.com

Figure 30.2

needs to (1) describe the facts that are legally significant to the issue in the memorandum of law, (2) provide any necessary background information and the procedural context underlying the memorandum of law, and (3) advance a theme that helps your client's position in the litigation.

> ### The Three Types of Facts in a Persuasive Facts Section
>
> 1. Legally significant facts relevant to the issue in the memorandum of law
> 2. Procedural facts that provide necessary background and context
> 3. Emotional facts that serve your persuasive theme

The Facts section in a trial court memorandum of law should present the facts persuasively. The Facts section should not be objective, like the Facts section in an office memo. The court should be inclined to decide the issue in your client's favor based on the Facts section alone. This does not mean, however, that you can misrepresent or ignore contrary facts that weigh against your argument. Avoiding contrary facts will hurt your credibility with the court, and, when your opponent points out the facts you have omitted, undermine your arguments. Instead of ignoring contrary facts, you should use legal writing techniques to portray the facts accurately and persuasively.

A. Categorize the Legally Significant Facts

The Facts section should describe all of the facts that are legally significant to the issue in your memorandum of law. To identify the legally significant facts, review the anchors from your applicable authorities. Then, review the facts of your case and note every fact that is connected to an anchor. Make a list of these legally significant facts; they will form the basis of your Facts section. This process should allow you to capture every relevant fact.

You need to identify all of the facts that are relevant to the anchors—even those that weigh against your argument. Do not omit contrary facts. Any fact included in the Analysis section of your CREAC must be included in your Facts section. If you identified a legally significant fact that you have not included in your Analysis, you may have missed an important argument. Once you have your list, you should categorize the helpful facts that you want to highlight and the contrary facts that you want to minimize.

B. Provide Procedural Context

Trial court documents are governed by rules of procedure. You should include facts that establish that your request to the court is procedurally proper. Moreover, you must describe the facts in procedurally appropriate terms.

For example, a motion to dismiss under Federal Rule of Civil Procedure 12(b)(6) should include procedural facts that show you have not yet filed a responsive pleading, which is required by the rule.[2] Moreover, you would limit the facts in the motion to the allegations in the complaint—because those are the only "facts" of record at that stage of the case. Thus, you would describe the facts as allegations, not evidence. Conversely, in a memorandum of law in support of a motion for summary judgment, you would establish that the facts you were relying upon were "undisputed," which is required by most summary judgment standards.[3]

C. Advance Your Theme Through Emotional Facts

Your theme is a comprehensive argument for why your client should prevail, not just on the issue in the memorandum of law, but in the entire case. Because a memorandum of law provides an opportunity to advocate for your client's position, you should include emotional facts in your Facts section that are at the heart of the dispute between the parties and advance your theme.

If facts that are not directly relevant to your legal issue could make the court sympathetic to your client, you should consider working those facts

---

2. *See* Fed. R. Civ. P. 12(b) ("A motion asserting any of these defenses must be made before pleading if a responsive pleading is allowed.").

3. *See* Fed. R. Civ. P. 56(a) ("The court shall grant summary judgment if the movant shows that there is no genuine dispute as to any material fact and the movant is entitled to judgment as a matter of law.").

into your Facts section. For example, imagine that you represent the plaintiff in a products liability case, and the defendant has moved to dismiss. Even if facts regarding how severely your client was injured do not impact whether the case should be dismissed, you would want to include those facts to give the court your client's perspective.

This technique requires subtlety. The court will not want to waste its time reading irrelevant facts. Thus, you should include only the most persuasive emotional facts to develop your theme and to help the court understand the case from your client's point of view.

D. Tell a Persuasive Story

After you identify the legally significant, procedural, and emotional facts that will make up your Facts section, you should weave them into a persuasive story. Although the Facts section in a plaintiff's document will likely include many, if not all, of the same facts as the defendant's document, the plaintiff and defendant should organize and characterize those facts very differently.

Your Facts section should be organized logically and use topic sentences and transitions between short paragraphs. But to make the section a persuasive story, you need to highlight the positive facts and minimize the negative facts. One of the best ways to do this is by taking into account the primacy and recency effects.[4] Readers pay more attention to information at the beginning and the end of a section of text; thus, where possible, you should begin and end your Facts section, and each paragraph within your Facts section, with helpful facts. You can minimize contrary facts by burying them in the middle of the Facts section and in the middle of paragraphs.

Another way to highlight positive facts and minimize negative facts is through word choice. For example, using party designations like "Plaintiff" and "Defendant" has a different impact than using the parties' names. Similarly, describing something as an "event" has a different connotation than "accident." Every word you use in your Facts section should be selected to present the facts as persuasively as possible for your side.

E. Include Citations to Litigation Documents

Because the Facts section of your memorandum of law advances your client's view of the facts, you need to support the facts with citations to litigation documents. Citations to litigation documents show that you have evidentiary support for your factual assertions, in the same way that citations to cases and statutes show that you have legal support for your arguments. Remember that opposing counsel will file a document telling the story from your opponent's point of view. For the court to evaluate each party's view of the facts, it needs to be able to verify the facts in the underlying factual documents.

---

4. These techniques are also discussed in Chapters 26 and 27.

Every sentence in your Facts section should be followed by a citation to the litigation document that establishes the facts described in that sentence. The citation format for litigation documents is covered by *Bluebook* Rules B7 and 10.8.3. These citations typically are enclosed in parentheses and include (1) the abbreviated name of the document and (2) a pincite to where the fact appears in the document. The abbreviations for litigation documents appear in *Bluebook* Table BT1. Litigation document citations should be as specific as possible to make it easy for the court to verify the facts you describe in the record. Your citation should include the specific page and, where possible, the specific paragraph or line number.

For example, in a memorandum of law in support of a motion to dismiss, you would need to cite the complaint. Here is a portion of a Facts section that includes citations to the complaint.

> Plaintiff admits that the box her helmet came in contains numerous warnings. (Compl. ¶23.) Among these warnings is the following language, "[i]f not fastened correctly, helmet chinstrap can come unbuckled." (Compl. ¶24.) Plaintiff alleges that the helmet came unbuckled during her accident because the chinstrap was pulled too tight and, therefore, not fastened correctly. (Compl. ¶¶3-7.)

For other types of motions, you need to cite to litigation documents, such as depositions, declarations, and affidavits. Here is an example of a paragraph from a Facts section followed by citations to a declaration; the first citation includes the page and line numbers of a deposition attached to the declaration as an exhibit.

> Plaintiff admitted that she saw the warnings on the helmet box and read them while she was in the store. (Jones Decl. Ex. A at 45:6-46:18.) The warnings are printed in large, bright red type. (Jones Decl. Ex. E at 2.) The warnings on Happy Helmet boxes are the same size and type as the warnings on boxes from the three other major bicycle helmet manufacturers. (Jones Decl. Exs. B, C, and D.)

F. Omit Arguments

Do not let legal arguments infiltrate your Facts section. If you present the facts persuasively, they may sound similar to your arguments. But you will connect your facts to the law in the Analysis section to create your legal arguments. Your Facts section should include only facts.

For example, in a products liability case where you represent a plaintiff who claims that her bike helmet was defective, the following facts would be persuasive:

- The plaintiff was wearing a helmet manufactured by the defendant when she was in a bike accident.
- The chinstrap of the helmet unbuckled during the crash.

- There are no warnings affixed to the helmet regarding how to properly buckle the chinstrap.

In contrast, the following statements consist of legal arguments that would not be appropriate in the Facts section because they connect facts and law:

- The risk of the chinstrap unbuckling was an inherent danger, and the defendant had a duty to warn consumers of dangers inherent in the bicycle helmet.
- The defendant was negligent in failing to warn that the chinstrap would come undone during a crash if it were buckled too tightly.

Finally, the last sentence of the Facts section should be a transition that sets up the arguments to come. Often, the best way to conclude your persuasive Facts section is with a sentence stating the relief you are requesting.

The following are examples of Facts sections for and against a motion to dismiss.

Facts section in Motion to Dismiss

On April 5, 2013, Plaintiff filed a Complaint alleging that Happy Helmets is legally obligated to include a warning label on its bicycle helmets explaining that the chinstrap could come unbuckled if fastened too tightly. (Compl. ¶3.) Plaintiff claims that she was injured when she hit a pothole while riding her bicycle, which caused her to lose control and flip over the handlebars. (Compl. ¶6.) As this occurred, Plaintiff alleges that the chinstrap of her helmet came unbuckled, causing the helmet to fall off. (Compl. ¶5.) Plaintiff claims that if the helmet had stayed on, she would not have been injured. (Compl. ¶2.) Plaintiff does not allege that the helmet in any way caused the accident.

This Facts section begins with a sentence establishing when the Complaint was filed. This sentence persuasively characterizes the parties by calling the defendant "Happy Helmets" but referring to the plaintiff only as "Plaintiff," rather than using her name.

To minimize facts regarding Plaintiff's injury, the writer states them concisely and places them in the middle of this paragraph. These facts are all characterized as "allegations" and followed by citations to the Complaint.

The first paragraph ends with a sentence that highlights a persuasive fact for Defendant, which is a fact that is missing from the Complaint. (For this reason, this sentence is not followed by a citation.)

Plaintiff admits that the box her helmet came in contains numerous warnings. (Compl. ¶23.) Among these warnings is the following language, "[i]f not fastened correctly, helmet chinstrap can come unbuckled." (Compl. ¶24.) Plaintiff alleges that the helmet came unbuckled during her accident because the chinstrap was pulled too tight and, therefore, not fastened correctly. (Compl. ¶¶3-7.) Because Plaintiff admits that Happy Helmets warned of the risk of the chinstrap coming unbuckled, the Court should grant Happy Helmets' Motion and dismiss Plaintiff's Complaint.

The second paragraph begins with a persuasive fact that describes an "admission" by Plaintiff that is persuasive for Defendant.

The last sentence is a transition that states the relief Defendant is requesting.

Facts section in Opposition to Motion to Dismiss

On November 11, 2012, Augustine Hemingway was severely injured when her bicycle helmet failed to protect her during a crash. (Compl. ¶5.) Ms. Hemingway was thrown over the handlebars of her bicycle after hitting

Because this Facts section is from Plaintiff's point of view, it begins with the date she was injured and describes the helmet's "failure." It also uses her name, rather than referring to her as "Plaintiff," to humanize her for the court.

Notice the persuasive word choice. In the preceding Facts
section the helmet "fell off," while in this one the helmet
"flew off."

a pothole. (Compl. ¶6.) Her helmet flew off during the crash, and she
suffered a severe concussion and numerous cuts and scrapes on her head
and face. (Compl. ¶5.) If her helmet had not come off, these injuries
would not have occurred. (Compl. ¶2.)

This Facts section describes the injuries suffered by Plaintiff, even though the injuries aren't directly relevant to the legal issue in the motion. This Facts section does not characterize the facts as "allegations."

There are no warnings on the helmet or chinstrap. (Compl. ¶3.) Moreover, there is no warning that users must take care not to make the chinstrap too tight because it can cause the chinstrap to come unbuckled
during a crash. (Compl. ¶3.) A warning on the box, which Ms. Hemingway discarded soon after purchasing the helmet and long before the accident, states only, "[i]f not fastened correctly, helmet chinstrap can come
unbuckled." (Compl. ¶¶23-25.) Because Defendant did not adequately
warn of the danger that resulted in severe injury to Ms. Hemingway, the
Court should deny Defendant's Motion to Dismiss.

Where Defendant's Facts section drew attention to the warning on the box, Plaintiff's Facts section focuses on the lack of warnings on the helmet itself.

This sentence uses the word "only" to minimize the value of the warning on the box.

The last sentence is a transition that states the relief Plaintiff is requesting.

3. STEP THREE: PREPARE A LEGAL STANDARD SECTION IF NECESSARY

In addition to the substantive legal issue in your memorandum of law, the
court's decision may depend on the legal or procedural standard governing
that type of motion. Certain motions have burdens or presumptions that can
impact the outcome. When preparing a motion with a special legal standard,
it would be helpful to you and the court to set out that standard—in a way
that is persuasive for your side—in a separate Legal Standard section before
the Argument. This Legal Standard section states only the procedural standard, not the rule that governs the substantive legal issue, which appears in
the Rule section of your CREAC.

For example, when a court considers a motion to dismiss under Federal
Rule of Civil Procedure 12(b)(6), it accepts the factual allegations in the complaint as true and views them in the light most favorable to the non-moving
party.[5] That legal standard overlays the specific legal question in a given motion: for example, whether the plaintiff has sufficiently alleged the elements
of a products liability cause of action. Through word choice and organization, you should present this Legal Standard as persuasively as you can.

---

5. *See, e.g., Daniels-Hall v. Nat'l Educ. Ass'n*, 629 F.3d 992, 998 (9th Cir. 2010) ("We accept as
true all well-pleaded allegations of material fact, and construe them in the light most favorable
to the non-moving party.").

For example, in a Rule 12(b)(6) motion to dismiss, the moving party would want to emphasize that the court is required to take only factual allegations—not legal conclusions—as true,[6] while the non-moving party would emphasize that the court must view the factual allegations in the light most favorable to the non-moving party. The parties will present the same legal standard, but each side should tailor that presentation to make it persuasive.

4. STEP FOUR: ADD PERSUASIVE ROADMAPS AND SUBHEADINGS TO GUIDE THE COURT

The purpose of your memorandum of law is to persuade the court. To do this, your document must be clear and cohesive. Thus, you should review your Argument section and point headings and then insert roadmaps, transitions, and headings where they will be useful to the court.

A. Draft Persuasive Roadmaps for Complex Arguments

If your trial court memorandum of law involves one or more complex issues with multiple subissues, you should draft at least one persuasive roadmap to introduce your arguments on each complex issue and to show how the issues relate. A persuasive roadmap sets up the structure of the argument that follows and provides crucial guidance for the court.

The roadmap begins with your Conclusion on the broadest issue. Then, it states your Conclusion on each subissue in the order that you will discuss the subissues. If your memorandum of law includes multiple complex issues, you should insert a persuasive roadmap for each main issue.

For example, if you have multiple CREACs with a point heading for each, put the roadmap before the first point heading to introduce the issues that follow. Or, for a document with one major point heading with multiple subissues, like the example below, put the roadmap after the main point heading to introduce the subissues that follow. The following is an example of a roadmap paragraph for a memorandum of law in opposition to a motion to dismiss.

I. The Court Should Not Dismiss Hemingway's Claim for Negligent Failure to Warn

The Court should deny Defendant's motion to dismiss. Hemingway's Complaint includes sufficient allegations that the risk of the chinstrap unbuckling was an inherent danger that triggered Defendant's obligation to warn. Further, Hemingway has demonstrated that Defendant did not include any warnings on the helmet or chinstrap that warned of this inherent danger. Last, Defendant will not be able to prove that the small

> This is a roadmap paragraph for the complex issue of negligent failure to warn. This issue has three subissues. The roadmap paragraph begins with the Conclusion on the main issue. Then, it states the Conclusion for the three subissues in the order those issues are discussed.

---

6. *See, e.g., Ashcroft v. Iqbal*, 556 U.S. 662, 678 (2009) ("[T]he tenet that a court must accept as true all of the allegations contained in a complaint is inapplicable to legal conclusions.").

warning that appeared on the helmet box was sufficient as a matter of law.

A. Hemingway Has Sufficiently Alleged That Defendant Was Obligated to Warn of the Inherent Danger of the Chinstrap Unbuckling.

[CREAC]

— Note that the language in the roadmap and the subheadings is similar, but not identical.

B. Defendant Failed to Affix Any Warnings to the Helmet or Chinstrap Regarding the Risk of Unbuckling.

[CREAC]

C. The Small Warning on the Box Was Not Sufficient as a Matter of Law.

[CREAC]

As you can see from this example, the sentences in the roadmap track the point headings for the subissues. Make sure, however, that the roadmap sentences and the point headings are not identical to avoid monotony.

A. Insert Persuasive Subheadings

Point headings help make a trial court memorandum of law persuasive because they present concise, readable arguments that stand out from the rest of the text. Point headings grab the reader's attention and provide the reader with a break. From reading Chapter 24, you should already have point headings that outline your Argument. Now, look through your Argument to see whether there are any stretches of two or more pages of text where no headings or subheadings appear. If so, consider inserting additional subheadings. You may want to include subheadings to break up a long Analysis section or to separate the Rule, Explanation, and Analysis sections.

You can add as many layers of subheadings as you think are necessary to guide and persuade the reader. The only limitation is that there must be at least two headings at each level of your outline. For example, if you added subheading A.1. below, you would also have to add subheading A.2.

A. Hemingway Has Sufficiently Alleged That Defendant Was Obligated to Warn of the Inherent Danger of the Chinstrap Unbuckling.
   1. Defendant was aware that the chinstrap could unbuckle if fastened too tightly.
   2. Hemingway could have loosened the chinstrap if the helmet contained an adequate warning.

Similarly, if you added subheading a. under A.2., you would also need to add subheading b.:

   2. Hemingway could have loosened the chinstrap if the helmet contained an adequate warning.
      a. Hemingway has alleged that she read and followed the other warnings printed on the helmet box.

b. Other helmet manufacturers include warnings on their chin-
   straps.

Like point headings, every subheading is a complete sentence that states a persuasive argument for your side. When taken together, the point headings and subheadings create a persuasive outline of your Argument.

5. STEP FIVE: WRITE A COMPELLING INTRODUCTION

The court will likely read the Introduction in your memorandum of law first. You can think of the Introduction as your opening statement. It tells the court what you are going to prove in the memorandum of law that follows. The Introduction should be concise and compelling. It should grab the court's attention and explain why your position is correct.

Try writing the Introduction last, after you have prepared the Argument and Facts sections. At that point, you are familiar with the anchors, your best arguments, and how to present them effectively. You also know the facts that are helpful and persuasive for your side. Moreover, you are comfortable with your theme and will be able to weave it through the Introduction.

An Introduction is typically only a paragraph or two. It should follow the general organization of your Argument—meaning that you present the points in the same order that you argue them. It should not include citations to factual documents or legal authorities. The following are Introductions that would work for the memoranda of law for and against the motion to dismiss involving the bicycle helmet.

Introduction for Memorandum of Law in Support of Motion to Dismiss

The Court should dismiss Plaintiff's Complaint for negligent failure to warn. Plaintiff admits that she saw the numerous warnings on the Happy Helmets box. Plaintiff admits that she read those warnings when she bought the helmet. And Plaintiff admits that there was a warning that stated that the chinstrap could come unbuckled if not fastened correctly. That warning is legally adequate. For all these reasons, Plaintiff's Complaint fails to state a claim as a matter of law and should be dismissed.

Introduction for Memorandum of Law in Opposition to Motion to Dismiss

The Court should deny Defendant's Motion to Dismiss because Augustine Hemingway has stated a viable claim for negligent failure to warn based on Happy Helmets' legally inadequate warnings. Happy Helmets is aware that if the chinstrap on one of its helmets is buckled too tightly, it can come undone during an accident. Yet, there is no warning on the helmet or chinstrap warning consumers not to buckle the chinstrap tightly. Indeed, even a consumer, like Augustine Hemingway, who reads all of the warnings on the box will have no idea that tightly buckling the chinstrap creates a risk that the helmet will fail so that it will provide no protection in the event of a bicycle crash. This failure is a risk, inherent in the helmet, that gives rise to a duty to warn. Because Defendant failed to adequately warn of this risk, its Motion to Dismiss should be denied.

6. STEP SIX: SCRUTINIZE AND REVISE

A trial court memorandum of law will be scrutinized by the court and opposing counsel. Use the following checklist to ensure that your document will hold up under this intense scrutiny.

- ☑ Does the caption follow the formatting rules that govern your document?
- ☑ Read the Introduction. Does it present a persuasive synthesis of your theme and Argument?
- ☑ Read the Facts section. Does it include all legally significant, procedural, and emotional facts that are relevant to the issue in the memorandum of law and support your theme?
- ☑ Does the Facts section include legally relevant contrary facts?
- ☑ Does the Facts section omit legal arguments?
- ☑ Does the Facts section tell a persuasive story from your client's point of view?
- ☑ Does the Facts section include a specific citation to a factual document for every fact or allegation that it includes?
- ☑ Read the point headings. Is every point heading a persuasive sentence?
- ☑ Do the point headings provide an outline of the points of your Argument?
- ☑ Does a point heading appear at least every two pages or so?
- ☑ Are there at least two point headings at every outline level?
- ☑ Read the Argument. Does every complex issue begin with a persuasive roadmap that introduces the subissues that follow?
- ☑ Does the document end with a separate Conclusion section that uses the customary language for your jurisdiction and a properly formatted signature block?

The following is an example of a trial court memorandum of law.

Example
Motion 30.1

UNITED STATES DISTRICT COURT
FOR THE SOUTHERN DISTRICT OF FLORIDA
CASE NO.: 11-3467-Civ-TUDOR/PHELIPPE

Kieran G. Mahoney

    Plaintiff,

    v.

Gold Coast Herald Tribune

    Defendant.

— The caption is properly formatted according to court rules.

DEFENDANT HERALD TRIBUNE'S MOTION TO DISMISS
PLAINTIFF'S COMPLAINT AND
INCORPORATED MEMORANDUM OF LAW

Defendant Gold Coast Herald Tribune respectfully requests that this Court dismiss Plaintiff Kieran G. Mahoney's Complaint for failure to state a claim upon which relief can be granted under Federal Rule of Civil Procedure 12(b)(6) and states the following in support:

— This is the legally operative language of the notice of motion.

INTRODUCTION

Kieran G. Mahoney became famous by appearing on the reality television show "The Real Wives of Dade County." Despite having courted publicity relentlessly to promote herself and the show, she is attempting to use a defamation claim to chill the Herald Tribune's ability to comment and opine on her life.

— The Introduction grabs the court's attention, advances the party's theme, and summarizes the arguments in the order they are made in the Argument section. It doesn't include citations to factual documents or legal authorities.

The Herald Tribune moves to dismiss Mahoney's Complaint for two reasons. First, the challenged statements were not defamatory as a matter of law. Instead, the statements were "rhetorical hyperbole," which is protected as pure opinion and cannot be the basis for a defamation claim. Further, Mahoney is a general public figure but has failed to plead a facially plausible claim that the Herald Tribune acted with actual malice—the required degree of fault. The Complaint alleges no facts that would establish that the Herald Tribune knew the statements in the column were false or acted with reckless disregard to their falsity. Accordingly, Mahoney's Complaint should be dismissed.

STATEMENT OF FACTS

Kieran G. Mahoney is a former "reality television star" who was a cast member of the popular reality television program "The Real Wives of Dade County." (Compl. ¶ 3.)

— The Statement of Facts weaves legally significant, procedural, and emotional facts into a persuasive story that advances the party's theme. It doesn't include any legal arguments.

"The Real Wives of Dade County" follows the lives of six women living in South Florida. (Compl. ¶ 2.) The show depicts the women's daily activities and interactions. (*Id.*)

From April 2011 to May 2012, Mahoney appeared regularly on the program, which airs on the Brave Television Network. (Compl. ¶ 3.) In addition to appearing on episodes of "Real Wives," Mahoney appeared at various media events to promote the program, and she frequently was the subject of media coverage that included discussion on radio and television talk shows and articles in newspapers, magazines, and blogs. (Compl. ¶ 12.)

On March 3, 2012, the Gold Coast Herald Tribune ran an item in its "Loose Lips" column about Mahoney. (Compl. ¶ 4.) Loose Lips is a celebrity gossip column that is written by Julie Lipkin. (Compl. ¶ 5.) Loose Lips often discusses reality television stars. (Compl. ¶ 6.) The column's tagline is "Entertainment News with a View." (Compl. ¶ 7, Ex. A.) The column appears on the Comics page of the Herald Tribune, next to Dear Abby, the horoscopes, comic strips, and Daily Jumble. (*Id.*) The March 3 column stated as follows:

> Mahoney a Charlatan in Chanel?
> A source close to Real Wives diva Kieran Mahoney says Mahoney is about to file for bankruptcy and is about to be investigated for tax fraud. Despite this, the bankrupt basketcase has been all over town pretending she can still handle the Miami lifestyle.

(*Id.*) Mahoney's Complaint alleges that, contrary to the information in the column, Mahoney did not file for bankruptcy and was never investigated by the IRS. (Compl. ¶ 10.) The Complaint alleges that the source of the information was likely a disgruntled former employee of Mahoney. (Compl. ¶ 11.)

On April 3, 2012, the Brave Network released a statement revealing its decision not to extend Mahoney's contract to appear on "Real Wives" for the next season. (Compl. ¶ 22.) The statement explained that "poor viewer response," a decline in ratings, and a desire to bring "fresh faces" to the cast were the reasons for its decision to not include Mahoney in the next season. (Compl. ¶ 23.) Mahoney alleges that her contract was not renewed because of the information in the Loose Lips column about her financial problems, despite the language in the Brave Network's statement to the contrary. (Compl. ¶ 25.)

A month after Brave's decision, Mahoney brought this action against the Herald Tribune alleging that the column was defamatory. (Compl. ¶ 1.) In particular, Mahoney alleges that the statements that she is a "charlatan" and a "bankrupt basket case" and that

---

The facts are organized persuasively to highlight the helpful facts that will serve the arguments that appear later in the memorandum of law.

Every sentence is followed by a citation to a litigation document. Because this is a motion to dismiss, all of the facts are allegations from the Complaint.

The facts are characterized persuasively for the Defendant. For example, it refers to "Loose Lips" as a column, rather than an article.

Negative facts are minimized by being placed in a less conspicuous place and described as allegations.

The facts include details like dates and quoted language, where relevant.

The Facts section avoids legal argument, pointing out instead where the Plaintiff's case lacks facts in support.

All facts relevant to the issue in the memorandum of law are included in the Statement of Facts.

she "is about to file for bankruptcy and is about to be investigated for tax fraud" were defamatory. (Compl. ¶ 14.) Because Mahoney fails to state a claim upon which relief can be granted, her Complaint should be dismissed.

— The Facts section concludes with a transition to the Argument.

LEGAL STANDARD

— The Legal Standard section describes the procedural standard for a motion to dismiss under Fed. R. Civ. P. 12(b)(6). This standard is stated persuasively, using words like "unless" and "only" to make it appear easy for a motion to dismiss to succeed. Authorities from this Court and higher courts are cited for support, including a case that resulted in the outcome requested in the memorandum of law, which is noted in a parenthetical.

A complaint should be dismissed under Federal Rule of Civil Procedure 12(b)(6) unless the plaintiff can present enough facts to state a claim for relief that is "plausible on its face." *Five for Entertainment S.A. v. Rodriguez*, 877 F. Supp. 2d 1321, 1326 (S.D. Fla. 2012) (granting motion to dismiss on defamation claim) (citing *Ashcroft v. Iqbal*, 566 U.S. 662 (2009)). "A complaint can only survive a 12(b)(6) motion to dismiss if it contains factual allegations that are 'enough to raise a right to relief above the speculative level, on the assumption that all the [factual] allegations in the complaint are true.'" *Id.* (citing *Bell Atl. Corp. v. Twombly*, 550 U.S. 544 (2007)).

ARGUMENT

— The Argument starts with a brief Conclusion to begin the roadmap.

The Court should grant the Herald Tribune's Motion to Dismiss. The Complaint fails to state a valid defamation claim under Florida law, and Mahoney is therefore not entitled to relief. Under Florida law, a plaintiff cannot succeed on a defamation claim unless she establishes the following five elements: (1) the statement was published; (2) the statement was false; (3) the statement was defamatory; (4) the defendant acted with actual malice, meaning knowledge or reckless disregard of the falsity on a matter concerning a public figure; and (5) the plaintiff suffered actual damages. *Jews for Jesus, Inc. v. Rapp*, 997 So. 2d 1098, 1106 (Fla. 2008).

— This persuasive roadmap paragraph includes the overarching Rule stating the elements of defamation.

Mahoney's Complaint fails for two reasons: (1) As a matter of law, the challenged statements are non-actionable rhetorical hyperbole, and (2) Mahoney is a public figure and the allegations in the Complaint establish that the Herald Tribune did not act with the required actual malice. Because both of these issues can be resolved as a matter of law based on the allegations in Mahoney's Complaint, the Complaint should be dismissed. *See Stewart v. Sun Sentinel Co.*, 695 So. 2d 360, 363 (Fla. Dist. Ct. App. 1997) ("Where the facts are not in dispute in defamation cases . . . pretrial dispositions are 'especially appropriate' because of the chilling effect these cases can have on freedom of speech.").

— The persuasive roadmap then states the Conclusion on each issue in the order the issues appear in the Argument.

— The roadmap ends with a transition that establishes that the relief requested is procedurally proper.

I. The Complaint Should Be Dismissed Because the Statements Were Rhetorical Hyperbole.

> This point heading is a concise, persuasive sentence that states the Conclusion on the first issue.

The Court should dismiss the Complaint because the challenged statements were not defamatory but instead were rhetorical hyperbole. The question "whether the complained of words are actionable expressions of fact or non-actionable expressions of pure opinion/ rhetorical hyperbole" is for the Court to decide as a matter of law. *Fortson v. Colangelo*, 434 F. Supp. 2d 1369, 1379 (S.D. Fla. 2006); *From v. Tallahassee Democrat, Inc.*, 400 So. 2d 52, 56 (Fla. Dist. Ct. App. 1981).

> The CREAC begins with a Conclusion.

> The Rule section begins with the most general rule, which defines procedurally whether the issue is one of law or fact. All rules are stated as persuasively as possible.

A. Defamation Cannot Be Premised on a Statement of Pure Opinion or Rhetorical Hyperbole That Discloses the Factual Basis for the Statement.

> Major issue I. contains one CREAC. To guide the court, there are subheadings to differentiate the Rule, Explanation, and Analysis sections. This first subheading states a broad rule.

Statements of pure opinion cannot be defamatory. *Fortson*, 434 F. Supp. 2d at 1379. "The distinction between fact and pure opinion/rhetorical hyperbole is a critical one; to be actionable, a defamatory publication must convey to a reasonable reader the impression that it describes actual facts about the plaintiff or the activities in which he participated." *Id.* A statement is pure opinion, rather than a mixed expression of opinion, when the facts that form the basis for the opinion are stated in the publication or available to the public. *From*, 400 So. 2d at 57 (citing Restatement (Second) of Torts §566); *see also Hay v. Indep. Newspapers, Inc.*, 450 So. 2d 293, 295 (Fla. Dist. Ct. App. 1984) ("Mixed opinion is based upon facts regarding a person or his conduct that are neither stated in the publication nor assumed to exist by a party exposed to the communication . . . . Pure opinion is protected under the First Amendment, but mixed opinion is not.").

> This Rule section describes the general rules persuasively through a combination of quoting and paraphrasing. To add weight to the Rule section, there are explanatory parentheticals with quoted language from the cases. The cases are a mixture of mandatory and persuasive authorities, selected because they are legally and factually similar to the present case and have favorable outcomes.

Pure opinion sometimes takes the form of "rhetorical hyperbole." *Fortson*, 434 F. Supp. 2d at 1378. The U.S. Supreme Court and the U.S. Court of Appeals for the Eleventh Circuit "have long recognized" that a non-literal assertion is not actionable defamation. *Horsley v. Rivera*, 292 F.3d 695, 701 (11th Cir. 2002). "Acknowledging that debate 'may well include vehement, caustic, and sometimes unpleasantly sharp attacks,' the Court nevertheless has decided that such attacks are constitutionally protected and those who make them are exempt from liability for defamation if the attacks are simply 'rhetorical hyperbole.'" *Horsley v. Feldt*, 304 F.3d 1125, 1131 (11th Cir. 2002) (citation omitted).

The Supreme Court has described rhetorical hyperbole as "imaginative expression" and "loose, figurative, or hyperbolic language." *Id.* (citing *Milkovich v. Lorain Journal Co.*, 497 U.S. 1, 20-21 (1990)). When a writer states an opinion using this kind of language, the statement "cannot reasonably be interpreted as stating actual facts" about the subject. *Milkovich*, 497 U.S. at 20, *quoted in Colodny v. Iverson, Yoakum, Papiano & Hatch*, 936 F. Supp. 917, 924 (M.D. Fla. 1996).

B.   The Medium, Context, and Language of a Statement Determine Whether It Is Rhetorical Hyperbole.

> The second subheading begins the Explanation section and states the three anchors the court will use to decide the issue in the memorandum of law.

A court determines whether a statement is rhetorical hyperbole by considering medium, context, and language. *Colodny*, 936 F. Supp. at 923. A statement that appears in an opinion piece or column, rather than a news article, is likely to be rhetorical hyperbole because the medium communicates that the statement is an opinion. *See id.* at 924 (holding that the context of a letter published in a "Commentary" section of a newspaper like a letter to the editor "unambiguously reveals that it is an opinion"); *see also Hay*, 450 So. 2d at 295 (holding that a statement published as a letter to the editor in a section of the newspaper titled "The Forum, Opinion," was pure opinion).

> The topic sentence describes the three anchors.

> This sentence persuasively explains the first anchor.

For example, one court held that statements in a sports column were rhetorical hyperbole, noting that they appeared in "a medium that fosters debate . . . and that routinely uses figurative or hyperbolic language." *Fortson*, 434 F. Supp. 2d at 1381. In *Fortson*, the statements about an NBA basketball player were in a column called "Hoop du Jour," which "held itself out as containing subjective content" and was a vehicle for the writer's "thoughts and opinions on the NBA." *Id.* Accordingly, "a reasonable reader is more likely to regard its content as opinion and/or rhetorical hyperbole." *Id.*

> This Explanation paragraph describes the details of a case that is a persuasive example of how a court has interpreted the first anchor. The facts of the present case will be compared to these facts in the Analysis section.

Further, a statement will be held to be rhetorical hyperbole when the language and context establish that the writer is stating an opinion, not a fact, or speaking figuratively, rather than literally. *See Feldt*, 304 F.3d at 1132 (holding that the "context" and "flavor" of the challenged statements made them rhetorical hyperbole); *Rivera*, 292 F.3d at 702 (holding that the circumstances of a television interview by Geraldo Rivera "instill upon a reasonable viewer the impression that the parties were exchanging dialogue at a non-literal level."); *Colodny*, 936 F. Supp. at 925 ("[T]he totality of the circumstances surrounding the 'fraud'

> This sentence persuasively describes the second and third anchors. They are closely related, so they are discussed together.

> The paragraph uses explanatory parentheticals to support the explanation of the second and third anchors.

5

statement clearly lead this Court to conclude that it was an expression of non-actionable, pure opinion.").

For instance, a court held statements to be hyperbole when "no reasonable reader" would take them in their "literal sense." *Fortson*, 434 F. Supp. 2d at 1382-83. In *Fortson*, the court held terms like "thugged out," "vacant lot," "meaningless mass," "gangstas and wankstas," and "attempted murder" were hyperbole when used to describe a basketball player and his actions. *Id.* at 1385. The court described the statements as epithets and slang and noted the terms were "a form of hyperbole typical in sports parlance." *Id.* at 1382-83. The court explained that the plaintiff's "assumption that reasonable people read words in a vacuum, according to their dictionary definition, is ill-founded. As the law recognizes, reasonable people read words contextually." *Id.* at 1385; *see also Colodny*, 936 F. Supp. at 925 (noting that the word "fraud" was "too imprecise, undefinable, and non-actionable" to "suggest to the ordinary reader that [the plaintiff] committed a crime").

> This paragraph describes the details of a case that is a persuasive example of how a court has interpreted the second and third anchors. Again, the facts of the present case will be compared to these facts in the Analysis section.

C. The Column in the Herald Tribune Was Rhetorical Hyperbole.

> The third subheading begins the Analysis section and states the Conclusion.

1. The underlying facts were disclosed to the reader.

> The Analysis section is broken up with another layer of subheadings. This subheading states the conclusion that the broad rule is satisfied.

The statements in the Herald Tribune column describing Mahoney as a "charlatan in Chanel" and "bankrupt basket case" were rhetorical hyperbole. First, the statements were "pure opinion," not a mixed opinion, because the column included the factual basis for the statements. *See From*, 400 So. 2d at 57. The column stated that the information came from "a source close to Mahoney." (Compl. ¶ 7, Ex. A.)

Further, the facts that were the basis for the statements, including that Mahoney was about to file for bankruptcy and was being investigated for tax fraud, were disclosed to the reader. (*Id.*) The opinion was not based on implied or undisclosed defamatory facts. (*Id.*) Similarly, in *Hay*, the court held that a statement was pure opinion when it was based on facts that were disclosed in the article. *Hay*, 450 So. 2d at 295.

> This Analysis paragraph shows the general rule is satisfied by comparing the facts of the present case to the facts and outcome of another case.

2. The statement appeared in the medium of a gossip column, which conveyed to the reader that it was rhetorical hyperbole.

> This subheading states the conclusion on the first anchor.

In addition, the medium in which the statement appeared—a gossip and entertainment column, rather than a news article—establishes that the statement was rhetorical

> This Analysis paragraph begins with a topic sentence explaining why the anchor is satisfied. It states the same idea as the subheading above it but isn't identical.

hyperbole. Like "Hoop du Jour" in *Fortson*, the Loose Lips column in the Herald Tribune is a medium where readers expect to encounter opinions and hyperbole. *See Fortson*, 434 F. Supp. 2d at 1381. The column has a brash, impudent style that suits the topics it covers: reality television and celebrity gossip. *See id.* at 1382 ("[C]ourts have recognized that sports commentaries in particular are likely to contain statements of opinion, rather than fact, because they serve as a 'traditional haven for cajoling, invective, and hyperbole.'"). Although the tagline for the column refers to the subject matter of the column as "entertainment news," the column is on the same page as the horoscopes, cartoon strips, and Daily Jumble—not news articles. (Compl. ¶ 7, Ex. A.) Loose Lips is not presented as news or fact-based reporting.

3. The context and language of the statement establish that it was not meant to be taken literally.

Last, the context and language of the statement establish that it was rhetorical hyperbole. The statement must be read in context—as a column written in a jokey voice that uses harsh language to convey the writer's disdain for the column's badly behaving famous subjects. *See Feldt*, 304 F.3d at 1133 ("Her comments were 'lusty and imaginative expression[s] of the contempt felt by [her] towards [Horsley].'") (alteration in original).

Readers of Loose Lips would not think that by calling Mahoney a "charlatan" and "bankrupt basket case" the Herald Tribune was stating actual facts regarding her financial and business activities or her mental health, just as the court concluded in *Fortson* that readers would not think that the plaintiff "engages in physically violent criminal activity" because the column claimed he was "thugged out." *See Fortson*, 434 F. Supp. 2d at 1382; *see also Rivera*, 292 F.3d at 702 (holding that no reasonable viewer would have concluded that Geraldo Rivera was "literally contending" that the plaintiff could be charged with a felony when he called him an "accomplice to murder").

The Loose Lips column used those terms figuratively, as exaggerated epithets, not factual statements. *See Fortson*, 434 F. Supp. 2d at 1385 ("[R]easonable readers . . . were no more likely to have believed that Fortson had actually tried to kill Cabarkapa than reasonable readers of the late 1920s were to have believed that 'Murderer's Row'—Ruth, Gehrig, and their Yankee teammates—had actually slayed opposing pitchers . . . . [T]he term 'murder' was obviously applied hyperbolically; and it was understood by the reasonable

---

— The paragraph includes a detailed comparison to a relevant case. It uses an explanatory parenthetical to add support to the analogy.

— This paragraph also acknowledges a fact that helps the opposing side in a way that minimizes its impact.

— This subheading states the conclusion on the second and third anchors.

— Again, this Analysis paragraph begins with a topic sentence explaining why the anchor is satisfied.

— This close comparison to the facts and outcome of a relevant case establishes that the second and third anchors support the Defendant's position.

— This additional case comparison is presented through a "see also" signal and explanatory parenthetical.

7

reader in that manner."); *DeMoya v. Walsh*, 441 So. 2d 1120, 1120-21 (Fla. Dist. Ct. App. 1983) (holding that calling plaintiff a "raving maniac" and "raving idiot" was pure opinion).

Accordingly, the Court should hold that as a matter of law the statements are non-actionable rhetorical hyperbole and dismiss Mahoney's defamation claim. *See From*, 400 So. 2d at 58 (affirming grant of motion to dismiss because statement was pure opinion).

> The CREAC ends with a short Conclusion and a citation that includes an explanatory parenthetical describing a favorable outcome.

II. The Court Should Dismiss Mahoney's Complaint Because It Fails to Allege Actual Malice.

> This point heading is a persuasive sentence that states the Conclusion on the second major issue.

In addition, the Court should dismiss Mahoney's Complaint because she is a public figure and has not pleaded actual malice. A defamation claim by a public figure will fail unless the plaintiff establishes "actual malice" on the part of the publisher by clear and convincing evidence. *Mile Marker, Inc. v. Peterson Publ'g, L.L.C.*, 811 So. 2d 841, 845 (Fla. Dist. Ct. App. 2002) (citing *N.Y. Times Co. v. Sullivan*, 376 U.S. 254 (1964)). "Under the actual malice test a public figure plaintiff must establish that the disseminator of the information either knew the alleged defamatory statements were false, or published them with reckless disregard despite awareness of their probable falsity." *Id.*

> The second major issue contains two subissues and thus, two CREACs. This roadmap paragraph sets up the two subissues in the order they are argued.

> These are overarching rules that apply to both CREACs for this major issue.

A. Mahoney Is a General Public Figure Because She Had Access to the Media and Volunteered to Be the Subject of Public Scrutiny.

> This subheading states the Conclusion for the first CREAC.

Mahoney is a general public figure. The Court decides as a matter of law whether a plaintiff is a public figure. *Mile Marker*, 811 So. 2d at 845. A general public figure is an individual who has achieved "pervasive fame or notoriety" in a community such that she "becomes a public figure for all purposes and in all contexts." *Gertz v. Robert Welch, Inc.* 418 U.S. 323, 351 (1974); *see also Don King Prods., Inc. v. Walt Disney Co.*, 40 So. 3d 40, 44 (Fla. Dist. Ct. App. 2010) (treating Don King as a general public figure).

> The first CREAC begins here with a Conclusion.

> The Rule section persuasively describes the general rules.

Two qualities distinguish public figures from private figures: (1) public figures "usually enjoy significantly greater access to the channels of effective communication and hence have a more realistic opportunity to counteract false statements then private individuals normally enjoy," and (2) they have "voluntarily exposed themselves to increased risk of injury from defamatory falsehood concerning them." *Gertz*, 418 U.S. at 344-45.

> The Explanation section begins with a summary of the anchors relevant to this subissue.

Courts consider these qualities to determine whether a plaintiff is a public figure. *See id.* For example, in *Rebozo*, the court held that Charles Rebozo was a general public figure because he had access to the channels of communication, including major news-papers and television networks, and he had voluntarily exposed himself to public scrutiny through his high-profile relationship with President Richard Nixon and work on Nixon's reelection campaign. *Rebozo v. Wash. Post Co.*, 637 F.2d 375, 379-80 (5th Cir. 1981); *see also Curtis Publ'g Co. v. Butts*, 388 U.S. 130, 154-55 (1967) (holding that individuals were public figures because they "commanded a substantial amount of independent public interest" and "had sufficient access to the means of counterargument to be able 'to expose through discussion the falsehood and fallacies of the defamatory statements'"); *Little v. Breland*, 93 F.3d 755, 758 (11th Cir. 1996) (holding that plaintiff was a public figure be-cause he had participated in "activities whose success depends in large part on publicity"); *Lampkin-Asam v. Miami Daily News, Inc.*, 408 So. 2d 666, 668 (Fla. Dist. Ct. App. 1981) (holding that author who sought "substantial" publicity was a public figure).

> — The details of multiple cases are used in this paragraph to explain how courts have interpreted these anchors. Some of the cases are discussed in the text, while others are summarized in citations with explanatory parentheticals.

As a cast member of the Brave Network reality television program "Real Wives of Dade County" Mahoney is a general public figure. The Complaint describes Mahoney as a "reality television star" and admits she had access to the channels of communication and voluntarily sought to be the subject of public scrutiny. (Compl. ¶¶ 3, 12.)

> — The Analysis begins with a concise thesis sentence.

Mahoney appeared frequently on television, made public appearances to promote her television show, and was written about in newspaper, magazine, and blog articles. (Compl. ¶ 12.) Like Charles Rebozo, who engaged in activities that were of great interest to the press, Mahoney chose to appear on a reality television show and promote that show in the media to garner public attention. *See Rebozo*, 637 F.2d at 379-80. Indeed, Mahoney brought this lawsuit because she alleges that she has suffered harm from not having her contract renewed to appear on the program. *See Lampkin-Asam*, 408 So. 2d at 668 (noting that the plaintiff sought substantial publicity, "including the very publicity which is the subject matter of this action"). Mahoney sought public exposure voluntarily; therefore, she is a general public figure, and this action should be dismissed.

> — The Analysis includes a detailed factual comparison to a relevant case to show how the anchors should be interpreted in the present case.

B. Mahoney Failed to Allege Actual Malice Because Her Complaint Admits the Article Was Not Published with Reckless Disregard.

> — This subheading states the Conclusion for the second CREAC.

Mahoney's Complaint fails to state a facially plausible claim that the Herald Tribune acted with actual malice. To plead actual malice, a plaintiff must allege that the publisher

> — The second CREAC begins here with a Conclusion.

9

knew the statements were false or published the statements with reckless disregard to whether they were false or not. *N.Y. Times Co.*, 376 U.S. at 279-80; *Lampkin-Asam*, 408 So. 2d at 668. The actual malice standard requires a plaintiff to prove that the defendant had a "high degree" of awareness of the probable falsity of the information. *Lampkin-Asam*, 408 So. 2d at 668-69 (the plaintiff must prove "the publication involved was deliberately falsified or published recklessly despite the publisher's awareness of probable falsity").

— The Rule section persuasively describes the broadest rules.

— The last sentence of this paragraph is the Explanation. The anchor for this rule is simple and doesn't require a discussion of the details of the case beyond this explanatory parenthetical.

Mahoney's claim should be dismissed because the Complaint admits that the Herald Tribune did not publish the column with any degree of reckless disregard for its truth. Mahoney admits that the column was based on information the author received from "a source close to Mahoney." (Compl. ¶ 7, Ex. A.) Even accepting Mahoney's allegations as true, the reliance upon the unnamed source establishes that the Herald Tribune had a basis for believing the information was true.

— The Analysis section begins with a thesis sentence.

Although Mahoney claims that this unnamed source is likely a disgruntled former employee, she does not allege any facts that would show by clear and convincing evidence that the Herald Tribune knew that this person was lying or that the Herald Tribune acted in reckless disregard of a high likelihood that this person was lying. (Compl. ¶ 10.) Instead, Mahoney's allegations indicate that the Herald Tribune believed the unnamed source's information to be true. *See Dockery v. Fla. Democratic Party*, 799 So. 2d 291, 297 (Fla. Dist. Ct. App. 2001) ("Plaintiff has failed to present any record evidence that would clearly and convincingly demonstrate that FDP *knew*, at the time that it published these statements, that Dockery was *not* under investigation by the federal government."). Thus, Mahoney has failed to sufficiently plead actual malice, and her Complaint should be dismissed.

— The comparison to a relevant case occurs only in a parenthetical. This use of a parenthetical is a strategic choice that is appropriate here because it focuses the argument on the lack of sufficient allegations in the plaintiff's complaint. It makes the argument appear simple and straightforward.

CONCLUSION

For the foregoing reasons, the Herald Tribune respectfully requests that the Court dismiss Mahoney's Complaint.

— The Conclusion section is a single sentence that uses customary language to repeat the request for relief.

DATED this 12th day of March, 2013.

Respectfully submitted,

/s/ Oscar Smalls
_____

Oscar Smalls
Counsel for
Defendant Gold Coast
Herald Tribune

— This signature block is properly formatted.

10

chapter 31

Appellate Briefs

An appellate brief is one of the most complex forms of persuasive legal writing. Appellate briefs are addressed to intermediate or highest-level courts. After a final decision or judgment by the trial court, the losing party files a notice of appeal. If a party loses at the intermediate appellate court, the party can ask the highest court to hear the next appeal in a writ of certiorari.

On an appeal, the parties file briefs on the merits. First, the losing party (now the "appellant" or "petitioner") files a brief asking the appellate court to review the decision of the court below and reach a different conclusion. Next, the prevailing party (now the "appellee" or "respondent") files a brief asking the court to affirm the lower court's decision. Last, the appellant files a reply brief. Once the briefs are submitted, the court may hold oral arguments.[1] After the intermediate appellate court renders its decision, the process may repeat, with the losing party asking the highest court to review the decision of the intermediate court.

Generally, new issues can't be raised on appeal. For an appellate court to decide an issue, that issue must have been decided in the lower court. Raising an issue at the trial court level so that it can be reviewed by an appellate court is called "preserving" the issue for appeal.

The format and substance of an appellate brief are governed by the appellate rules of procedure and local rules of court. This chapter will provide general guidance for preparing an appellate brief, but you should always follow the specific rules that govern your document.

Writing an Appellate Brief

1. Create a template based on the requirements of the appellate rules of procedure and local rules
2. Research the standard of review
3. Prepare a persuasive Issue Presented

---

1. See Chapter 37 for a discussion of how to prepare for oral argument.

4. Draft your Facts section, including procedural history
5. Write a forceful Summary of Argument
6. Create a complete, cohesive document
7. Set aside, then revise

1. STEP ONE: CREATE A TEMPLATE BASED ON THE REQUIREMENTS OF THE APPELLATE RULES OF PROCEDURE AND LOCAL RULES

The appellate rules of procedure and local court rules determine the format for an appellate brief. These rules vary from court to court. A court can reject any document that does not comply with its rules, so you must follow them closely. Most appellate briefs include at least the following parts:[2]

Appellate Brief

1. Cover with caption
2. Table of Contents
3. Table of Authorities
4. Issues Presented
5. Facts section, including procedural history
6. Summary of Argument
7. Standard of Review
8. Argument
9. Conclusion section
10. Signature block

Put your appellate brief together by creating a template that follows the applicable font size, type, and spacing requirements, keeping in mind that the rules may be different than those for trial court documents. Also, take notice of the page or word limit, and calendar the deadline when the brief is due.

A. Create the Cover

Appellate briefs have a cover that is similar to the caption on a trial court memorandum of law. The cover typically includes (1) the court, (2) the case number, (3) the name of the case, (4) the title of the document, and (5) the name of the court below that rendered the decision being appealed. In some courts, the cover will also include the name and contact information of the lawyers representing the party filing the document.

Court rules differ regarding the spacing, orientation, and organization of the information on the cover. In federal court, the cover's color depends on which party files the brief. The appellant's brief has a blue cover, and the

---

2. *See, e.g.,* Fed. R. App. P. 28. The names for these parts vary from jurisdiction to jurisdiction.

No. 06-14836-DD

——

In the United States Court of Appeals
for the Eleventh Circuit

——

LEAGUE OF WOMEN VOTERS OF FLORIDA, ET AL.,

Plaintiffs-Appellees,

v.

SECRETARY OF THE STATE OF FLORIDA, ET ANO.,

Defendants-Appellants.

——

**ON APPEAL FROM THE UNITED STATES DISTRICT COURT
FOR THE SOUTHERN DISTRICT OF FLORIDA**

THE HONORABLE PATRICIA A. SEITZ

——

**BRIEF OF PLAINTIFFS-APPELLEES LEAGUE OF WOMEN VOTERS
OF FLORIDA, ET AL.**

——

WENDY R. WEISER	ERIC A. TIRSCHWELL	ELIZABETH S. WESTFALL
RENÉE PARADIS	CRAIG L. SIEGEL	JENNIFER MARANZANO
The Brennan Center for	ERIN A. WALTER	Advancement Project
Justice at NYU School	Kramer Levin Naftalis &	1730 M St., NW Suite 910
of Law	Frankel LLP	Washington, DC 20036
161 Ave. of the Americas	1177 Ave. of the Americas	Phone: (202) 728-9557
New York, NY 10014	New York, NY 10036	
Phone: (212) 998-6730	Phone: (212) 715-9100	

Attorneys for Plaintiffs-Appellees

Figure 31.1

appellee's brief has a red cover.[3] Court websites often provide a template for
a properly formatted cover. Figure 31.1 shows an example of a cover for a
brief filed in the U.S. Court of Appeals for the Eleventh Circuit.

B. Fill in the Parts of the Brief

Next, you should create a heading for each part of the brief in the order
required by the rules. Once you have a complete template, you should fill in
the parts of the brief as you prepare them. You can begin by inserting into the
Argument section your persuasive CREAC(s) and point headings. You may
want to prepare the sections out of order; some sections will be easier and less
time consuming than others.

——

3. Fed. R. App. P. 32(a)(2).

2. STEP TWO: RESEARCH THE STANDARD OF REVIEW

The standard of review is the level of deference an appellate court gives to the decision of a lower court. Because the standard of review frames the appellate court's analysis, an appellate brief must describe the applicable standard(s) of review before addressing the substantive arguments. Court rules establish where the standard of review appears in a brief. Typically, it is included at the end of the statement of facts, in a separate section before the Argument, or at the beginning of each CREAC.

The standard of review that will apply to an issue depends on whether the issue is an issue of law, an issue of fact, a mixed question of law and fact, or an evidentiary ruling. The standard of review may also be determined by a case's procedural posture. Generally, appellate courts give less deference to lower courts on legal issues and more deference on factual issues and evidentiary rulings. The most common standards of review from the least deferential to the most deferential are de novo, clearly erroneous, substantial evidence, and abuse of discretion.

You should research the standard(s) of review that will apply to the specific issues in your brief. Look for a binding case that is procedurally and substantively similar to your case. For instance, if you were preparing an appellate brief challenging a grant of summary judgment on a claim for misappropriation of trade secrets, you would want to cite a case for the standard of review that involved an appellate court within your jurisdiction reviewing a summary judgment decision in a trade secret case.

You should present the standard of review persuasively for your side. Sometimes this task will be easy. A standard of review that is deferential to a lower court decision that you want the court to affirm is obviously helpful. But even when the standard is not so helpful, you can present it persuasively by selecting a case that applied the standard of review and reached a favorable outcome for your side. If you can find such a case, you should note the favorable outcome in a parenthetical.

The following examples show how the appellant and appellee could present the standard of review persuasively in an appeal after a grant of summary judgment in a trade secrets case:

> Appellant's Standard of Review (challenging grant of summary judgment)
>
> This Court reviews the district court's grant of summary judgment de novo, viewing the facts and drawing all reasonable inferences in favor of the non-moving party. *See Kendall Holdings, Ltd. v. Eden Cryogenics, LLC*, No. 12-3258, 2013 WL 1363728, at *7 (6th Cir. April 5, 2013) (reversing summary judgment on claim for misappropriation of trade secrets). "The court does not 'weigh the evidence and determine the truth of the matter but...determine[s] whether there is a genuine issue for trial.'" *Id.* (alteration in original).

Appellee's Standard of Review (asking appellate court to affirm summary judgment)

This Court reviews a grant of summary judgment de novo. *See Stratienko v. Cordis Corp.*, 429 F.3d 592, 597 (6th Cir. 2005) (affirming grant of summary judgment on claim for misappropriation of trade secrets).

3. STEP THREE: PREPARE A PERSUASIVE ISSUE PRESENTED

The Issue Presented, also called the "Statement of the Issues," sets out the issue or issues that the court will decide on appeal. The Issue Presented in an appellate brief is persuasive, unlike the Question Presented in an office memo. Your Issue Presented should be a leading question that communicates your client's position and persuasive theme to the court.

An Issue Presented can have a variety of formats, but one common format is similar to the under-does-when formula that you use to write the Question Presented in an office memo. For an Issue Presented, you can use the "did-when" format:

1. The Issue Presented begins with a clause starting with "did" that asks whether the lower court's decision was correct. For the appellant, this clause usually asks whether the court acted "improperly," and for the appellee, this clause usually asks whether the court acted "properly."
2. Then, it has a "when" clause that summarizes the most persuasive, legally significant facts.

For example, the following are Issues Presented for the opposing sides in the appeal of a trade secrets case:

Did the trial court improperly grant summary judgment when Gene Showers filed suit for trade misappropriation within four years of learning that Oscar Industries had wrongly acquired his detailed drawings of a self-cleaning juicer and used those drawings to manufacture a competing product? — The first part of the Issue Presented for the appellant asks whether the trial court improperly granted summary judgment.

The second part describes the legally significant facts that are persuasive for the appellant and advances the appellant's persuasive theme that Oscar Industries misappropriated Showers' trade secrets.

Did the trial court properly grant summary judgment when there was undisputed evidence that in 2004—more than five years before filing suit—Gene Showers was notified in writing that Oscar Industries may have been given access to conceptual artwork for Showers' juicer? — The first part of the Issue Presented for the appellee asks whether the trial court properly granted summary judgment.

The second part describes the legally significant facts that are persuasive for the appellee and minimizes facts that would be persuasive for the appellant.

These Issues Presented are persuasive because they induce the reader to an-swer "yes." There generally should be an Issue Presented for every major issue addressed in your brief. The major issues are often those with capitalized, Ro-man numeral headings—I., II., III., etc.

4. STEP FOUR: DRAFT A PERSUASIVE FACTS SECTION, INCLUDING PROCEDURAL HISTORY

An appellate brief includes a persuasive statement of facts, which is also called "the statement of the case." The Facts section should be a persuasive story that includes legally significant, procedural, and emotional facts. In addition, because the appellate court needs to know what happened to the case in the lower court and what rulings are being appealed, the Facts section should include a procedural history with dates.[4] The facts in this section of the appel-late brief must be followed by citations to the Record on Appeal.

A. Use Persuasive Topical Subheadings

One technique that can be helpful when preparing a Facts section for an ap-pellate brief is to include short subheadings to guide the reader. Topical sub-headings break up a long statement of facts, organize the facts persuasively, and advance your theme. These subheadings are usually not complete sen-tences. Instead, they are fragments that highlight persuasive factual topics.

For example, in a summary judgment appeal on the statute of limitations in a trade secrets case, the following could be the subheadings for each party's brief:

Appellant's Brief (challenging trial court's
grant of summary judgment)

A. Showers' Innovative Design for a Self-Cleaning Juicer
B. Oscar Industries' Misappropriation of Showers' Design
C. Showers' Suit for Trade Secret Misappropriation
D. Trial Court Proceedings

Appellee's Brief (asking appellate court
to affirm summary judgment)

A. The Trial Court Grants Oscar Industries' Motion for Summary Judg-ment
B. Showers' First Notice of His Claim in May 2004
C. Showers' Delay in Filing Suit

Even though the facts are omitted in these examples, the reader can un-derstand each party's persuasive theme from the subheadings alone. These Facts sections are organized differently because the appellant organized the

---

4. *See, e.g.*, Fed. R. App. P. 28(a)(6).

facts around his trade secrets and the alleged misappropriation, while the appellee organized the facts around the motion for summary judgment and the statute of limitations issue. Both parties used subheadings to highlight facts that are persuasive for their positions; neither party just listed the facts chronologically.

B. Include Citations to the Record

The facts in an appellate brief must appear in the Record on Appeal, which includes the case documents filed in the lower court and the transcript of any proceedings.[5] Every sentence in the Facts section should be followed by a citation to the Record. The citation format for the Record on Appeal is covered by *Bluebook* rules B7.1.1 and B7.1.2. Citations to the Record are typically enclosed in parentheses and include a pinpoint citation to the page in the Record where the fact appears. The following is a portion of a Facts section with citations to the Record on Appeal:

> On November 11, 2002, Gene Showers conceived the idea of a self-cleaning juicer. (R. at 18.) He described the idea in his "Invention Journal" as follows: "MAJOR INNOVATION! Juicer that cleans itself through a pulp recycling mechanism." (R. at 57.) He followed that written entry with a simple drawing of a pulp recycling mechanism. (R. at 60.)

5. STEP FIVE: WRITE A FORCEFUL SUMMARY OF ARGUMENT

A section called the Summary of Argument often precedes the Argument section in an appellate brief. Federal Rule of Appellate Procedure 28(a)(7) requires the Summary of Argument to be "a succinct, clear, and accurate statement of the arguments made in the body of the brief…." The Summary of Argument should be concise—usually no more than one page. In the Summary of Argument you should distill your argument to its most important points, weave in your persuasive theme, and argue to the court why you should prevail.

The Summary of Argument in the brief prepared by Laurence Tribe, Kathleen Sullivan, and Brian Koukoutchos for Respondent Michael Bowers in the *Bowers v. Hardwick* case displays the type of concise and forceful writing that makes a Summary of Argument persuasive:

SUMMARY OF ARGUMENT

> The State of Georgia would extend its criminal law into the very bedrooms of its citizens, to break up even wholly consensual, noncommercial sexual relations between willing adults. And the State contends before this

---

5. *See, e.g.*, Fed. R. App. P. 10(a).

Court that it may freely do so without giving any good reason. All that Respondent argues is that a Georgia citizen is entitled by the Constitution to demand not only a warrant of the Georgia police officer who would enter his bedroom, but also a substantial justification of the Georgia legislature when it declares criminal the consensual intimacies he chooses to engage in there.

No less justification is acceptable in a society whose constitutional traditions have always placed the highest value upon the sanctity of the home against governmental intrusion or control. Nor is the mere invocation of contestable moral views sufficient to defend a law that so thoroughly invades individuals' most intimate affairs.

Thus the law challenged here must be subjected to heightened scrutiny, and it may be upheld upon remand only if the State of Georgia offers a more powerful justification than the one it has offered here: namely, the tautology that the State has criminalized the private acts at issue because a majority of Georgia's legislators disapprove of them.[6]

6. STEP SIX: CREATE A COMPLETE, COHESIVE DOCUMENT

Although you have now prepared most of your appellate brief, it is not complete. An appellate brief includes many discrete parts, but it should read like a cohesive document with a unified voice and theme. To create this cohesive document, you should prepare all of the required parts and then insert introductory roadmaps, transitions, and headings where necessary to guide the reader.

For instance, an appellate brief begins with a Table of Contents that lists each required section as well as the Argument point headings and subheadings.[7] These point headings provide an outline of your Argument. When you create your Table of Contents, review this outline to make sure that your point headings are persuasive, readable, and logically organized. In addition, you should consider whether the point headings sufficiently convey the substance of your persuasive argument. The Table of Contents is one of the first parts of your brief that the court will read, so use it to persuade.

Additionally, your brief will need a Table of Authorities that lists every cited authority.[8] Compiling this Table of Authorities gives you an opportunity to assess whether you have included sufficient legal authorities in your brief and cited them correctly.

---

6. Brief for Respondent at 4, *Bowers v. Hardwick*, 478 U.S. 186 (1986) (No. 85-140), 1986 WL 720442.

7. *See, e.g.*, Fed. R. App. P. 28(a)(2).

8. *See, e.g.*, Fed. R. App. P. 28(a)(3).

You will also need a short Conclusion section and signature block at the end of your brief. And you may need to prepare a section establishing the basis for the appellate court's jurisdiction[9] and include a Certificate of Compliance stating that the brief is within the word limit.[10]

Do not underestimate how long it will take to complete these parts of the brief. Although these sections may seem simple, preparing them can be painstaking and time intensive. Further, make sure you prepare each section with the goal of making it as persuasive and professional as possible.

Once you have a complete document, you should read it from beginning to end. Look for long blocks of text of two or more pages and consider inserting subheadings as breaks. Then, add roadmaps or transitions where necessary to guide the court and create cohesion.

7. STEP SEVEN: SET ASIDE, THEN REVISE

Due to the complexity and importance of an appellate brief, you should leave enough time to set it aside before you begin the revising process. Your credibility as an advocate depends on how you have developed the substance of your arguments and how professionally you present those arguments to the court. Because an appellate brief has so many components, you will need considerable time to revise your brief.

Use the following checklist to ensure that your document is complete.

- ☑ Review the rules governing your document. Have you included every section that the rules require in the proper order?
- ☑ Does the cover follow the formatting rules that govern your document?
- ☑ Read the Table of Contents. Does it present a logical outline of your argument?
- ☑ Read the Issue Presented. Is it a leading question that persuasively suggests the answer you want the court to reach?
- ☑ Read the Facts section. Is it organized persuasively to advance your theme?
- ☑ Does the Facts section include a citation to the Record on Appeal for every fact it includes?
- ☑ Read the Summary of Argument. Does it summarize your major points and forcefully advance your theme?
- ☑ Read the Standard of Review. Is it presented persuasively for your side by, if possible, citing a case with a favorable outcome?
- ☑ Read the brief from beginning to end. Does it have a cohesive voice and persuasive theme?

The following is an example of an appellate brief.

---

9. *See, e.g.*, Fed. R. App. P. 28(a)(4).
10. *See, e.g.*, Fed. R. App. P. 32(a)(7)(C).

Example
Appellate Brief
31.1

No. 13-11112-PL

**IN THE UNITED STATES COURT OF APPEALS
FOR THE ELEVENTH CIRCUIT**

—The Cover is properly formatted according to court rules.

Kieran G. Mahoney,

Plaintiff-Appellant,

v.

Gold Coast Herald Tribune,

Defendant-Appellee.

**APPEAL FROM THE UNITED STATES DISTRICT COURT FOR THE
SOUTHERN DISTRICT OF FLORIDA**

APPELLANT KIERAN G. MAHONEY'S INITIAL BRIEF

Gus T. Fline
Fla. Bar No. 992828
FLINE, POCH, & SMIL, P.A.
1300 S. Bayshore Dr., Suite 86
Miami, FL 33132
Telephone: (305) 444-8888
gtf@fpslaw.com

*Counsel for Plaintiff-Appellant
Kieran G. Mahoney*

TABLE OF CONTENTS

The Table of Contents lists every part of the brief and all of the persuasive headings and subheadings that appear in the Statement of Facts and the Argument. Checking that the pages listed are correct should be one of the final proofreading tasks.

TABLE OF AUTHORITIES

— The Table of Authorities organizes and lists every legal authority cited in the brief with a properly formatted citation. This is a time consuming section of the brief to prepare and should be proofread many times.

STATEMENT OF THE ISSUES

I. Did the district court improperly grant the Gold Coast Herald Tribune's Motion to Dismiss when Kieran G. Mahoney stated a facially plausible claim for defamation on the basis that the Herald Tribune's article was a mixed expression of fact and opinion that was explicitly and implicitly based on false and defamatory facts?

II. Did the district court improperly grant the Herald Tribune's Motion to Dismiss when Ms. Mahoney adequately alleged actual malice because the Herald Tribune acted with reckless disregard when it purposefully avoided learning that its single unnamed source was lying?

STATEMENT OF THE CASE

This is a defamation case against the Gold Coast Herald Tribune for false statements published about Kieran G. Mahoney.

I. The Herald Tribune's Defamatory Statements

On March 3, 2012, the Herald Tribune included an article in its entertainment news section, "Loose Lips," that reported on Ms. Mahoney's financial and mental health:

> Mahoney a Charlatan in Chanel?
> A source close to Real Wives diva Kieran Mahoney says Mahoney is about to file for bankruptcy and is about to be investigated for tax fraud. Despite this, the bankrupt basket case has been all over town pretending she can still handle the Miami lifestyle.

(R. at 3, ¶ 4.)

The information in the article is false. (R. at 4, ¶ 10.) Ms. Mahoney did not file for bankruptcy, was never investigated for tax fraud, and is not a "basket case." (*Id.*) The Herald Tribune did not attempt to confirm the story with Ms. Mahoney before publishing the article. (R. at 4, ¶ 12.)

Although the source of the false information is unnamed in the article, Ms. Mahoney alleged that she believes the source to be her former personal trainer, Brock Goodin. (*Id.*) Ms. Mahoney had a falling out with Mr. Goodin and fired him as her trainer just three days before the article appeared in the Herald Tribune. (*Id.*)

II. Ms. Mahoney's Contract Is Not Renewed

In the month following publication of the Herald Tribune article, the Brave Network decided not to renew Ms. Mahoney's contract to appear on its reality program

1

Margin notes:
— The Statement of the Issues includes a persuasive Issue Presented for every major issue—meaning every issue at the Roman numeral level of the outline—argued in the brief. The issues are presented as leading questions that communicate the client's position and persuasive theme. They use the "did-when" format.

— The Statement of the Case contains the factual and procedural history and the rulings presented for review. This section tells the persuasive story of the case from Ms. Mahoney's perspective, using legally significant, procedural, and emotional facts.

— The facts are organized under persuasive topical subheadings.

— The facts begin with a fact that is helpful to Ms. Mahoney, and the facts are characterized persuasively for her throughout. For example, Loose Lips is described as an "article" in the "entertainment news section," rather than a gossip column.

— Every fact is followed by a citation to the Record on Appeal.

— Negative facts are minimized by being placed in the middle of facts that are persuasive for Ms. Mahoney.

"The Real Wives of Dade County." (R. at 7, ¶ 22.) "Real Wives" followed the daily lives of six wealthy women living in South Florida. (R. at 2, ¶ 2.) The Brave Network claimed that Ms. Mahoney's contract was not renewed out of a desire to add "fresh faces" to the cast, but the real reason the contract was not renewed was that the article made it appear that Ms. Mahoney could no longer afford the glamorous, expensive lifestyle that is the focus of the show. (R. at 8, ¶¶ 23, 25.)

— Because the facts are from Ms. Mahoney's point of view, they are presented as true, rather than as allegations.

Ms. Mahoney is a divorced mother of two. (R. at 3, ¶ 6.) Before appearing on the show, she was a stay-at-home mom who had never been on television or performed publicly. (*Id.*) She is not an actress or celebrity. (*Id.*) Since the article was published, Ms. Mahoney has suffered considerable financial harm, including the loss of income from the show and related promotional appearances. (R. at 9, ¶ 35.)

— The facts conclude with a persuasive fact for Ms. Mahoney.

III. Procedural History and Rulings Presented for Review

On February 18, 2013, Ms. Mahoney filed a Complaint against the Herald Tribune stating a cause of action for defamation. (R. at 1.) The Herald Tribune responded to Ms. Mahoney's Complaint by moving to dismiss under Fed. R. Civ. P. 12(b)(6). (R. at 15.) The district court granted the motion on July 17, 2013. (R. at 52.) The district court dismissed the defamation claim on the basis that (1) the challenged publication was pure opinion and rhetorical hyperbole, and (2) the Complaint failed to allege the actual malice required because Ms. Mahoney is a public figure. (R. at 55.)

— This section provides the procedural history of the case from Ms. Mahoney's point of view. To humanize her, the brief refers to her as Ms. Mahoney. Every sentence is followed by a citation to the Record on Appeal.

Ms. Mahoney timely filed her Notice of Appeal on August 8, 2013. (R. at 70.) Ms. Mahoney appeals the decision of the district court on the bases that the defamatory statements were not pure opinion and the Complaint sufficiently alleged actual malice.

SUMMARY OF ARGUMENT

Ms. Mahoney's Complaint for defamation states a claim for relief and should not have been dismissed. Defamation is intended to redress precisely the harm Ms. Mahoney suffered in this case. Ms. Mahoney was the subject of a newspaper article based on information from a single unnamed source that stated that she was going to file for bankruptcy and was being investigated for tax fraud. The article also described her as a "charlatan" and a "basket case." All of these facts are false and defamatory, and the district court's decision should be reversed.

— The Summary of Argument distills the persuasive theme and arguments in the brief into a succinct and clear statement. It uses simple and direct language to explain to the court why Ms. Mahoney should prevail. It does not include citations to the Record or legal authorities.

First, the district court improperly held that the Herald Tribune's article was rhetorical hyperbole. The article is both explicitly and implicitly based on false and

— The Summary of Argument uses "first" and "second" to mirror the organization of the arguments in the Argument section.

defamatory factual allegations regarding Ms. Mahoney's financial situation. The reasonable reader would have taken these statements literally, and the statements are therefore not protected pure opinion. At a minimum, the article contains a mixed expression of opinion and fact, and the jury should decide whether the harmful content is defamatory.

Second, the district court improperly held that Ms. Mahoney has not adequately pleaded actual malice, which is required because she is a public figure. In fact, the Complaint alleges that the Herald Tribune acted with actual malice by purposefully avoiding the truth that its single unnamed source was a disgruntled former employee who was motivated to lie. Viewing the allegations in the Complaint in the light most favorable to Ms. Mahoney, this Court should hold that the Complaint states a facially plausible claim for defamation and should not have been dismissed.

— The Summary of Argument concludes with a transition to the Argument.

STANDARD OF REVIEW

This Court reviews de novo the grant of a Rule 12(b)(6) motion to dismiss. *Speaker v. U.S. Dep't of Health & Human Servs.*, 623 F.3d 1371, 1379 (11th Cir. 2010) (reversing grant of motion to dismiss). The Court accepts the allegations in the complaint as true and construes them in the light most favorable to the plaintiff. *Id.*

— The Standard of Review is presented persuasively for Ms. Mahoney. It cites mandatory authorities and notes any favorable outcomes in explanatory parentheticals.

To state a facially plausible claim, a plaintiff needs to plead only "factual content that allows the court to draw the reasonable inference that the defendant is liable for the misconduct alleged." *Id.* at 1380 (citing *Ashcroft v. Iqbal*, 566 U.S. 662 (2009)). "The Court has instructed us that the rule 'does not impose a probability requirement at the pleading stage,' but instead 'simply calls for enough fact to raise a reasonable expectation that discovery will reveal evidence of' the necessary element." *Id.* (quoting *Watts v. Fla. Int'l Univ.*, 495 F.3d 1289, 1295-96 (11th Cir. 2007)).

— Words like "only" make it appear easy for Ms. Mahoney to satisfy the pleading standard and survive a motion to dismiss.

ARGUMENT

The Court should reverse the district court's decision granting the motion to dismiss Ms. Mahoney's defamation claim. The Complaint adequately pleads the elements of defamation: the statement was published, false, and defamatory; the defendant acted with actual malice; and the plaintiff suffered actual damages. *See Jews for Jesus, Inc. v. Rapp*, 997 So. 2d 1098, 1106 (Fla. 2008). When the allegations are viewed in the light most favorable to Ms. Mahoney—as is required on a motion to

— The Argument section begins with a persuasive roadmap paragraph. The paragraph starts with a general Conclusion. Then, it states the overarching rule of the elements of a defamation claim. It ends with a specific Conclusion that states the two major issues that will be argued in the Argument section.

3

dismiss—they establish that the challenged statements were defamatory, and the Herald Tribune acted with actual malice.

I. The Complaint Stated a Claim for Defamation Because the Challenged Statements Were False, Defamatory Statements of Fact, Not Rhetorical Hyperbole.

— The Roman numeral point heading concisely states the Conclusion on the first issue.

The Court should reverse the district court's decision because the Herald Tribune's false statements were not rhetorical hyperbole. Instead, they were mixed expressions of fact and opinion that relied upon defamatory facts and created a false factual assertion.

— The CREAC begins with a Conclusion that includes more detail than the Conclusion in the point heading.

A. Mixed Expressions of Fact and Opinion Are Properly the Basis of a Defamation Claim.

— This subheading signals the start of the Rule section. It states the rule persuasively for Ms. Mahoney.

To be defamatory, a statement must be a false statement of fact. *Keller v. Miami Herald Publ'g Co.*, 778 F.2d 711, 715 (11th Cir. 1985). Mixed expressions of fact and opinion are also actionable. *Johnson v. Clark*, 484 F. Supp. 2d 1242, 1247 (M.D. Fla. 2007) ("The law, however, distinguishes between pure expressions of opinion, which are constitutionally protected, and mixed expressions of opinion, which, like factual statements, are not."). A mixed expression of opinion occurs when the challenged statement is based on defamatory facts. *Id.*

— The rules are organized from general to specific. The Rule section uses a mixture of paraphrasing and quoting to present the rules persuasively. Explanatory parentheticals add detail.

1. The Jury Decides Whether a Mixed Expression Was Defamatory.

— Because this Rule section is long and complex, there are additional subheadings. This subheading highlights a narrow rule that is persuasive for Ms. Mahoney.

Whether a mixed expression of opinion is defamatory is a question for the jury. *Id.* ("Where the court finds that the statement in question is of mixed opinion and fact and reasonably capable of defamatory interpretation, then a jury issue is presented."); *E. Air Lines, Inc. v. Gellert*, 438 So. 2d 923, 927 (Fla. Dist. Ct. App. 1983) ("If Ashlock's statement would likely be reasonably understood by ordinary persons as a statement of an undisclosed existing defamatory fact, then it was properly the jury's function to determine whether a defamatory meaning was attributed to it by recipients of the communication . . . ."), *abrogated on other grounds by Ter Keurst v. Miami Elevator Co.*, 486 So. 2d 547, 550 (Fla. 1986).

— Explanatory parentheticals quote key language from cases that describe and apply the narrow rule.

2. A Statement Is a Mixed Expression When It Is Explicitly or Implicitly Based on False Factual Allegations.

— This subheading signals the beginning of the Explanation section. It emphasizes the anchors that are persuasive for Ms. Mahoney.

To determine whether a statement is a mixed expression of opinion, the Court looks at the statement in its totality and considers "whether the speaker accurately presented the underlying facts of the situation before making the allegedly defamatory remarks." *Zambrano v. Devanesan*, 484 So. 2d 603, 606-07 (Fla. Dist. Ct. App.

— The Explanation begins with a topic sentence that persuasively summarizes the anchors.

1986); *see also E. Air Lines, Inc.*, 438 So. 2d at 927 (citing Restatement (Second) of Torts §566, cmt. c) ("It is the court's function to determine from the context 'whether an expression of opinion is capable of bearing a defamatory meaning because it may reasonably be understood to imply the assertion of undisclosed facts that justify the expressed opinion about the plaintiff or his conduct.'").

A statement is not protected as pure opinion when it creates a "false assertion of fact." *Anson v. Paxson Commc'ns Corp.*, 736 So. 2d 1209, 1211 (Fla. Dist. Ct. App. 1999) (quoting *Milkovich v. Lorain Journal Co.*, 497 U.S. 1, 18-19 (1990)). The U.S. Supreme Court has stated, "[e]ven if the speaker states the facts upon which he bases his opinion, if those facts are either incorrect or incomplete, or if his assessment of them is erroneous, the statement may still imply a false assertion of fact." *Milkovich*, 497 U.S. at 18-19.

> This paragraph provides a more specific description of the anchors and uses key language from a major case to explain one of the anchors persuasively.

Accordingly, courts have held that statements that imply the existence of false and defamatory facts—especially facts regarding the plaintiff's ability to perform his or her profession—are actionable. *See Zambrano*, 484 So. 2d at 607; *E. Air Lines, Inc.*, 438 So. 2d at 928. In *Zambrano*, the court held that the defendants' statements that a doctor "had deserted his responsibilities and duties; that he had walked away from his private practice, and his hospital on-call schedule, without prior notice; and that he had acted in an unprofessional and unethical manner" were not protected as rhetorical hyperbole because they contained factual allegations about the plaintiff and the defendants did not accurately present the underlying facts. *Zambrano*, 484 So. 2d at 606. Similarly, the court in *Eastern Airlines, Inc.* held that statements accusing a pilot of being "paranoid" and claiming that he was still flying jets only because it was "awfully hard to fire anyone these days" were defamatory because they implied "that the plaintiff suffers from a mental affliction incompatible with his ability to carry out the responsibilities of his occupation." *E. Air Lines, Inc.*, 438 So. 2d at 927-28.

> This paragraph uses details from positive cases, including the facts, holdings, and key language, to explain one of the anchors persuasively.

B. The Article Was a Mixed Expression of Fact and Opinion.

The Herald Tribune's article was actionable defamation, not rhetorical hyperbole. The statements in the article were mixed expressions of fact and opinion that both stated and implied that they were based on false and defamatory facts.

> This subheading signals the beginning of the Analysis section. It concisely states that the rule described in heading A. is satisfied in this case.

> This paragraph states the broad thesis and incorporates the brief's persuasive theme.

1. The Article Includes False Factual Statements.

First, the Loose Lips article is not rhetorical hyperbole because "the statements on their face contain factual allegations." *Zambrano*, 484 So. 2d at 607. The article

> This subheading briefly applies the first anchor to the present case.

> The paragraph begins with a topic sentence summarizing how the first, most persuasive, anchor supports the Conclusion.

5

contains two false factual allegations: (1) that Ms. Mahoney filed for bankruptcy, and (2) that she was investigated for tax fraud. (R. at 4, ¶ 10.) Like the factual statements in *Zambrano* that the plaintiff had left his medical practice and the hospital's on-call schedule without notice, these false factual statements about Ms. Mahoney are actionable defamation, not pure opinion. *See Zambrano*, 484 So. 2d at 607; *see also Keller*, 778 F.2d at 717 ("[T]o be actionable, [a publication] must be false and consist of a statement of fact."); *LRX, Inc. v. Horizon Assocs. Joint Venture*, 842 So. 2d 881, 885 (Fla. Dist. Ct. App. 2003) ("The Horizon letter, as a matter of law, was not pure opinion, where it contains false assertions of fact.").

    Indeed, like the statements in *Zambrano*, the false factual allegations regarding Ms. Mahoney's finances related to her ability to perform her profession. *See Zambrano*, 484 So. 2d at 607. The "Real Wives" show depicts the daily lives of wealthy women. (R. at 2, ¶ 2.) By falsely representing that Ms. Mahoney was having financial problems, the Herald Tribune attacked her ability to perform her profession—which is defamatory. *See Madsen v. Buie*, 454 So. 2d 727, 730 (Fla. Dist. Ct. App. 1984) ("[T]he statements made by appellee in her letter clearly attack appellant's ability to perform adequately within his profession and therefore . . . constitute libel per se.").

2. The Article Is Based on Undisclosed, Defamatory Facts.

    Second, the Loose Lips column is not rhetorical hyperbole because it contains accusations about Ms. Mahoney that are based on undisclosed defamatory facts. The article cannot be pure opinion because it describes Ms. Mahoney as a "charlatan" and a "basket case," but presents no facts to support or explain these descriptions. *See Johnson*, 484 F. Supp. 2d at 1251 ("[I]t is certainly Defendant's 'opinion' that Mr. Johnson had engaged in 'spin,' lying, and 'betrayal' of the heirs, but the Original Letter either does not contain factual support for the opinion, or the 'facts' upon which the opinion is based themselves might reasonably be determined to be either untrue, incomplete, or incorrectly interpreted."). The implication that undisclosed facts show Ms. Mahoney to be a fraud or mentally unstable is defamatory. *See Milkovich*, 497 U.S. at 18 ("[E]xpressions of 'opinion' may often imply an assertion of objective fact.").

    The Herald Tribune cannot couch its false defamatory statements as "opinions" or "hyperbole" to avoid a defamation claim. *See Anson*, 736 So. 2d at 1210-11. Like in *Anson*, where the court held that statements describing the plaintiff as a "drug using

---

— This paragraph analogizes the facts in this case to the facts of a factually and legally similar case with a favorable outcome.

— An explanatory parenthetical provides additional support by showing the present case is similar to another case with a favorable outcome.

— The analogy continues with greater specificity in this paragraph.

— Again, an explanatory parenthetical provides additional support by showing the present case is similar to another case with a favorable outcome.

— This subheading briefly applies the first anchor to the present case.

— The paragraph begins with a topic sentence persuasively summarizing how the analysis of the second anchor supports the Conclusion.

— This explanatory parenthetical demonstrates that the facts of a case with a favorable outcome are similar to the facts in the present case.

— This paragraph refutes a counterargument.

teenage homosexual prostitute" could be defamatory even if they were opinions or "talk radio schtik," the statements calling Ms. Mahoney a "charlatan" and a "basket case" are defamatory because they imply the existence of undisclosed facts regarding her conduct and mental health. *See id.* at 1211 ("[L]abeling the statements as opinion does not necessarily shield the defendants from an action for defamation.").

> —Analogizing to a case with a favorable outcome adds legal support to help refute the counterargument.

3. The Article's Medium, Context, and Language Establish That It Is Actionable Defamation, Not Rhetorical Hyperbole.

> —This subheading briefly refutes a counterargument.

Last, the Herald Tribune's statements are not rhetorical hyperbole based on the medium, context, or words used in the article. The medium of the article was the "entertainment news" section of a newspaper, not a letter to the editor or the opinion page. *Colodny v. Iverson, Yoakum, Papiano & Hatch*, 936 F. Supp. 917, 924 (M.D. Fla. 1996). *But see Johnson*, 484 F. Supp. 2d at 1251 (holding that statements in a letter to the editor were mixed expressions of opinion and fact, not pure opinion).

> —The paragraph begins with a topic sentence preemptively refuting the strongest counterargument.
>
> —This paragraph provides factual and legal support to refute the counterargument.

The article was not printed in the context of an emotional debate concerning an issue of public concern, but was instead a short gossipy piece about a reality television program. *See Horsley v. Feldt*, 304 F.3d 1125, 1132 (11th Cir. 2002) ("The context of Gandy's statements and their flavor convince us that they are rhetorical hyperbole. Gandy and Horsley were engaged in heated debate on the highly controversial topic of abortion and the emotionally-charged subject of the Nuremberg Files and the murder of abortion providers."); *Horsley v. Rivera*, 292 F.3d 695, 702 (11th Cir. 2002) ("Horsley and Rivera were engaged in an emotional debate concerning emotionally-charged [sic] issues of significant public concern.").

> —This paragraph uses explanatory parentheticals to distinguish mandatory authorities with unfavorable outcomes.

The language in the article is straightforward and literal. It states that Ms. Mahoney is going to file for bankruptcy and is being investigated for tax fraud. It does not use the kind of over-the-top invective that would not be taken literally by any reasonable reader. *See Fortson v. Colangelo*, 434 F. Supp. 2d 1369, 1381-83 (S.D. Fla. 2006) ("[C]ourts have recognized that sports commentaries in particular are likely to contain statements of opinion, rather than fact, because they serve as a 'traditional haven for cajoling, invective, and hyperbole.'"). For example, in *Fortson*, the column described a basketball player as a "meaningless mass" and characterized his actions as "attempted murder." *Id.* at 1385. The language here is not so extreme. The article describes Ms. Mahoney as a diva, a charlatan, and a basket case, but it also states alleged facts about Ms. Mahoney in the typical style of a newspaper article.

> —This paragraph makes an affirmative argument to preemptively refute a counterargument and distinguish a factually and legally similar case with an unfavorable outcome.

Thus, when viewed in their totality and in the light most favorable to Ms. Mahoney, the statements in the Herald Tribune article are not rhetorical hyperbole. The Court should reverse the district court's decision granting the Herald Tribune's Motion to Dismiss.

— The CREAC ends with a Conclusion on the major issue and a reprise of the request for relief.

II. The Complaint Alleges Actual Malice Because It Pleads That the Herald Tribune Purposefully Avoided the Truth by Relying on a Single Untruthful Source.

— The Roman numeral point heading concisely states the Conclusion on the second issue.

Ms. Mahoney's Complaint adequately alleges that the Herald Tribune acted with actual malice because it recklessly published false information from a source it knew had a reason to lie. A public figure has a claim for defamation when the publisher acted with actual malice. *N.Y. Times Co. v. Sullivan*, 376 U.S. 254, 279-80 (1964). "If a false and defamatory statement is published with knowledge of falsity or a reckless disregard for the truth, the public figure may prevail." *Harte-Hanks Commc'ns, Inc. v. Connaughton*, 491 U.S. 657, 688 (1989) (affirming that newspaper acted with actual malice).

— The CREAC begins with a Conclusion that includes more detail than the Conclusion in the point heading.

— The Rule section uses a mixture of paraphrasing and quoting to present the rules persuasively. An explanatory parenthetical describes a favorable outcome.

Reckless disregard is established when the defendant had a "high degree of awareness of probable falsity." *Id.*; *see Dunn v. Air Line Pilots Ass'n*, 193 F.3d 1185, 1197-98 (11th Cir. 1999). Reckless disregard can be established by showing that the publisher purposefully avoided learning the truth. *Harte-Hanks Commc'ns, Inc.*, 491 U.S. at 691 ("Although failure to investigate will not alone support a finding of actual malice, the purposeful avoidance of the truth is in a different category.").

— The rules are organized in the Rule section from general to specific. This paragraph describes the narrower rules.

When a defendant publishes the false information of an informant, "recklessness may be found where there are obvious reasons to doubt the veracity of the informant or the accuracy of his reports." *Id.* at 688 (quoting *St. Amant v. Thompson*, 390 U.S. 727, 732 (1968)). In *Harte-Hanks Communications, Inc.*, the U.S. Supreme Court held that a newspaper had acted with actual malice when it "used a single source as the basis for a highly improbable story" and purposefully avoided evidence that would reveal the truth. *Levan v. Capital Cities/ABC, Inc.*, 190 F.3d 1230, 1243 (11th Cir. 1999) (distinguishing a case where all of the evidence supported the published statements as "precisely the opposite" of *Harte-Hanks*) (citing *Harte-Hanks Commc'ns, Inc.*, 491 U.S. at 691-92). Similarly, a Florida court held that the evidence created a jury issue on actual malice when a television news program aired a program that relied upon an "unidentified informer," despite knowing that the

— The Explanation section begins with a topic sentence that persuasively describes an anchor.

— The details of an important case are used to persuasively explain the anchor.

— A mandatory authority with an unfavorable outcome is minimized by being discussed in a parenthetical in the middle of a paragraph.

— An additional case with a favorable outcome is used to add support to the persuasive explanation of the anchor.

informer's credibility was "greatly suspect." *S. Air Transp., Inc. v. Post-Newsweek Stations, Fla., Inc.*, 568 So. 2d 927, 928 (Fla. Dist. Ct. App. 1990).

Here, the Herald Tribune acted with actual malice when it purposefully avoided learning the truth regarding the statements it printed from an unnamed source. Ms. Mahoney has sufficiently alleged that because the unnamed source was likely a disgruntled former employee, a personal trainer she fired three days before the story ran, the Herald Tribune had "obvious reasons" to doubt his veracity. *See Harte-Hanks Commc'ns, Inc.*, 491 U.S. at 691.

The Herald Tribune is just like the defendant in *Harte-Hanks*—both newspapers reported stories based on information from one unreliable source while avoiding obvious information to the contrary. *See id.* The Herald Tribune did not even attempt to confirm the story with Ms. Mahoney, likely because it knew she would establish its falsity. (R. at 4, ¶ 12.) This purposeful avoidance constitutes actual malice, and because Ms. Mahoney has adequately pleaded this claim, the Court should reverse the district court's decision granting Defendant's Motion to Dismiss.

> — The Application begins with a sentence that states the thesis on this issue.
>
> — This sentence uses facts to show how the anchor supports the Conclusion on this issue. It also integrates a quotation of key language from a case with a favorable outcome.
>
> — This paragraph provides legal support for the anchor by analogizing the facts of the present case to the facts of a case with a favorable outcome.
>
> — The CREAC ends with a Conclusion on the second issue and a reprise of the request for relief.

CONCLUSION

The Court should reverse the district court's decision to grant the Herald Tribune's Motion to Dismiss.

> — The Conclusion uses customary language to repeat the request for relief.

Date: June 5, 2013

Respectfully Submitted,

/s/ Gus T. Fline
————————————
Gus T. Fline
Counsel for Appellant
Kieran G. Mahoney

> — The signature block is properly formatted.

9

part VII

Other Legal Communication

chapter 32

Introduction to Other Forms of Legal Communication

In addition to writing memos and motions, attorneys communicate with judges, clients, colleagues, and opposing counsel in other ways. Attorneys write correspondence, including letters, emails, and text messages. Judges, with the assistance of their clerks and interns, write judicial opinions. And after all the necessary papers have been written, attorneys present oral arguments to the court.

Each type of legal communication has principles and conventions for the new legal writer to learn—these are discussed and demonstrated in the following chapters. But like the legal writing formats you have already learned, these other forms of legal communication provide an opportunity to demonstrate your competence, credibility, professionalism, and attention to detail. Understanding these new and still evolving forms of legal communication will make you into a legal writer who is ready for the challenges of the day-to-day practice of law.

chapter 33

Letters

Attorneys write letters to judges, opposing counsel, clients, clerks, witnesses, and many others. For instance, many attorneys prepare client advice letters to convey the same objective legal analysis that is found in an office memo. Attorneys also frequently prepare persuasive letters to opposing counsel regarding discovery disputes or other issues.

A letter can be more formal than an email message and may be necessary when it is not possible or appropriate to communicate electronically. The format and conventions of proper letter writing may be unfamiliar because we rarely write letters for personal correspondence. But as an attorney, any letter you send will reflect your professionalism. Thus, your letters should be written thoughtfully and display a careful attention to detail. Moreover, because letters can be legally significant documents, a letter must be an accurate record of when, where, and how it was sent, as well as being precise regarding the substantive facts and law.

Professional letters are typically printed on letterhead and structured as shown in Figure 33.1.[1]

Usually, the text of a letter is single spaced with nonindented paragraphs that are separated with a blank line between each paragraph. Letters that are longer than one page should have a heading on subsequent pages that includes the page number. Often, this page number is formatted as "Page 2 of 8" to help the reader keep track of all the pages of the letter.

The Components of a Professional Letter

1. The correct date
2. An accurate description of the method of transmission
3. A properly formatted recipient name and address
4. A useful re: line
5. An appropriate greeting
6. A professional style that is tailored to the recipient
7. A customary closing

---

1. If you are preparing a professional letter that is not on letterhead, the sender's address should appear above the date.

LETTERHEAD

Date

<u>VIA METHOD OF TRANSMISSION</u>

Recipient Name
Recipient Address

Re: Line
PRIVILEGE DESIGNATION, IF APPLICABLE

Salutation:

Body of letter in non-indented single spaced paragraphs with a blank
line between each paragraph.

Closing,

Signature

Enclosure
cc: Names of cc recipients

Figure 33.1

1. THE CORRECT DATE

A professional letter must be dated correctly. Often, an attorney will begin
drafting a letter days before she sends it. If the attorney enters the date that
she starts working on the letter, rather than the date that she mails it, the
letter will not be an accurate record of when it was sent.

Develop a practice to ensure that letters are always dated correctly. Some
attorneys avoid entering the date until the letter is ready to be finalized and
sent, others manually update the date each day that they work on the letter,
and others insert the date as a field in Microsoft Word so that the date
updates automatically.

A letter's date can be legally significant. For example, the date of a letter may establish when a party received notice of a legal right or when a party fulfilled a legal obligation. Letters exchanged during a case are usually stored chronologically in a correspondence file, and they create a timeline of litigation events. A letter with the wrong date can create practical and ethical problems because it misrepresents when the communication occurred.

2. AN ACCURATE DESCRIPTION OF THE METHOD OF TRANSMISSION

The VIA line on a professional letter describes the method used to send the letter. Because letters can be legally significant case events, every letter must accurately state how it was transmitted. A letter sent by U.S. Mail would have the following VIA line:

VIA U.S. MAIL

Attorneys routinely send letters using methods other than the U.S. Postal Service, and a single letter may be sent using multiple methods. For example, an attorney may write an enclosure letter for a box of documents. The letter will be included in the box that will be sent by FedEx, but the attorney may also send the letter as an attachment to an email to inform the recipient that the box is on its way. In that case, the VIA line would state as follows:

VIA EMAIL & FEDERAL EXPRESS

By accurately reflecting how a letter was transmitted, you preserve the letter as a trustworthy record.

3. A PROPERLY FORMATTED RECIPIENT NAME AND ADDRESS

Every letter must include the recipient's name and address. In a formal professional letter, the letter should also include the recipient's job title.

For example, in a letter addressed to a judge, the recipient's name should be written as "The Honorable __[name]__ , "and the next line should identify the full name of the court before the court's address. For example,

The Honorable Thelton E. Henderson
U.S. District Court for the Northern District of California
Phillip Burton Federal Building & United States Courthouse
450 Golden Gate Avenue
San Francisco, CA 94102

Other titles that should be used include Clerk of Court, Esq., General Counsel, Dr., and business titles like Senior Vice President of Development.

4. A USEFUL RE: LINE

Similar to the subject line of an email, a professional letter should have a re: line that informs the recipient of the general subject of the letter. Typically, letters written during litigation put the case name and number in the re: line. For example,

Re: *Miller v. Schmidt*, No. C10-288228

A more detailed description of the subject of the letter can be included in the re: line, as long as it can be stated concisely and will be helpful to the recipient. For example,

Re: Scheduling Manley Deposition in *Miller v. Schmidt*, No. C10-288228

If the letter is protected by the attorney-client privilege, that information should be noted after the re: line, as follows:

PRIVILEGED ATTORNEY-CLIENT COMMUNICATION

5. AN APPROPRIATE GREETING

The appropriate greeting depends on the level of formality in the letter. Typically, letters are used for more formal correspondence. Thus, a professional letter will usually use the highest level of formality and have a greeting that includes a salutation, an honorific, and a colon. For example,

Dear Mr. Huizinga:	Dear Ms. Baily:
Dear Judge Hur:	Dear Chief Justice Abrams:

When a letter is addressed to a judge, the appropriate honorific is Judge or Justice, unless the person is the Chief or Presiding Judge or Justice, in which case that title should be used.

6. A PROFESSIONAL STYLE THAT IS TAILORED TO THE RECIPIENT

When you sign a letter as an attorney, you are putting your reputation and credibility on the line. For this reason, you should never send a letter that is inaccurate or intemperate. Every letter has the potential to become a matter of public record. Letters exchanged in litigation are often attached to court filings. When that happens, the court, the clients in the case, and the public all have access to the letter.

A. Avoid Legalese

The principles of good writing apply especially to formal letters. Like any legal document, a professional letter should use concise, plain English—not legalese. A letter should also reflect the voice, personality, and professionalism of its author. And it should be written in a readable style appropriate to its audience. When writing to a judge, the style should be deferential; when writing to opposing counsel, the style should be civil; and when writing to a layperson, the style should be accessible.

A professional letter can include pleasantries that are appropriate to the situation and the relationship between the writer and the recipient. But a letter should not adopt mannered or stilted phrases just because they are common in professional correspondence. Weak wording, like "we write to inform you that," "it is important to note that," "in light of the fact that," and "with regard to," do not belong in a professional letter any more than they belong in a legal memo or brief.

B. Consider the Recipient's Knowledge of the Law

The tone and style of a professional letter should be tailored to the recipient's sophistication and knowledge of the law. A letter that is written to a non-lawyer should use language that is comprehensible to a layperson. This type of letter should use quoted language from legal sources sparingly, if at all, and it should not include detailed citation information, which will not be useful or understandable to a non-lawyer. In contrast, a letter to a lawyer or judge should use the relevant language from legal sources and should include the correct citation information.

Any professional letter should be scrupulously accurate regarding the facts and law it describes. Further, any letter that provides legal advice or states a legal conclusion should describe the facts and law that are the basis for the advice. By doing so, the letter memorializes what the attorney knew at the time the letter was prepared.

C. Use Pronouns Thoughtfully

A letter should use pronouns thoughtfully to reflect the relationship between the writer and recipient. A letter addressed to a client will sound cooperative when it uses "we" to describe the actions being taken as part of the representation. For example, writing to a client that "we need to prove the following elements" sounds like the attorney and the client have a common goal, but "you need to prove the following elements" sounds like the attorney is giving the client a difficult assignment. Also, letters often use the plural "we" and "our" when they are written by an attorney who works for a firm or in an office with other lawyers to show that the letter reflects the position of all the lawyers working on the matter.

D. Adopt a Readable Format and Organization

An effective professional letter is readable and its purpose is clear. The most important information in a letter should usually appear at the beginning of the letter and may be repeated at the end of the letter. For instance, a client advice letter should usually state the attorney's conclusion in one of the first few paragraphs.

Professional letters should use short sentences and paragraphs whenever possible because they are easier to read. Letters should also include bulleted and numbered lists when they will assist the reader. Longer letters should include headings and signposts to guide the reader and to break up the text.

E. Proofread

A letter must be proofread carefully. Although typographical and proofreading errors are not acceptable in any legal document, recipients may have some understanding regarding errors that appear in email messages sent quickly from mobile devices. The same understanding does not extend to formal letters. Never send a letter that has misspellings, typos, grammar problems, or other correctable errors.

7. A CUSTOMARY CLOSING

Just as letters usually have formal greetings, they also have formal closings. Professional letters typically end with a sentence or two that wraps up the letter on a positive note, often encouraging the recipient to contact the writer with any questions. Then, the letter includes a formal closing. The most common closings used in legal letter writing are as follows:

Sincerely,
Very truly yours,
Respectfully,

When a letter is addressed to a judge, it should close with "Respectfully." Otherwise, any polite, formal closing is appropriate.

After the closing and signature, the letter should indicate whether there are any enclosures or carbon copy ("cc") recipients. Again, these details are important to ensure that the letter is an accurate record of what was sent and to whom.

8. EXAMPLES OF PROFESSIONAL LETTERS

The following examples demonstrate two types of professional letters. The first is an advice letter to a client that presents the same legal analysis that appears in Example Memo 16.1 in Chapter 16 and Example Email 34.5 in Chapter 34. The second is a letter to opposing counsel regarding a discovery dispute.

STERN, SOGARD & MURANO, LLP

5 CALIFORNIA STREET, 34TH FLOOR | SAN FRANCISCO, CA 94111 | PHONE: 415-333-4444

January 22, 2013 — Correct date reflecting when letter was sent

VIA U.S. MAIL — Method of transmission

Ms. Despina Blackhurst
278 Queensbridge Way
San Jose, CA 95002

— Properly formatted recipient's name and address

Re: Analysis of open and notorious element for adverse possession claim

— Useful re: line including concise summary of the subject of the letter

PRIVILEGED ATTORNEY-CLIENT COMMUNICATION — Privilege designation

Dear Ms. Blackhurst: — Formal greeting with Dear, honorific, and a colon

This letter summarizes our analysis of whether we will be able to establish the element of an adverse possession claim that requires your use of the small parcel to have been "open and notorious."

— The letter begins by stating its purpose.

As described below, we conclude that your use likely satisfies the open and notorious element because your shed and "No Trespassing" signs provided the owner of the parcel with constructive notice of your adverse possession. This letter, however, is limited to our analysis of this one element. For an action to quiet title to succeed, we would have to prove every element of adverse possession.

— The Conclusion is stated early in the letter.

— The use of "we" reflects that this letter is from all of the lawyers working on the matter.

Facts

— Headings guide the reader and break up the text.

You purchased a piece of property in North Lake Tahoe from your uncle in June 2005, believing that the property included both a large parcel and a smaller parcel across an alley from the larger parcel. You live in a house on the large parcel. On the small parcel, you installed a shed where you store snow removal equipment. You used a combination lock to secure the shed. In October 2010, you discovered that teenagers were hanging out in the shed. You chased them away and changed the lock's combination. You also posted "No Trespassing" signs on the small parcel.

— The letter describes the facts that are the basis for the legal analysis.

In June 2012, Aaron Krieger, the owner of the property adjacent to the small parcel, claimed that, according to county records, he owned the small parcel. He told you that he had been living in Norway for the past seven years and had been renting out the property. Now, you seek to quiet title by proving that you acquired the parcel through adverse possession.

Page 2 of 3 — Page number

<u>California Adverse Possession Law</u> — This heading signals the explanation of the law.

To establish adverse possession in California, we need to prove five elements:

(1) actual occupation that is sufficiently open and notorious to give the owner reasonable notice; — The letter uses a numbered list to make the rule easier to understand.

(2) possession hostile to the owner's title, which includes possession that occurred through mistake;

(3) a claim that you have title to the property;

(4) continuous and uninterrupted possession for five years; and

(5) payment of all property taxes.

The purpose of the open and notorious element is to give the owner actual or constructive notice of the adverse possession. To be open and notorious, the use of the property must be visible to the true owner and others. When a use is open and notorious, it raises the presumption that the owner had notice of the adverse possession. But the owner is not required to have actual notice of the adverse use. And an owner cannot defeat an open and notorious use by ignoring it.

Courts decide whether an adverse use is sufficiently open and notorious by looking at the facts of the case, including the condition of the land, where it is located, and how it should be used. Courts have also considered whether the adverse claimant enclosed, maintained, and improved the property.

For example, in a case called *Nielsen v. Gibson*, where the adverse claimants fenced, irrigated, improved, and built a go-cart course on a property, the possession was sufficiently open and notorious. Similarly, in the case *Lobro v. Watson*, where for twenty-five years the adverse claimants occupied the property and made improvements at their own expense, including fencing the lot, replacing the roof, and planting trees and flowers, the court held that the use was open and notorious. — The letter describes relevant cases, but does not include citations because they would not be helpful to the client who is not a lawyer.

In contrast, in *Klein v. Caswell*, possession of a vacant lot was not sufficiently open and notorious where the land was not improved or regularly cultivated and where there was conflicting evidence about how much the claimants used the property. In that case, one claimant testified that she occasionally visited the property over a twenty-two-year period for picnics, and at one time, she asked a neighbor to keep the lot cleaned up. But several neighbors who frequently passed the lot said that it always appeared neglected, the same as other unoccupied, vacant lots in the area. The court held that this "slight use" was not sufficient.

Page 3 of 3

<u>Analysis of Whether Use Was Open and Notorious</u>
By installing and maintaining a locked shed on the small parcel and hanging "No Trespassing" signs on the shed after you discovered that teenagers were using it without your permission, you likely used the property in a way that was sufficiently open and notorious to provide reasonable notice to Krieger of your adverse possession. Like a fence or a go-cart course, your shed and signs were visible to Krieger. The shed and signs showed him that you were occupying, maintaining, and improving the parcel, like in the *Nielsen* and *Lobro* cases, where the claimants installed fences, planted flowers, and otherwise improved the properties they were adversely possessing.

— This heading signals the start of the analysis.

In addition, your use of the property was active and not occasional. Your use of the small parcel goes beyond the occasional picnic in *Klein* that was held to be an insufficient use. Further, there will not be conflicting evidence about your use of the property like there was in that case.

— The letter includes a discussion of contrary authority and a potential counterargument.

Krieger may argue that he did not have actual notice of your use because he was in Norway during the five years that you used the property. Actual notice, however, is not required. Krieger cannot defeat your open and notorious use by willfully ignoring it. In *Nielsen*, the court rejected a similar argument by an owner who had been in Ireland during the period of adverse possession. Based on this analysis, we think that a court would likely hold that your use of the property satisfied the open and notorious element for adverse possession.

<u>Next Steps</u>
You will hear from us soon regarding our analysis of the other adverse possession elements. As always, please let us know if you have any questions or would like to discuss this in person or on the phone. You can call me directly at (415) 888-9999.

— This heading signals a discussion of what will happen next.

— The letter concludes on a positive note and encourages the client to contact the attorney with any questions. As a courtesy, it includes the attorney's direct phone line.

Very truly yours,

— Formal closing

/s/ Rebecca McCarthy

Rebecca McCarthy

Sample
Letter 33.2

STERN, SOGARD & MURANO, LLP

5 CALIFORNIA STREET, 34TH FLOOR | SAN FRANCISCO, CA 94111 | PHONE: 415-333-4444

January 22, 2013 — Correct date reflecting when letter was sent

VIA U.S. MAIL — Method of transmission

Ms. Mary Rivers, Esq. — Properly formatted recipient's name and address
The Rivers Law Group
278 San Carlo Way, Suite 800
San Jose, CA 95002

Re: Discovery issues in *Miller v. Schmidt*, No. C10-288228 — Useful re: line including concise summary of the subject of the letter, case name, and number

Dear Ms. Rivers: — Formal greeting with Dear, honorific, and a colon

Thank you for granting an extension of time through today for Sarah Schmidt to respond to Plaintiff's First Set of Interrogatories and First Set of Requests for Production. Ms. Schmidt's responses are enclosed. — Polite tone, reflecting civil relationship with opposing counsel. Short sentences are used when possible.

As I mentioned in the voicemail that I left for you yesterday, we would like to schedule Charlie Manley's deposition as soon as possible. We have been happy to work with you on a deposition schedule that is convenient for everyone involved, but five months have passed since we noticed this important deposition and it has yet to be scheduled. If Mr. Manley is not made available in the next month, we will be forced to move to compel. Please let me know by 5 p.m. Friday, January 25, when Mr. Manley's deposition can go forward. — The use of "we" reflects that this letter is from all of the lawyers working on the matter. / The letter is concise and direct, but uses passive voice here to avoid sounding too confrontational.

I look forward to hearing from you. Please let me know if you have any questions. — Positive wrap-up

Very truly yours, — Formal closing

/s/ Rebecca McCarthy

Rebecca McCarthy

Enclosures — Notification of enclosures

cc: Brandon Henderson, Esq. — Carbon copy recipient

chapter 34

Email

In many law offices, email is the primary mode of communication. Most attorneys spend much of their time reading and writing email messages. Although many of us regularly use email for personal correspondence, a professional email should have certain qualities that distinguish it from a personal email message.

> ### The Qualities of a Professional Email
> 1. A "to" line that includes only the correct and necessary recipients
> 2. A subject line that is brief, substantive, and specific
> 3. A greeting that is professional
> 4. A format and writing style that is simple and direct
> 5. An appropriate closing and signature block
> 6. Attachments that are properly titled and attached
> 7. A concern for privilege and privacy

1. A "TO" LINE THAT INCLUDES ONLY THE CORRECT AND NECESSARY RECIPIENTS

The first step in preparing an effective professional email is to email only the proper recipients. Attorneys often send emails that discuss sensitive, confidential, or privileged information. Including an unintended recipient on an email to a client could destroy the attorney-client privilege for that message and make it discoverable. Further, incorrectly addressing an email can lead to confusion and embarrassment for the attorney. Be careful when using the "reply all" command in email; it often leads to unintended recipients.

2. A SUBJECT LINE THAT IS BRIEF, SUBSTANTIVE, AND SPECIFIC

Every professional email should have a subject line that concisely describes the substance or purpose of the message. An effective subject line notifies the recipient of the message's contents and allows the sender and recipient to sort the email into a folder and search for it later.

The subject line should be brief. Attorneys often read emails on their phones, and a long subject line is hard to understand when viewed on a small screen. A concise subject line has the best chance of catching the recipient's attention.

The subject line should describe the substance of the email with enough detail to distinguish it from other messages. Identifying the case or matter that a message concerns in the subject line is helpful. By doing so, the sender and recipient can file the message with other messages about the same case. Because colleagues may exchange thousands of emails about a single case, an email with a subject line that includes only the case name can easily be lost. Thus, the better practice is to include the case or matter name and a brief description of the specific topic covered by each message.

For instance, suppose you are working on the case *Abrams v. Hall* and need to send an email to another attorney working on the case concerning edits to a motion to compel. The following subject line is too vague to be effective:

Subject: Abrams v. Hall

A better subject line would be as follows:

Subject: Abrams v. Hall: Edits to motion to compel

This subject line is effective because it identifies both the case and the specific issue discussed in the email.

3. A GREETING THAT IS PROFESSIONAL

There are many acceptable greetings for email correspondence. The relationship between the sender and recipient, the subject of the email, and the circumstances surrounding the correspondence determine what greeting is most appropriate. Table 34.1 describes the most common email greetings and when to use them.

4. A FORMAT AND WRITING STYLE THAT IS SIMPLE AND DIRECT

Although attorneys send emails on an infinite number of topics, the following principles of organization and style can make any email more effective.

A. Lead with the Most Important Information

The main point of an email should appear in the first few sentences of the message. Often, a recipient will not read an email closely at first. Instead, the recipient will skim the message quickly to get the gist and plan to come back

Greeting	Usage	Table 34.1
Dear Mr. Jones: Dear Ms. Ali:	This greeting uses a salutation, an honorific, and a colon. This is the most formal greeting format and the standard for professional letters. An email that uses this format is akin to a formal letter being transmitted electronically. Use this greeting when you are writing a formal email and need to show deference to the recipient. For instance, this greeting would be appropriate if you are writing an email to a judge's clerk or a new client. Note that the honorific Ms. should be used instead of Mrs. or Miss for female recipients, unless you have been advised that the particular recipient prefers something other than Ms.	
Dear Sam, Dear Farrah,	This greeting uses a salutation, the recipient's first name, and a comma. This greeting is common in email correspondence. It reflects that email messages often require less formality than professional letters because they are exchanged between people who are familiar with each other. This greeting would be appropriate when emailing opposing counsel. It preserves some formality by using "Dear," but acknowledges that the sender and recipient are on a first-name basis.	
Sam, Farrah,	This greeting uses the recipient's first name and a comma. This greeting is common in email correspondence when the sender and recipient know each other well and often exchange emails. It would be appropriate when emailing a colleague.	
No greeting	An email without a greeting is appropriate when the sender and recipient exchange multiple emails in the same chain. The lack of repeated greetings makes the email chain shorter and easier to read. For formal emails requiring deference to the sender, however, the better approach is to repeat the greeting even for later emails in a chain.	

to the message at a later time if it requires more attention. Accordingly, the most important information in the email should be located in the first paragraph or the first sentence of a paragraph to guarantee that the recipient notices that information during the initial skim.

B. Distill the Substance of the Email into Short Components

The format for a professional email should be compact and easy to read on a small screen. The best format for the body of an email is usually short, single-spaced, nonindented paragraphs that are separated by a blank line. In addition, when an email needs to list information, use bullets or numbers to set the information apart and make it easy to read.

An email that uses short sentences and paragraphs to convey information will be more effective than an email that is written with long, complex sentences and paragraphs. If an email is long and unwieldy, it may be more efficient to discuss the issues in person or on the phone. And if an email needs to communicate a complicated legal analysis, it may be more helpful to write the analysis in a formal memorandum and attach that document to a short email message that briefly summarizes the memo's contents.

C. Make It Easy for the Recipient to Respond

If an email requires the recipient to answer a question, it should ask the question in a way that makes it easy for the recipient to answer. The question should be direct and, when possible, ask for a simple answer. Further, the question should not be buried in the middle of a message where the recipient may not notice it. Short questions in short messages are more likely to elicit quick responses, as are messages that include only a question or two, rather than a long list.

For instance, imagine that you are emailing a senior attorney about a hearing in the case you are working on together. The following question is too vague and open ended to allow for a simple response:

How should we handle staffing for the upcoming hearing?

In contrast, the senior attorney can easily answer the following question with a yes or no:

Should I plan to appear at the upcoming hearing?

Often, the key to writing an effective email is to put yourself in the position of the recipient. By doing so, you will make it more likely that you receive a prompt and direct response.

D. Be Careful About Tone

Email messages often have a less formal tone than business letters because email allows us to exchange messages very quickly, almost like a face-to-face conversation. Further, because we may use email extensively for personal reasons, we are comfortable writing email messages.

But as with any written communication, conveying the appropriate tone in an email can be difficult. Emails cannot include gestures, facial expressions, or vocal cues (and professional emails should never include emoticons or "textese" like LOL, TTYL, BRB). Thus, emails can be easily misinterpreted. In the professional context, therefore, erring on the side of formality is safer. Although you can certainly include personal touches in professional emails—for instance, by wishing the recipient well—avoid sarcasm, exclamations, and overly emotional responses.

The tone of an email reflects how formal, familiar, and friendly the message appears to the recipient. Aside from its content and the greeting and closing, the tone of an email is most affected by word choice, pronoun use, and sentence structure. An effective email calibrates its tone to accurately reflect the purpose of the message and the relationship between the sender and recipient.

The words used in an email have an obvious impact on tone as they describe the substance of the message. Before using an incendiary or provocative word in an email, consider whether it is appropriate. Often, an email written in the heat of the moment will seem too strong once you have had some time to consider the proper tone. Moreover, certain words can make an email feel more or less formal. For instance, although contractions should appear sparingly in formal legal documents like memos or motions, they can be appropriate for email messages.

Similarly, the use of pronouns impacts the tone of an email by characterizing the relationship between the sender and recipient. For instance, when writing an email to opposing counsel regarding a discovery dispute, the use of "you" can give the message an appropriately accusatory or adversarial tone. In contrast, when writing an email to a client, it may be preferable to use "we" to convey that the sender and recipient are working toward a common goal.

Consider the following two examples, which provide the same information, but have different tones because of their word choice:

As I mentioned in my email last Monday, we need to discuss the best day for the Morton deposition.

> This sentence has a friendly tone. It describes something that "we" need to "discuss," which sounds collaborative. The use of the word "best" sounds positive and non-threatening. This sentence would be appropriate in an email to a client.

You have failed to respond to the email I sent last Monday regarding scheduling the Morton deposition.

> This sentence has a harsher tone. It accuses the recipient of failing to do something. It also creates a sharp distinction between "you" and "I." This sentence could be appropriate in an email to an opposing counsel.

Last, short sentences make an email easy to read on a small screen, but short sentences can also sound terse and give a message a harsh tone. For instance, responding to a question with a one-word answer, like "no," can sound unintentionally brusque to the recipient. An email should balance the need for brevity with a concern for how that brevity will appear to the recipient out of context.

E. Proofread

Like all legal writing, email messages should use proper grammar and punctuation and be free of spelling and other typographical errors. An error in the subject line or body of an email is unprofessional and hurts the sender's credibility. In addition, a spelling or typographical error may make it harder to use the search function to find the email later.

F. Use a Professional Format

Email messages should use a font that is conservative and professional in type, size, and color. In particular, the font type should be one typically used in professional writing, including Arial, Calibri, Georgia, Times New Roman, Verdana, or something similar. The font size should be between 10- and 12-point. The color should be black or dark blue.

5. AN APPROPRIATE CLOSING AND SIGNATURE BLOCK

At the end of an email message, inviting the recipient to call with any questions is often a good idea. Like the salutation, the closing and signature block should be tailored to the relationship between the sender and recipient.

The closing needs to be appropriate for the purpose and tone of the message. There are a number of closings that are appropriate for professional emails. The most common closings are as follows:

Best regards,	Thank you,
Regards,	Very truly yours,
Sincerely,	

When the sender and recipient have exchanged multiple emails in a single chain, the closing does not need to be repeated for each message.

An email signature block should be short, simple, and professional. Its purpose is to provide the recipient with the sender's basic contact information, not to convey the quirks of the sender's personality. Generally, the most important information to include in a professional signature block is the sender's full name, employer, business address, and direct phone number. A professional signature block should use a conservative font type, size, and color.

The following is an example of an appropriate signature block:

Vishal Lee
Parker, Van Nort, and Granville, LLP
2416 Nobel Drive
Miami, FL 33133
(555) 123-4567

As with salutations and closings, when the sender and recipient have exchanged multiple messages in a single chain, repeated signature blocks can be omitted to avoid making the chain longer than necessary. Similarly, an attorney's signature block should not include an inspiring or amusing quotation. Adding a quotation to a signature block makes every message longer and creates the risk of irritating the recipient. Last, an attorney should not include "Esq." after his or her name in the signature block. Esquire is an honorific to show deference or respect to someone else, rather than a title to adopt for yourself.

6. ATTACHMENTS THAT ARE PROPERLY TITLED AND ATTACHED

Attorneys often send email attachments. Before attaching a document, give the document a useful, descriptive title that will mean something to the recipient. Then, make sure that the document has the correct file extension (.docx, .pdf, etc.) to allow the recipient to open it and make edits as appropriate. Most important, always attach the attachment. To avoid sending a message without the attachment, consider attaching the document first, before writing the rest of the message. If you do send a message without its attachment, quickly send a short follow-up message—with the attachment—stating that the document is attached.

7. A CONCERN FOR PRIVILEGE AND PRIVACY

Any email has the potential to become a public document. Email messages can easily be forwarded to unintended and unforeseen recipients. Even emails covered by the attorney-client privilege or attorney work-product protection could be discovered or disclosed in later litigation between the attorney and the client. For this reason, be extremely careful about discussing sensitive topics over email. Never send an email that your gut tells you is inappropriate or unwise.

When sending an email that is protected by the attorney-client privilege, include a privilege label, such as "PRIVILEGED ATTORNEY-CLIENT COMMUNICATION," at the top or bottom of the message. In addition, before sending a privileged message, take care to check that no recipients included on the message would destroy the privilege. For instance, including an expert witness on an email to a client will mean that the message is no longer privileged because there is no privilege between an attorney or client and an expert.

When corresponding with recipients with whom there is no privilege, an attorney should be aware that the email could become a public document. For example, emails exchanged between opposing counsel are routinely attached to motions that are filed with the court during discovery disputes. Such emails will impact an attorney's professional reputation with the recipient, the court, and anyone else who reads the message.

Many law offices have boilerplate language that they include on all messages regarding how an email should be treated if it is inadvertently received by the wrong person. To the extent possible, make sure that any such disclaimers are professionally formatted and designed to take up no more room than necessary.

8. EXAMPLES OF EFFECTIVE EMAILS

The following are examples of professional emails. They demonstrate the different levels of formality that attorneys use when preparing email messages. The first is an email to a clerk of court. The second is an email to opposing counsel. The third is an email to a client. The fourth is an email to a colleague. The fifth example is an advice email to a client conveying the same legal analysis that appears in Example Memo 16.1 in Chapter 16 and Example Letter 33.1 in Chapter 33.

Formal email to a judge's calendar clerk

Example
Email 34.1

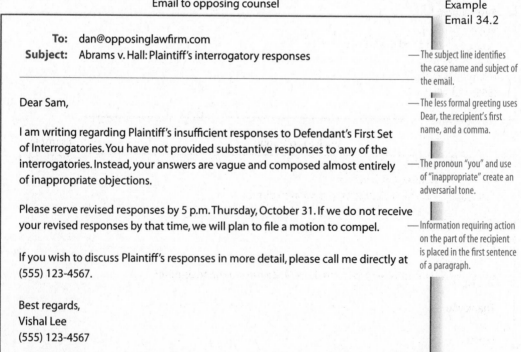

To: clerk@court.com
Subject: Abrams v. Hall (Case No. 12-1113): Response to request to reschedule telephone hearing on motion to compel

— The subject line identifies the case by name and number and briefly describes the purpose of the email.

Dear Ms. Ali:

— The formal greeting uses an honorific and a colon.

Thank you for your message regarding rescheduling the telephone hearing on the motion to compel in Abrams v. Hall. The attorneys for Defendant Travis Hall are available on August 1, 2015, at both 11 a.m. and 3:30 p.m. for the hearing.

— The body of the email is short, simple sentences in a single-spaced, non-indented paragraph.

Please let me know if you have any questions. My direct line is (555) 123-4567.

— The last paragraph offers to have the recipient contact the sender directly and includes a phone number.

Best regards,
Vishal Lee
Parker, Van Nort, and Granville, LLP
2416 Nobel Drive
Miami, FL 33133
(555) 123-4567

— The email ends with a formal closing with complete signature block.

Email to opposing counsel

Example
Email 34.2

To: dan@opposinglawfirm.com
Subject: Abrams v. Hall: Plaintiff's interrogatory responses

— The subject line identifies the case name and subject of the email.

Dear Sam,

— The less formal greeting uses Dear, the recipient's first name, and a comma.

I am writing regarding Plaintiff's insufficient responses to Defendant's First Set of Interrogatories. You have not provided substantive responses to any of the interrogatories. Instead, your answers are vague and composed almost entirely of inappropriate objections.

— The pronoun "you" and use of "inappropriate" create an adversarial tone.

Please serve revised responses by 5 p.m. Thursday, October 31. If we do not receive your revised responses by that time, we will plan to file a motion to compel.

— Information requiring action on the part of the recipient is placed in the first sentence of a paragraph.

If you wish to discuss Plaintiff's responses in more detail, please call me directly at (555) 123-4567.

Best regards,
Vishal Lee
(555) 123-4567

Email to client

> **To:** farrah@client.com
> **Subject:** Abrams v. Hall: Motion to compel analysis
>
> ———————————————————————————————
>
> PRIVILEGED ATTORNEY-CLIENT COMMUNICATION
>
> Dear Farrah,
>
> We have analyzed whether we should file a motion to compel Plaintiff to provide revised interrogatory responses. We think that the Court is likely to grant the motion, and even if the motion is denied, it will educate the Court about Plaintiff's discovery abuses.
>
> The Court is likely to grant the motion for two reasons:
> (1) Three of Plaintiff's responses include only objections. The Court has held in previous cases that such responses are inappropriate; and
> (2) Plaintiff's responses to all 10 interrogatories total only 14 pages. Given that Defendant's responses to Plaintiff's interrogatories were more than 60 pages long, we have a strong argument that Plaintiff's responses are insufficient.
>
> Please let me know if you would like to discuss this analysis further in person or on the phone. You can always call me directly at (555)123-4567. We would like to begin drafting the motion as soon as possible.
>
> Best regards,
> Vishal Lee
> Parker, Van Nort, and Granville, LLP
> 2416 Nobel Drive
> Miami, FL 33133
> (555) 123-4567

— The subject line identifies the case name and purpose of the email.

— Privilege label

— This informal greeting is appropriate when the attorney and client have a familiar, well-established relationship.

— The first sentence gives the email a friendly tone. The next paragraph states a conclusion using "we" to create a connection between the attorney and the client.

— A numbered list makes the substance of the email easy to read.

— The email ends with an offer to discuss further in person or by phone and includes a direct phone number.

Email to colleague

> **To:** denise@lawfirm.com
> **Subject:** Abrams v. Hall: Edits to motion to dismiss
>
> ———————————————————————————————
>
> Denise,
>
> When will you be finished inputting the edits to the motion to dismiss?
>
> Thank you,
>
> Vishal

— The subject line identifies the case name and subject of the email.

— The informal greeting uses the recipient's first name and a comma.

— The body of the email is a simple, direct question.

— The email ends with an appreciative closing and no signature block.

Advice email to client
Note: This is the same legal analysis that appears in Example Memo 16.1 in Chapter 16 and Example Letter 33.1 in Chapter 33.

Example
Email 34.5

To: despina.blackhurst@email.com
Subject: Analysis of open and notorious element
Attachment: August28_Letter.pdf

— The attachment is attached and properly titled.

PRIVILEGED ATTORNEY-CLIENT COMMUNICATION

Dear Despina,

We have analyzed whether your use of the small parcel likely satisfies the open and notorious element for adverse possession. A court would probably determine that because your shed and "No Trespassing" signs provided the owner with constructive notice of your adverse possession, your use was sufficiently open and notorious.

— The first substantive paragraph of the email provides the attorney's conclusion. The email uses "we" to reflect that this is advice from the team of attorneys working on the case.

Facts
- You purchased a piece of property in North Lake Tahoe from your uncle in June 2005, believing that the property included both a large parcel and a smaller parcel across an alley from the larger parcel.
- You live in a house on the large parcel.
- On the small parcel, you installed a shed where you store snow removal equipment. You used a combination lock to secure the shed.
- In October 2010, you discovered that teenagers were hanging out in the shed. You chased them away and changed the lock's combination. You also posted "No Trespassing" signs on the small parcel.
- In June 2012, Aaron Krieger, the owner of the property adjacent to the small parcel, claimed that, according to county records, he owned the small parcel.
- He told you that he had been living in Norway for the past seven years and had been renting out the property.

— Headings guide the reader and break up the text of this long email.

— The facts that are the basis for the analysis are presented as a bulleted list, which is easy to read.

California Adverse Possession Law
Adverse possession has five elements:
1. actual occupation that is sufficiently open and notorious to give the owner reasonable notice;
2. possession hostile to the owner's title, which includes possession that occurred through mistake;
3. a claim that you have title to the property;
4. continuous and uninterrupted possession for five years; and
5. payment of all property taxes.

— The elements are presented in a numbered list written in plain language.

The purpose of the open and notorious element is to give the owner actual or constructive notice of the adverse possession. To be open and notorious, the use of the property must be visible to the true owner and others. When a use is open and notorious, it raises the presumption that the owner had notice of the adverse possession. But actual notice is not required. And an owner cannot defeat an open and notorious use by willfully ignoring it.

Courts decide whether an adverse use is sufficiently open and notorious by looking at the facts of the case, including the condition of the land, where it is located, and how it should be used. Courts have also considered whether the adverse claimant enclosed, maintained, and improved the property.

Relevant cases

Our analysis is based on three cases that are factually and legally similar to your situation. They are summarized below:

Nielsen v. Gibson: The adverse claimants fenced, irrigated, improved, and built a go-cart course on a property. The court held the possession was sufficiently open and notorious.

Lobro v. Watson: For 25 years the adverse claimants occupied the property and made improvements and additions at their own expense, including fencing the lot, replacing the roof, and planting trees and flowers. The court held that the use was open and notorious.

Klein v. Caswell: The court held that possession of a vacant lot was not sufficiently open and notorious where the land was not improved or regularly cultivated and where there was conflicting evidence about the extent that the claimants used the property. One claimant testified that she occasionally visited the property over a 22-year period for picnics, and at one time, she asked a neighbor to keep the lot cleaned up. But several neighbors who frequently passed the lot said that it always appeared neglected, the same as other unoccupied, vacant lots in the area. The court held that this "slight use" was not sufficient.

— The relevant cases are summarized in separate, short paragraphs. Citation information is omitted because it would not be helpful to the client.

Analysis

By installing and maintaining a locked shed on the small parcel and hanging "No Trespassing" signs on the shed after you discovered that teenagers were using it without your permission, you likely used the property in a way that was sufficiently open and notorious to provide reasonable notice to Krieger of your adverse possession.

— The analysis is presented in short paragraphs.

Like a fence or a go-cart course, your shed and signs were visible to Krieger. The shed and signs showed the owner that you were occupying, maintaining, and improving the parcel, like in the *Nielsen* and *Lobro* cases, where the claimants installed fences, planted flowers, and otherwise improved the properties they were adversely possessing.

In addition, your use of the property was active and not occasional. Your use of the small parcel goes beyond the occasional picnic in *Klein* that was held to be an insufficient use. And there will not be conflicting evidence about your use of the property like there was in that case.

Krieger may argue that he did not have actual notice of your use because he was in Norway during the five years that you used the property. A similar argument was rejected in *Nielsen*, where the owner was in Ireland during the adverse possession. Krieger cannot defeat your open and notorious use by claiming he did not have actual notice.

Based on this analysis, we think that a court would likely hold that your use of the property satisfied the open and notorious element for adverse possession.

Next steps

Please note that this analysis is limited to one element required for adverse possession. For an action to quiet title to succeed, we would have to prove all five elements. You will hear from us soon regarding our analysis of the other adverse possession elements.

The letter we received last week from Krieger's attorney, which we discussed yesterday on the phone, is attached.

— The email describes the attached document.

As always, please let me know if you have any questions or would like to discuss this in person or on the phone.

Very truly yours,
Rebecca McCarthy
Stern, Sogard & Murano, LLP
(415) 888-9999

— The sender's direct phone number is included in the signature block.

chapter 35

Messaging and New Technology

The technology available to attorneys to communicate with their clients, adversaries, and colleagues is constantly evolving. Many attorneys now correspond over text message from their cellphones and instant message from their computers or tablets. Because communication is one of an attorney's primary tasks, attorneys should be enthusiastic about these expanding forms of communication.

As you use these new technologies, and any others that may soon be invented, you should remember that your written correspondence, in any format or medium, is a reflection of your credibility and professionalism. Consider the following three principles of professional correspondence when using new messaging technology.

> **Principles of Professional Correspondence When Using New Technology**
> 1. Err on the side of formality
> 2. Pause before pressing send
> 3. Be vigilant regarding confidentiality

1. ERR ON THE SIDE OF FORMALITY

Messaging makes it easy to communicate quickly and informally, which can be helpful to a busy attorney. But you should hesitate before dispensing with the typical formalities of written correspondence, including the use of titles, honorifics, and complete sentences. These formalities help to establish the boundaries of the professional relationship. Communicating with your clients or colleagues in the same style that you communicate with your friends may undermine your professional credibility.

When you are writing in your professional capacity, err on the side of maintaining the formalities that demonstrate your prudence, maturity, and reliability. Do not feel that you have to match the informality of the person on the other side of the conversation. Even if you receive a very informal message (for example, one that uses text abbreviations or emoticons), you should respond with the level of formality appropriate to the legal profession.

2. PAUSE BEFORE PRESSING SEND

Messaging allows for written correspondence to happen in real time with very little lag. The efficiency of communicating over text and instant message has many benefits for attorneys. But it also it makes it easy to send a message in haste that you may regret.

Attorneys are expected to exercise good judgment. Part of this good judgment is taking a moment, when necessary, to weigh the options before making a decision. Do not let the speed of messaging technology force you to act more quickly than you would like. Instead, if you need more time to respond, you can usually say that. There is nothing to gain from responding quickly with an answer that you later decide was incorrect.

3. BE VIGILANT REGARDING CONFIDENTIALITY

An attorney has an ethical duty to maintain a client's confidential information.[1] You should, therefore, make sure that any technology you use for correspondence does not jeopardize the confidentiality of your clients' information. Be as vigilant regarding the privacy of your professional communications over text and instant message as you are for emails and letters.

---

1. *See, e.g.*, ABA Model Rule of Professional Conduct 1.6.

chapter 36

Judicial Opinions

At this point in law school, you have likely read judicial opinions from courts of all levels and many jurisdictions. A judicial opinion sets forth the reasons and the authorities for a decision. Judges write opinions for two main purposes: to explain the court's rationale and to provide consistency in the law by following and setting precedent. In addition, judges write opinions to communicate with the parties, their attorneys, and the public. Although judges are the authors of opinions, they frequently receive assistance in drafting the opinions from their judicial clerks and judicial interns. As a result, you could have the opportunity to write an opinion early in your law school career.

Judicial opinions share many of the characteristics of a legal memorandum. Both should present a fair and objective view of the facts and the law, both present a sound legal analysis, and both typically follow the logical CREAC organization.[1] As a result, the process for writing a judicial opinion and a legal memo are similar.

But memos and opinions have one major difference: While a legal memo predicts the most likely answer to a legal question, a judicial opinion provides the answer authoritatively. As a result, an opinion will not use qualifying language, such as "probably" or "likely" in its Analysis or Conclusion. Instead, an opinion will definitively state the answer to the legal question as it renders a decision in a legal dispute.

Writing a Judicial Opinion

1. Identify the issue(s) for analysis
2. Outline and draft each part
3. Proofread to perfection

---

1. STEP ONE: IDENTIFY THE ISSUE(S) FOR ANALYSIS

The first step toward drafting a judicial opinion is making sure that you understand the specifics of the case before you. When you are writing an opinion

---

1. Review the *Knapp v. Ball* opinion in Chapter 5 for one example of an opinion that follows the CREAC format.

for an intermediate appellate court or supreme court, you will have persuasive briefs from the parties and an extensive record to review.

The appellate record will have numerous documents from the lower court, such as deposition transcripts, affidavits, a trial transcript, and lower court orders. These documents provide a starting point for understanding the case, and you will need to carefully read and reread each page of the record to grasp the nuances of the case before you. In addition, you will need to conduct your own research and analysis—using the parties' briefs as a starting point—to ensure that you apply the law fairly and reach an impartial decision.

For cases at the trial court level, you can start to identify the issue or issues you need to analyze by reviewing the point headings from the parties' motions. A good point heading should explicitly state the legal issue. For example, a Defendant's Motion to Dismiss an adverse possession case could have the following two point headings:

I. The Motion To Dismiss Should Be Granted Because Plaintiff Cannot Establish That She Occupied Defendant's Land In An Open And Notorious Manner.
II. Plaintiff Rarely Trespassed On Defendant's Land And Therefore Cannot Establish That She Continuously Possessed The Land As California Law Requires.

After reviewing the point headings and independently researching and reviewing the law, you would discover that California law requires five elements for an adverse possession claim, including "open and notorious possession" and "continuity of possession." After fully reviewing the record to make sure no other issues need to be analyzed, you would conclude that your opinion needs to address these two elements in a Discussion with two separate CREACs.

But suppose the point headings above were less clear regarding the issues to be analyzed. Your task might be more challenging, but you would reach the same result. After reviewing the facts in the record and the applicable law, you would discover that an adverse possession claim has five elements. After ruling out three elements that are not in dispute following a thorough review of the record and applicable law, you would identify the two issues that are identified in the specific point headings above.

For cases at the appellate court level, the point headings could also provide you with the starting point to identify the issues for analysis. But you will have an even better indicator of the precise legal issue before you: the question presented. All briefs begin with a question presented of some form. The exact style and title for the question presented varies between courts—some court rules require an "Issue Presented" or "Statement of the Issues." But whatever the name, this statement should set forth the precise issue for review.

For example, consider the following "Legal Issue" statements from the State and Defendant in a Minnesota criminal case.[2]

---

2. *State v. Wiggins*, 788 N.W.2d 509, 509 (Minn. Ct. App. 2010).

APPELLANT'S LEGAL ISSUE

Did the police officer seize Wiggins—when she had him put his hands behind his head and told him, to move his legs—and then search him—when she pulled up his sagging pants and found a gun—without the requisite reasonable and articulable suspicion to seize and search?[3]

APPELLEE'S LEGAL ISSUE

A police officer saw marijuana in an automobile. Before searching the car, she had appellant get out and put his hands behind his head. As appellant got out, his pants were at his knees. The officer pulled the pants up and noticed something hard in appellant's pocket. Appellant said he did not know what it was. The officer reached into the pocket and seized a loaded pistol. Was the pistol seized lawfully?[4]

A careful reading of these two issue statements reveals two precise issues: whether the search of appellant was lawful and whether the seizure of the pistol was lawful. A review of the applicable law confirms that courts analyze these two legal issues separately. And a review of the record shows that both issues are in dispute. So each issue would merit a separate CREAC in the opinion's Discussion.

2. STEP TWO: OUTLINE AND DRAFT EACH PART

A. Review Samples to Create a Template

Courts use different formats for their orders and opinions depending on their level and jurisdiction. In general, each opinion will provide a case caption, an Introduction, a Facts section, a Discussion with a CREAC-style analysis of each issue, and a Decision. Depending on the complexity of each of these sections, an opinion may include headings, along with subheadings within the sections. When preparing to draft a judicial opinion, review several examples from your judge and your court to create an exact template for the opinion—from the case caption to the final Decision. Opinions are public records, and you can find opinions from many courts—for free—on the courts' websites.[5]

---

3. Appellant's Brief at 3, *Wiggins*, 788 N.W.2d 509 (No. A09-1987), 2010 WL 3779216.

4. Respondent's Brief at 1, *Wiggins*, 788 N.W.2d 509 (No. A09-1987), 2010 WL 3779218.

5. For example, through a simple web search, opinions from the Massachusetts Supreme Judicial Court and the Massachusetts Appeals Court can be found here: http://www.massreports.com/SlipOps/Default.aspx, and orders and opinions from the Texas Supreme Court can be found here: http://www.supreme.courts.state.tx.us/historical/recent.asp. Keep in mind that most of the opinions in your casebooks are edited to be shorter than the originals, so most will not give you an accurate idea of the many parts in an opinion as it is issued by a court.

As an example, the following represents a basic outline of a Minnesota search and seizure opinion that is discussed throughout this chapter of the *Handbook*.

- Case caption
- Introduction
- Facts
- Issue Statement
- Analysis beginning with roadmap
  - CREAC on seizure issue
  - CREAC on search issue
- Decision

B. Introduction

The Introduction at the start of a judicial opinion briefly describes what the case is about. This section should introduce the parties, procedural history, key facts, precise legal issue(s), and the outcome of the case. The Introduction is often only a paragraph or two, so the challenge is to summarize the key information in a concise yet complete way. The following example by Judge Vance E. Salter of the Florida Third District Court of Appeal is succinct and straightforward as it introduces the case's key details.

> Marisol Alonso appeals an order denying a motion for new trial based on alleged misconduct by certain jurors. Ms. Alonso is the personal representative for the estate of Kristine Fernandez, original plaintiff in a severe (and ultimately fatal) motor vehicle collision and rollover case. After a three-week trial, the jury returned a verdict in favor of appellee Ford. We affirm the denial of the motion for new trial.
>
> The issues raised by the appellant are (1) an allegation of premature deliberations by certain members of the jury, (2) an allegation that one member, Juror S., suffered a "high blood pressure headache" and "went along with a defense verdict in this case only because he was fearful of having a stress-induced stroke caused by his severe hypertension," and (3) an allegation by Juror S. that another juror, Juror K., "smelled like a batch of beer," and seemed to Juror S. to have been intoxicated at one or more points during the trial. Of these, only the third issue merits extended analysis as a basis for the motion denied by the trial court.[6]

Annotations:
- Nature of the case
- The parties include plaintiff-appellant Alonso and appellee Ford.
- The case history and the Conclusion are described in these two sentences.
- Here, the Court details the issues that the appellant raised on appeal with specific quotes from the record.
- The Court then explains why it will fully analyze only one of the issues.

The above example provides a traditional opening to an appellate opinion. But judges—unlike law students—do not have to follow a strict format for their writing assignments. The following Introduction to a dissent from a denial of certiorari written by Chief Justice Roberts has drawn attention for

---

6. *Alonso v. Ford Motor Co.*, 54 So. 3d 562 (Fla. Dist. Ct. App. 2011).

its creativity. Even so, the Introduction provides all the necessary information: the nature of the case, the parties, the key facts, the issue, the procedural history, and Roberts' conclusion.

> North Philly, May 4, 2001. Officer Sean Devlin, Narcotics Strike Force, was working the morning shift. Undercover surveillance. The neighborhood? Tough as a three-dollar steak. Devlin knew. Five years on the beat, nine months with the Strike Force. He'd made fifteen, twenty drug busts in the neighborhood.
>
> Devlin spotted him: a lone man on the corner. Another approached. Quick exchange of words. Cash handed over; small objects handed back. Each man then quickly on his own way. Devlin knew the guy wasn't buying bus tokens. He radioed a description and Officer Stein picked up the buyer. Sure enough: three bags of crack in the guy's pocket. Head downtown and book him. Just another day at the office.
>
> That was not good enough for the Pennsylvania Supreme Court, which held in a divided decision that the police lacked probable cause to arrest the defendant. The court concluded that a "single, isolated transaction" in a high-crime area was insufficient to justify the arrest, given that the officer did not actually see the drugs, there was no tip from an informant, and the defendant did not attempt to flee. I disagree with that conclusion, and dissent from the denial of certiorari. A drug purchase was not the only possible explanation for the defendant's conduct, but it was certainly likely enough to give rise to probable cause.[7]

C. Facts

In cases where the facts are not too complex, a judge may choose to weave all of the legally significant facts into the Introduction and Discussion. For instance, both of the previous opinion excerpts above did not include separate Facts sections. But when the relevant facts of a case are particularly involved, you may need to include a separate Facts section with a heading. Whichever format you choose, keep in mind a judge's obligation to remain impartial. So while you should take into account the parties' version of events, the Facts section must present the story of the case objectively.

In addition, an opinion must set forth all the legally significant facts. Because the holding in a case depends on the facts, omitting a key fact could affect the way that courts apply and interpret the precedent. As a result, a judicial opinion should include every legally significant fact and any fact that is necessary to provide context.

Finally, a Facts section must be organized logically. Like a Facts section for an office memo,[8] the Facts section can be organized by chronology or by topic.

---

7. *Pennsylvania v. Dunlap*, 555 U.S. 964, 964 (2008) (Roberts, C.J., dissenting from denial of cert.).

8. Refer to Chapter 14 for a review.

It should also consist of short, focused paragraphs with topic sentences and transitions that guide the reader through the story of the case.

D. Discussion

The Discussion section sets forth the law and rationale for a decision. This section may begin with a separate issue statement, and it will include a CREAC-style analysis for each legal issue. If the opinion addresses more than one legal issue, the Discussion should include a roadmap paragraph and headings to help the reader follow the analysis of each issue.

i. Issue Statement

The Discussion in the opinion for the Minnesota search and seizure case began with the following issue statement:

ISSUE

Did the police officer seize or search Wiggins unconstitutionally when she ordered him out of the car and pulled up his sagging pants?

This issue statement introduces the idea that the opinion will analyze the search and seizure issues separately. Because the opinion addresses two distinct issues, Judge Kevin G. Ross of the Minnesota Court of Appeals provided a roadmap at the start of the Discussion, before sections with the headings, "The Seizure" and "The Search."[9]

ii. Roadmap

A roadmap in a judicial opinion introduces the CREAC analyses that follow. A roadmap can be one or more paragraphs, and it begins with a general Conclusion. It then states the overarching rule for the minor issues analyzed in each CREAC and shows how the issues relate to each other. For example, the roadmap in the search and seizure opinion details the state and federal constitutional provisions that protect against unreasonable searches and seizures.

iii. Standard of Review

In addition, a roadmap provides a logical point for addressing the standard of review. Once a case reaches an appellate court, the question before the appellate panel of judges is often not the same as it was when the trial court decided it. The standard of review determines how much deference the appellate court should give to the lower court's judgment. In some cases, the appellate court is required to defer to the trial court's judgment because the trial court is the finder of fact.

For example, under the abuse of discretion standard, the appellate court will reverse only if the decision below was based on an erroneous conclusion

---

9. *Wiggins*, 788 N.W.2d at 509.

of law or where the record contains no evidence on which the judge could have rationally based the decision.[10] The de novo standard, in contrast, requires the appellate court to show no deference to the lower court's finding and review the judgment anew. To determine the standard of review in your case, begin by reviewing the parties' briefs. Then, even when the parties do not dispute the standard of review, conduct your own research to confirm that the standard cited by the parties is correct.

Because the standard of review determines how the court will analyze the facts and law in your case, describing the standard of review at the start of the opinion makes sense. If you do not include a roadmap in your opinion, then include the standard of review in the Rule section of your CREAC.

iv. CREAC-Style Analysis

After the roadmap, the Discussion in a judicial opinion will discuss each legal issue using a CREAC-style analysis. The CREAC in a judicial opinion does not look exactly the same as the traditional CREAC that you will use for an office memo.

The major difference is that judicial opinions cannot use any qualifying language, such as "probably" and "likely" because they need to decisively render a judgment. As you draft the CREAC for each issue in your opinion, make sure that your Conclusions are stated authoritatively. For example, the first Conclusion for the seizure analysis in the Minnesota case begins authoritatively:

> Wiggins was seized when the officer ordered him from the car and instructed him to raise his hands.

In addition, the Analysis in a judicial opinion should include no hedging. The Analysis in a traditional CREAC not only includes qualifying language but it also includes a counter-analysis, where the writer objectively describes the legal arguments that do not support the Conclusion.

Similarly, a judicial opinion can and should describe the losing party's arguments. But the court must address the failed arguments in a way that authoritatively dismisses them. Under the analysis of the search in the Minnesota case, Judge Ross details a few arguments that the defendant unsuccessfully made or could have made. Judge Ross then decisively describes why those arguments fail:

> Wiggins argues that affirming the district court would encourage officers to trample the privacy of young people who participate in the baggy-pants fashion trend. The concern is unwarranted. Our holding arises from the unique facts here....
>
> Wiggins has not made and the facts would not support the claim that the officer's raising of his pants was a pretext to explore for contraband

---

10. *See, e.g., Deitchman v. E.R. Squibb & Sons, Inc.,* 740 F.2d 556, 563-64 (7th Cir. 1984).

in his pockets; the officer had no motive to look for justification to search because she had already concluded that a pat-search was justified and she intended to conduct one immediately after Wiggins's pants were suitably rearranged....

Wiggins raises other arguments that mistakenly assume that the officer's touching of his pants constituted a search. We do not address these arguments.[11]

The Analysis fairly summarizes the failed arguments while explaining why the arguments fail under the law.

E. Decision

For each issue under review, you will draft two Conclusion statements to follow the CREAC organization. The Decision section of an opinion formalizes your Analysis and Conclusion by stating the court's holding. Because the holding sets precedent, it must clearly describe the scope of the court's decision. The Decision below from the search and seizure case describes the key facts that support the court's final ruling:

DECISION

Police lawfully detained Wiggins after reasonably suspecting that he and others were exchanging illegal drugs. The officer reasonably ordered Wiggins to raise his hands and reasonably decided to adjust his excessively sagging pants. The adjustment did not constitute a search and was not conducted in a manner that raises any constitutional concerns.[12]

3. STEP THREE: PROOFREAD TO PERFECTION

A judicial opinion not only represents the work of the judge or justice who authors the opinion, it also represents the work of the court. The quality of both the analysis and the writing will reflect upon the credibility of the judiciary. As a result, making sure that the analysis and writing are flawless is of paramount importance.

The editing process for a judicial opinion is intense. Several judicial clerks and judges may work together on numerous drafts to refine the analysis before declaring it sound. Once the editing phase is complete, a careful proofreading will commence. The proofreading will check every detail—ensuring that every letter, space, comma, and period is in its proper place. A thorough proofreading will include checking citations for format and accuracy, and it will include reviewing every word, sentence, and paragraph for spelling, gram-

---

11. 788 N.W.2d at 515.
12. *Id.*

mar, and style. Finally, the proofreading phase will check for any remaining typographical and formatting errors. The goal is to turn out an accurate, sound, and well-written opinion that helps maintain the integrity of the judicial process.

4. EXAMPLE OF AWARD-WINNING OPINION WRITING

In the search and seizure case discussed throughout this chapter, Judge Ross[13] found that a police officer did not violate a defendant's constitutional rights. The officer discovered a handgun in the defendant's pocket after "she hoisted up his sagging pants that had dropped to hang around his knees."[14]

STATE v. WIGGINS
7788 N.W.2d 509 (2010)

Opinion

ROSS, Judge.

This case requires us to determine the constitutionality of a novel police procedure which, as far as we can tell, has never been reviewed on appeal by this court or any other. An officer investigating a suspected drug deal directed appellant Frank Wiggins from a car, ordered him to raise his hands high overhead, and then discovered a handgun in his pocket when she hoisted up his sagging pants that had dropped to hang around his knees. Wiggins appeals from his conviction of possession of a firearm by an ineligible person. We must decide whether the unique wardrobe assist was a search subject to constitutional regulation and, if not, whether it was the kind of seizure-related contact otherwise prohibited by the Fourth Amendment. Because we hold that the officer's tactic was neither a search nor an unreasonable touching during a lawful investigative detention, we affirm.

— This Introduction paragraph describes the defendant and the search and seizure that led to this appeal. It also sets forth the precise legal issue before the appellate court.

— The holding is stated in clear, decisive terms.

Facts

St. Paul police officer Kara Breci and her partner were on patrol on a November 2008 afternoon in a high drug-activity area when they noticed a car parked with its engine idling in a White Castle parking lot. Officer Breci had seen many drug deals, and several things in addition to the location aroused her suspicion that she was witnessing another one. The driver and a man later identified as appellant Frank Wiggins sat in the front seat, and a third man approached and entered the back seat without any food from the restaurant. No one in the car appeared to be

— The Facts section tells the story of the case chronologically, first explaining why officers stopped the defendant and asked him to step out of his car. The section sets forth the facts in an impartial and straightforward manner.

---

13. The Green Bag, http://www.greenbag.org, recognized the opinion for "exemplary legal writing" in 2010.

14. *Wiggins,* 788 N.W.2d at 509.

eating. The back-seat occupant began to look down at his lap. As the officers walked to the car they saw the rear occupant drop a plastic bag to the floor. They asked the man what the bag contained, and he replied, "Some weed." Wiggins seemed nervous to Officer Breci while her partner was questioning the rear occupant.

The officers ordered the men out of the car. Officer Breci directed Wiggins to raise his hands above his head. Wiggins wore loose-fitting jeans, which, when he stood, were hanging down around his knees. Officer Breci decided to pat-frisk Wiggins for weapons. But first, she pulled his pants up. As she lifted Wiggins's pants, she felt a hard object in his front pocket. She asked Wiggins what it was, and he responded that he did not know. The officer surmised that it was a handgun and removed a .380 caliber pistol from Wiggins's pocket.

— Next, the story continues the chronology by describing why and how one police officer searched the defendant.

Because Wiggins had prior violent-crime convictions, the state charged him with possession of a firearm by an ineligible person. Wiggins moved the district court to suppress the gun evidence, arguing that the seizure of the car and its occupants was unsupported by reasonable suspicion and that the officer conducted an unconstitutional frisk when she hoisted his pants. The district court denied Wiggins's motion to suppress, reasoning that the officers lawfully approached the car and ordered the occupants out based on their seeing the marijuana, that Officer Breci reasonably chose not to direct Wiggins to reach for his own pants out of concerns for her own safety, and that Officer Breci did not search Wiggins but instead found the gun by accident as she was "help[ing] him get his pants into a decent position."

Wiggins waived his right to a jury trial and submitted the case to the district court on stipulated facts, preserving for appeal his challenge to the stop and alleged search. *See State v. Lothenbach*, 296 N.W.2d 854, 857-58 (Minn. 1980); Minn. R. Crim. P. 26.01, subd. 4. The district court found Wiggins guilty of possession of a firearm by an ineligible person. Wiggins appeals, challenging the district court's denial of his pretrial suppression motion.

*— The **Facts** section then details the state's criminal case against the defendant and the procedural history that led to the appeal.*

Issue

Did the police officer seize or search Wiggins unconstitutionally when she ordered him out of the car and pulled up his sagging pants?

— The issue statement references both the search and seizure issues.

Analysis

Wiggins argues that the district court failed to vindicate his state and federal constitutional rights by denying his motion to suppress the gun evidence that resulted from the officer's alleged search. The United States and Minnesota constitutions guarantee the right of persons not to be

— The roadmap devotes two paragraphs to introducing the legal issues of search and seizure.

subjected to "unreasonable searches and seizures." U.S. Const. amend. IV; Minn. Const. art. I, §10. Evidence seized in violation of this guarantee generally must be suppressed. *State v. Jackson*, 742 N.W.2d 163, 177-78 (Minn. 2007). Wiggins correctly argues that in limited circumstances the supreme court has interpreted the state constitution to provide greater protection than the Fourth Amendment provides. *See In re Welfare of B.R.K.*, 658 N.W.2d 565, 577 (Minn. 2003) ("[W]e are free to interpret the Minnesota Constitution as affording greater protection against unreasonable searches and seizures than the United States Constitution, but do not do so cavalierly."). But Wiggins does not contend that this is such a circumstance, and we will analyze his constitutional claims under a single standard. When reviewing a district court's pretrial suppression ruling on undisputed facts, we consider the facts independently and decide de novo whether the undisputed facts warrant suppression as a matter of law. *State v. Othoudt*, 482 N.W.2d 218, 221 (Minn. 1992).

> — First, the roadmap provides the broadest search and seizure rules from the highest authorities: the federal and state constitutions.

> — By providing the broad rules first, the roadmap puts the search and seizure issues that are analyzed below in context.

> — The roadmap sets forth the de novo standard of review here.

Wiggins retreats somewhat from his argument to the district court, conceding now that the police lawfully approached the parked car and looked inside and that, on observing the bag of marijuana in plain view in the rear passenger compartment, they could also order the three occupants out to search the car. Wiggins challenges only the police conduct that occurred after he left the car. He argues that police unlawfully seized and pat-searched him without having a reasonable, articulable suspicion that he was involved in criminal activity and that he was armed and dangerous. His arguments do not persuade us.

> — The roadmap ends by stating the appellant's arguments, which the appellate court must resolve. The summary serves as a thesis for the analysis that follows.

The Seizure

Wiggins was seized when the officer ordered him from the car and instructed him to raise his hands. A person has been "seized" when, "in view of all of the circumstances surrounding the incident, a reasonable person would have believed that he was not free to leave." *In re Welfare of E.D.J.*, 502 N.W.2d 779, 781 (Minn. 1993). A reasonable person would not have believed that he was free to leave after a police officer discovered illegal drugs in his car and ordered him to get out and to raise his hands. So Wiggins was seized and we must decide whether the seizure was lawful.

> — The **Conclusion** paragraph begins and ends with the court's precise Conclusion, which includes a description of the precise legal issue.

> — The seizure **Rule** from a state supreme court case provides the context necessary to explain the legally significant terms in the Conclusion.

To lawfully seize a person temporarily to investigate a crime, a police officer must have a reasonable, articulable suspicion that the person was or will be engaged in criminal activity. *Terry v. Ohio*, 392 U.S. 1, 21-22 (1968); *State v. George*, 557 N.W.2d 575, 578 (Minn. 1997). This is not a high standard, *State v. Timberlake*, 744 N.W.2d 390, 393 (Minn. 2008), and we apply it in view of the totality of the circumstances from an objectively reasonable officer's perspective, *Appelgate v. Comm'r of Public Safety*, 402 N.W.2d 106, 108 (Minn. 1987). In doing so, we recognize that trained law enforcement officers may interpret circumstances using infer-

> — The rule **Explanation** uses federal and state cases to describe how to interpret whether a seizure is unlawful. The court states the Rule and the Explanation objectively, describing the anchor that reasonable suspicion depends on the circumstances.

ences and deductions beyond the competence of untrained persons. *State v. Richardson*, 622 N.W.2d 823, 825 (Minn. 2001).

Wiggins argues that the bag of marijuana found in the passenger compartment cannot justify his detention because spotting the drugs would not reasonably lead an officer to suspect that Wiggins was involved with them. Wiggins casts the episode with himself as the uninvolved occupant of a car in which someone else's contraband just happened to be discovered in the back seat. But his characterization misses the bigger scene: police came upon a stopped and idling car in a fast-food restaurant's parking lot in an area known to them as a place of drug dealing; they observed that the car was occupied by three men having no apparent business with the restaurant, including a man who wandered up to the car and into the back seat; and they watched Wiggins sitting nervously when the back-seat occupant told the officers that the bag he had tried to hide on the floor contained "some weed." These circumstances would lead a reasonable officer to suspect that Wiggins was engaging in a drug deal. The seizure and brief investigative detention that arose from that suspicion therefore did not violate the Fourth Amendment or article I, section 10 of the Minnesota Constitution.

— The **Analysis** begins by briefly summarizing Wiggins' arguments to show how he views the circumstances.

— The transition "but" marks the start of the court's objective **Analysis** of how police view the circumstances. The details here show why police had reasonable suspicion to seize the defendant.

— The Court ends its seizure analysis by restating the **Conclusion**.

The Search

[Analysis omitted.]

Decision

Police lawfully detained Wiggins after reasonably suspecting that he and others were exchanging illegal drugs. The officer reasonably ordered Wiggins to raise his hands and reasonably decided to adjust his excessively sagging pants. The adjustment did not constitute a search and was not conducted in a manner that raises any constitutional concerns.

— The **Decision** section authoritatively summarizes the specific Conclusions on the search and seizure issues before providing the overall Conclusion. The Court provides a fact-based reason for each Conclusion.

Affirmed.

chapter 37

Oral Arguments

Oral argument gives you the opportunity to convince the court that your argument should prevail. This practice—of standing at a court podium and having a formal conversation with the judges deciding your case—allows you to emphasize and elaborate on the best arguments in your motion or brief. Oral argument also gives you a chance to respond to and rebut opposing counsel's arguments and to address specific questions that a judge may have about your position.

Whether you are arguing before a trial court judge or Supreme Court Justices, oral argument also provides you with an opportunity to build your professional reputation. At oral argument, you should demonstrate to the court, your client, and your colleagues that you are meticulously prepared. A well-prepared advocate knows the facts, the record, and the law and can seamlessly cite to each throughout an argument. A well-prepared advocate also can communicate a credible argument without any embellishment of the facts or law.

Additionally, a well-prepared advocate should zealously defend a client's position—but with the restraint necessary to show the proper respect for the judicial process. A respectful advocate will show deference to the judges, civility to opposing counsel, and reverence to the customary rules of decorum.

Specific practices for oral argument will vary depending on the court. A trial court argument on a motion could take just a few minutes and draw only a few questions from the judge. An argument before the U.S. Supreme Court typically lasts 30 minutes and includes multiple questions from most of the Justices. For every argument, you should acquaint yourself with the particular court's rules and practices. To prepare for oral argument, you can start by developing a plan and following the strategy outlined in this chapter.

Oral Arguments

1. Develop a plan
2. Prepare for a conversation, not a speech
3. Follow rules of decorum

---

1. STEP ONE: DEVELOP A PLAN

Start preparing for oral argument by developing a strategy. Review your brief and opposing counsel's brief to think about how you can fine tune your theme and arguments. Consider what arguments you want to emphasize and what points in opposing counsel's brief you need to address. Then, develop an outline for your argument that includes your (1) greeting, (2) opening roadmap, (3) an outline of your major arguments and authorities, and (4) conclusion. If you are the movant or appellant, you also will need to plan for a rebuttal. Your outline will serve as the notes you need to present an effective oral argument.

A. Greeting

The greeting that starts your oral argument will provide a formal introduction to you and your case. The customary greeting begins, "May it please the court." This formal opening shows deference to the court. Next, you should provide your name and your client's name. Deputy Solicitor General Gregory Garre's argument in *Hepting v. AT&T* before the United States Court of Appeals for the Ninth Circuit in 2008 provides a typical greeting, which is transcribed below:

> Thank you, Judge Pregerson, and may it please the court. My name is Gregory Garre, and I'm appearing here today on behalf of the United States.

In some cases, you might appear with co-counsel for oral argument with each of you arguing a distinct issue. The first speaker should introduce both attorneys and explain the issue that each of you will address. The greetings for both attorneys could follow this format:

> First attorney (Jones):

> Good morning, your Honors, and may it please the court. I am Melody Jones, and I'm here with co-counsel John Day on behalf of the appellant, pharmacist Jody Levinson. I will argue that Dr. Levinson fulfilled her duty to the customer. And Mr. Day will argue that there is no duty extended to remote plaintiffs.

> Second attorney (Day) (following first attorney's completed oral argument):

> Thank you, and may it please the court. I am John Day, here on behalf of Dr. Levinson.

B. Opening Roadmap

After the greeting, you should launch into your argument beginning with an opening roadmap that provides an overview of the major points you want to make. The roadmap should begin with a conclusion referencing the relief that you seek. Then, the roadmap should briefly describe the essential arguments you plan to make in the order you plan to make them.

The roadmap should be concise yet thorough. Keep in mind that while you should be prepared to address each of your arguments in detail, you may run out of time because of judges' questions. As a result, the roadmap gives you the first and best opportunity to summarize the major reasons why the court should grant the relief you seek. Here's an example of a roadmap for a case relating to whether the pharmacist has a duty to warn customers of drugs' side effects.

> This case is about a pharmacist, Dr. Levinson, who fulfilled her duty as a pharmacist by correctly filling a customer's prescription and answering all the customer's questions. This court should affirm summary judgment in favor of Dr. Levinson because the trial court correctly determined that no genuine issue of material fact exists relating to Dr. Levinson's careful fulfillment of her duty as a pharmacist. Three points demonstrate why Dr. Levinson fulfilled this duty.
>
> First, Dr. Levinson did everything she was required to do under the Missouri statute, pharmacy regulations, and case law. And according to these authorities, there is no duty to warn pharmacy customers about side effects.
>
> Second, the duty to warn patients about side effects belongs to the physician.
>
> Third, requiring pharmacists to warn customers about every possible adverse reaction would be unduly burdensome and unnecessarily extend the pharmacists' duty.

This roadmap provides a concise overview of the advocate's three best arguments. The first two points are based on statutory and case law; the third invokes a policy consideration that begins to incorporate the theme that extending the duty to warn would have unworkable consequences.

In the opening to *Hepting v. AT&T*, Deputy Solicitor General Garre provides a clear roadmap that also emphasizes three major points and incorporates a theme: protecting national security. *Hepting* was a class-action lawsuit that alleged constitutional violations in connection with the government's alleged warrantless surveillance programs.[1] Here is a transcript of Garre's opening:

> Your Honors, the nation's top officials' whose job it is to assess and protect foreign intelligence have determined that litigating this action could result in exceptionally grave harm to the national security of the United States. They've reached that judgment because litigating this action would require the adjudication of three central facts, each of which directly implicates state secrets: first, whether or to what extent any secret intelligence gathering relationship exists between AT&T and the government; second, whether or to what extent any alleged surveillance activities have taken place; and

---

1. *See Hepting v. AT&T*, 439 F. Supp. 2d 974 (N.D. Cal. 2006).

third, whether or to what extent any particular communications have been intercepted.

As the director of national intelligence and the director of the National Security Agency have explained in the public and non-public declarations filed with this court, litigating those central facts could compromise the sources, methods, and operational details of our intelligence gathering capabilities, and equally important, could disclose potential gaps in those capabilities.

To watch a YouTube video of the oral argument in *Hepting v. AT&T*, scan the QR code or go to http://bit.ly/149L99W.

C. Argument

i. Create an Outline of Your Arguments

Immediately following the roadmap, you should be prepared to elaborate on your first major argument. You should also be prepared to be interrupted by a stream of questions—relating to your first argument or any other issue raised in the briefs. The following strategy for developing an outline will allow you to do both.

Your argument outline will provide you with the notes you need to make an effective presentation. The outline should not follow the same organization you used in your brief. For instance, you do not need to begin by reciting your Facts section or by reading the Rule and Explanation sections from your brief. The judges have read your brief, and they are familiar with the facts and the law. Your roadmap will have provided the necessary overview of the case, so this part of your oral argument should focus on elaborating on the arguments in your brief's Analysis section that you summarized in the roadmap.

In addition, your oral argument outline should not be a series of sentences and paragraphs similar to what you have in your brief. This format would inhibit eye contact and your ability to have a conversation with the judges about your case. Instead, list the major points you want to make and only those notes that are necessary for you to describe your argument.

The extent of notes that attorneys use for oral argument varies widely. Some attorneys will jot down only a few phrases and case names. Others will have a comprehensive, bulleted outline that details the facts and holdings of key cases and the specific points to address for each argument. They key is to practice with your notes and develop a system that allows you to describe your arguments effectively and move easily between your major points without reading your argument word for word.

As a starting point, create an outline that lists each of your major arguments. Then, below each argument, provide a list of the points you want to make, along with supporting authority. For example, an outline for an oral argument could follow this basic format:

Argument 1
- Point A
  - Supporting authority
- Point B
  - Supporting authority
- Point C
  - Supporting authority

Argument 2
- Point A
  - Supporting authority
- Point B
  - Supporting authority

Suppose a judge asks you a question about Argument 1, Point B when you are addressing Point A. This outline would allow you to move to your notes for Point B to answer the question. Then, you could transition back to Point A or move on to Point C, depending on the progression of your argument.

Try to take a balanced approach as you fill in your outline, providing only the details necessary for you to describe your arguments. The following example provides a detailed outline for four points under the first argument on the pharmacist's duty to warn. The notes summarize the argument and then provide a list of legally significant facts and authorities as support.

First, Dr. Levinson fulfilled the duty required by Missouri law because there is no duty to warn pharmacy customers about side effects.
- Did everything required under Missouri law:
  - Correctly filled customer's prescription
  - Personally offered to discuss medication with her
  - Confirmed the dosage
  - Answered all her questions
  - Addressed all her concerns
- Missouri statute §388.010: Practice of pharmacy requires that pharmacists counsel customers "about the safe and effective use of drugs."
  - Does not reference side effects
- Missouri board of pharmacy regulation 4 C.S.R. 220 requires pharmacists to "personally offer to discuss matters" and to discuss issues deemed significant in the pharmacist's professional judgment.
  - Cannot practically include discussing every possible adverse reaction with every customer

- *Horner* and *Krug* cases both demonstrate no duty to warn pharmacy customers about side effects.
  - *Krug*: Physicians are learned intermediaries who act between the drug manufacturer and the patient, and physicians have the duty to warn patients about side effects.
  - *Horner*:
    - Distinguishable facts b/c customer died of overdose
    - Referenced side effects, interactions in one footnote, relating to Washington state case (which held that imposing a duty to warn about side effects would interfere with the physician-patient relationship)

ii. Create an Outline of Your Authorities

In addition to creating an outline for each major argument you want to address, you should create an outline with additional details about each authority you want to use. This list of authorities should include your best cases as well as any unhelpful authorities that opposing counsel may use or that the judges may ask you about. The list should include quotations of relevant constitutional and statutory provisions and brief summaries of the relevant facts and law of pertinent cases. For instance, the previous argument outline probably does not give the speaker enough information about the *Horner* or *Krug* cases to answer a tough question about the cases. Having a separate outline of authorities would allow the attorney to check the notes for the cases, respond to a question, and move back to the major argument.

Keeping your notes to a minimum will allow you to appear organized before the court. An attorney who has to rifle through a disheveled stack of papers to respond to a judge's question on a particular argument or a particular case does not appear well prepared. To organize their materials for

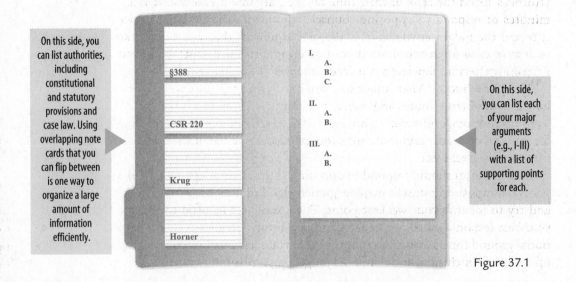

On this side, you can list authorities, including constitutional and statutory provisions and case law. Using overlapping note cards that you can flip between is one way to organize a large amount of information efficiently.

§388

CSR 220

Krug

Horner

I.
  A.
  B.
  C.

II.
  A.
  B.

III.
  A.
  B.

On this side, you can list each of your major arguments (e.g., I-III) with a list of supporting points for each.

Figure 37.1

oral argument, some attorneys like to use a folder with their authorities listed on one side and their arguments listed on the other. This method allows you to keep your notes and your thoughts organized and to move seamlessly between your points (see Figure 37.1).

Whether you use this folder method or develop a different way to organize your notes, you should appear organized, well prepared, and professional during your argument.

D. Conclusion

Keep track of your time as you move through your argument to make sure that you have time to complete your argument and conclude. For the conclusion, ask the court again for the relief that you seek and thank the judges for their time. An example of a closing statement in the duty to warn case is the following:

> For these reasons, I respectfully request that this court affirm the grant of summary judgment in favor of Dr. Levinson and find that she fulfilled her duty as a pharmacist and that no extension of this duty is required. Thank you for your time.

If you run out of time before you reach your conclusion, make sure you show respect for the court's schedule and conclude as quickly as possible. A simple conclusion could suffice: "We ask that you affirm summary judgment. Thank you, your Honors." The key is to provide a formal, respectful closing to your argument.

E. Rebuttal

If you are the movant or appellant, you will get the last word in oral argument. How much time you should devote to rebuttal is a strategic decision. Most attorneys spend the bulk of their time on their argument and reserve a few minutes to respond to opposing counsel's argument. The general practice is to tell the judges at the start of the oral argument that you would like to reserve time for rebuttal. After your greeting, provide a short statement describing the time allocation you desire, such as: "I would like to reserve two minutes for rebuttal." Then, make sure you honor this time allocation. If you have a total of ten minutes and reserve two minutes for rebuttal, you should wrap up your oral argument within eight minutes. If you fail to reserve time for rebuttal or if your argument runs too long, you may forfeit the opportunity to make a rebuttal.

Your rebuttal should respond to opposing counsel's oral argument. Take notes on opposing counsel's major arguments and on the judges' questions, and try to identify your weakest point. Then, use your rebuttal to provide your best response based on the facts and law. If time permits, offer an additional ground for the court to grant the relief you seek. Finally, make sure to offer a brief conclusion, and thank the judges—again—for their time.

2. STEP TWO: PREPARE FOR A CONVERSATION, NOT A SPEECH

Having a limited set of notes should help you prepare to have a conversation with the judges. Oral argument is not an opportunity to give a speech or lecture. Instead, you should prepare to answer a wide array of questions from the judges. Make sure that you know your record, facts, and law well enough to be able to cite to specific facts in the record when answering questions. In addition, make sure you can cite to specific authorities, the relevant language in each, and their citations. To prepare to answer questions, consider any weak points in your argument and try to anticipate what the judges might ask. Make a list of potential questions and draft answers that you could use in response.

A. Expect Tough Questions, Easy Questions, and Hypotheticals

Generally, judges' questions fall into one of three basic types. First, judges will likely ask you questions that delve into weak points in your argument. Be prepared to highlight key facts, to distinguish unhelpful authorities, and to describe your position fairly and persuasively. Second, judges may ask hypothetical questions. For instance, in the duty to warn example, a judge could ask a hypothetical exploring the consequences of extending pharmacists' duty to warn.

Third, a judge might ask you a friendly question that allows you to state one of your most persuasive arguments or cite to one of your most helpful cases. Take care to recognize this type of question as a lifeline. A judge might ask a friendly question to explore a point that was interrupted earlier, or a judge might want you to offer a particular argument to communicate the point to a colleague on the bench. To help you recognize this type of question, keep in mind that the judges are not your adversaries. Oral argument provides you the chance to have a conversation with the judges and to help them see your view of the case.

In the *Hepting* oral argument you reviewed earlier, Deputy Solicitor General Garre responds to an array of questions. The first question, which comes directly after he provides his roadmap, is a friendly one. Garre responds with a direct answer and uses citations and explanations of multiple cases in support. Throughout the 30-minute argument, Garre responds to a variety of questions, each time offering a direct answer supported by authority. In this way, he engages in an effective conversation with the judges that advances his position.

The following transcript excerpt provides examples of tough, friendly, and hypothetical questions in *Florida v. Jardines*, the U.S. Supreme Court case addressing whether police violated the Fourth Amendment when they took a trained drug-detection dog to the door of a private home.[2] The advocate for the government is again Gregory Garre.

---

2. *Florida v. Jardines*, 133 S. Ct. 1409 (2013).

Justice Ginsburg: Suppose—suppose the house had on the lawn, no dogs— Hypothetical Question
allowed?

Mr. Garre: I think that would be different, Your Honor. It would be—and
that's a way in which the house is different than a car. Homeowners
can restrict access to people who come up to their front door by putting gates or a sign out front.

Justice Scalia: Well, that's right. And there's such a thing as what is called— Friendly Question
the curtilage of a house. As I understand the law, the police are en-
titled to use binoculars to look into the house if—if the residents leave
the blinds open, right?

Mr. Garre: That's right.

Justice Scalia: But if they can't see clearly enough from a distance, they're— Friendly Question
not entitled to go onto the curtilage of the house, inside the gate, and
use the binoculars from that vantage point, are they?

Mr. Garre: They're not, Your Honor.

* * *

Justice Kagan: Mr. Garre, this is what we said in *Kyllo*. And I'm just going— Tough Question
to read it. We said, "We think that obtaining by sense-enhancing tech-
nology any information regarding the interior of the home that could
not otherwise have been obtained without physical intrusion into a
constitutionally protected area constitutes a search, at least where, as
here, the technology in question is not in general public use." So what
part of that do you think separates your case from this one? In other
words, what part of that language does not apply in this case?

Mr. Garre: Well, first of all, Franky's nose is not technology. It's—he's
using—he's availing himself of God-given senses in the way that dogs
have helped mankind for centuries.

Justice Kagan: So does that mean that if we invented some kind of little— Hypothetical Question
machine called a, you know, smell-o-matic and the police officer had
this smell-o-matic machine, and it alerted to the exact same things
that a dog alerts to, it alerted to a set of drugs, meth and marijuana
and whatever else, the police officer could not come to the front door
and use that machine?

Mr. Garre: Your Honor, I think the contraband rationale would be the
same. It would be different in that you don't have technology in this
case. And I think that's an important distinction because, as we read
Kyllo, the Court was very concerned about advances in technology, and
that's just not true for a dog's nose.[3]

---

3. Transcript of Oral Argument at 6, 16-17, *Florida v. Jardines*, 133 S. Ct. 1409 (No. 11-564),
available at http://www.supremecourt.gov/oral_arguments/argument_transcripts/11-564.pdf.
Transcripts and audio from oral arguments before the U.S. Supreme Court are available on the
Court's website: http://www.supremecourt.gov.

B. Prepare a Response

When asked a question, take a moment to consider your answer before launching into your response. Then, start your response with a direct "yes" or "no" answer. Next, provide the facts and authority necessary to support your answer. If you don't understand a question, ask the judge to repeat the question, or offer your understanding: "Your Honor, I believe you are asking me _____." Then, pause and allow the judge to agree or rephrase the question before offering your answer.

Be mindful of your time when answering questions. If you run out of time in the middle of a question, ask for a moment to respond: "Your honor, I see my time is up. May I have a moment to answer your question and conclude?" Then, if allowed, provide a concise answer and an abbreviated conclusion.

C. Practice Seamless Transitions Between Arguments and Questions

An oral argument is a conversation with the judges. To have an effective conversation, you can neither read your notes aloud for the entire argument nor give a memorized speech. Instead, you should think about your argument as a set of distinct points or subarguments—all of which lead to your ultimate conclusion.

For example, in the outline for the argument on the pharmacist's duty to warn, the attorney details four major bullet points for her first argument. She has a major bullet point listing helpful facts and three more bullets referencing authorities with notes on how each authority helps her position. Each of these arguments is distinct but contributes to supporting the major argument that the pharmacist had no duty to warn customers about side effects.

> First, Dr. Levinson fulfilled the duty required by Missouri law because there is no duty to warn pharmacy customers about side effects.
> - Did everything required under Missouri law:
> - Missouri statute §388.010: practice of pharmacy requires that pharmacists counsel customers "about the safe and effective use of drugs."
> - Missouri board of pharmacy regulation 4 C.S.R. 220 requires pharmacists to "personally offer to discuss matters" and to discuss issues deemed significant in the pharmacist's professional judgment.
> - *Horner* and *Krug* cases both demonstrate no duty to warn pharmacy customers about side effects.

This organization allows the attorney to transition seamlessly between her major points. For example, suppose the attorney has just started describing the helpful facts when a judge asks a question about the *Horner* case, which the attorney needs to distinguish. The attorney could glance at the fourth bullet point before answering the question.

Because all of the points are related, the attorney could then transition to any one of the four major bullet points in her outline to continue to support her argument. For example, after answering the question about *Horner*, she could transition with the following: "In addition, the *Krug* case supports the argument that pharmacists have no duty to warn customers of side effects because . . . ." Or she could move back to her second point with this transition: "The *Horner* case deals with Section 388.010, which states . . . ." By organizing your argument outline into a set of distinct—but related—points, you can prepare yourself to seamlessly transition between each.

Not all transitions are effective, however, particularly when they fail to show the proper deference to the court. Keep in mind that you want to follow the judge's lead when making your argument. You should invite questions because you want to make sure that you have adequately satisfied any concerns a judge may have about your position. Do not become frustrated if you are interrupted. For example, if a judge interrupts your first argument to ask a question, you might want to return to your first point by stating: "As I was saying . . . ." But this transition reflects a mild annoyance at the interruption. Instead, use transitions to show how your arguments build upon one another to support your conclusion.

D. Memorize Your Opening and Closing

Having a conversation with the judges requires eye contact. Try to memorize most or all of your greeting and opening roadmap so that you can establish eye contact with each of the judges or justices from the start. In addition, try to memorize your conclusion so you can finish your argument in the same effective fashion. Even if you need to write out the opening and closing verbatim in your outline to feel comfortable for your oral argument, try reciting most of your opening and closing without looking down at your notes.

E. Practice to Refine Style

To ensure that you maintain eye contact throughout the presentation, practice using your notes and looking up toward the judges. Watching yourself in a mirror or recording yourself with your phone, tablet, or computer will show you how much—or how little—eye contact you make. It also will help you become mindful of this important oral argument technique. In addition, repeated practice and review of your oral argument will help you gain confidence and reduce nervousness.

Practicing with a colleague also will help your preparation and confidence. Use the list of potential questions you created and ask a colleague to practice drilling you as you practice your oral argument. Work on your transitions between different arguments. Consider how each of your distinct arguments is related so you can easily transition between them and create a seamless presentation.

F. Prepare for the Unexpected

Remember that any topic raised in the parties' briefs is open for debate during oral argument. Although your goal is to be prepared for any question, the court may ask you a question that you did not expect, or opposing counsel may make an argument or give an answer that you did not anticipate. In such instances, you want to have the ability to respond accurately and with confidence.

Thus, in addition to the outlines of your arguments and authorities, you should bring to your argument copies of the parties' briefs, any relevant factual documents, and the cited statutes and cases. You should arrange these materials so that they appear organized and are easy for you to reference. Many attorneys put these documents in a binder with tabs. These materials will help you provide a thoughtful response if an unexpected issue arises during your argument.

3. STEP THREE: FOLLOW RULES OF DECORUM

Every court will have its own rules of professional conduct. But in general, these rules require that you show deference to the court, civility to opposing counsel, and respect for the judicial process. The checklist below provides a good starting point for conducting yourself according to the customary rules of decorum:

- ☑ Arrive early. Be ready to begin when the judges are ready, whether that time is 15 minutes early or one hour late.
- ☑ Adhere to timekeeping requirements without being reminded by the judge.
- ☑ Dress in court attire, which means wearing a dark, conservative suit.
- ☑ Be meticulously prepared.
- ☑ Be respectful by addressing the judge as "Your Honor."
- ☑ Be civil toward opposing counsel.
- ☑ Show an appropriate level of seriousness; jokes are seldom proper.
- ☑ Stand up straight at the podium, with organized notes and no pen in hand; limit hand gestures.
- ☑ When a judge starts talking, stop talking immediately.
- ☑ Invite questions from the judges.
- ☑ At the close of argument, thank the judges for their time.

part VIII

Research and Citation

chapter 38

Introduction to Legal Research and Citation

Lawyers must be skillful researchers. The following chapters explain how legal research and the related skill of legal citation provide the foundation for the objective and persuasive documents you are learning to prepare. Every legal analysis depends on legal research. Before a memo, motion, brief, letter, email, or judicial opinion containing legal analysis can be prepared, you must first conduct accurate and thorough legal research. Then, for that research to be useful to the document's audience, the legal sources must be cited correctly.

In practice, legal research and citation tasks are frequently assigned to junior lawyers. Employers expect law students and recent graduates to be practice ready in research and citation. The following chapters present principles of legal research and legal citation that will enable you to become effective at these important skills. These chapters will guide you as you research and cite legal authorities while writing the documents discussed throughout this book.

chapter 39

Legal Research Basics

1. THE PROCESS OF LEGAL RESEARCH

As a legal researcher, you must balance the pressures of accuracy, thoroughness, efficiency, and economy. When doing legal research, you do not get credit for trying. You must always find the correct answer and understand that answer completely. Further, you must conduct your research efficiently and economically. Lawyers are expected to juggle multiple projects at once, and charges for your research time and resources will often be passed along to cost-conscious clients. Thus, your approach to every research question should be thoughtful and well organized.

The only way to become an effective legal researcher is through practice. There is rarely just one way to research a legal question. Some lawyers develop strong preferences for certain sources, formats, and methods. But if your research is accurate, thorough, efficient, and economical, your supervisors and clients will likely not be concerned with the details of how you did it. In law school, you have the opportunity to practice your research skills without the pressure of a paying client. Thus, you need to do enough legal research to discover which methods, techniques, and approaches work best for you. During this period of experimentation as your research skills develop, you should aim to understand the process of legal research, not just look for the "right" answer to each particular question.

2. THE SOURCES FOR LEGAL RESEARCH

Recall from Chapter 4 that there are two types of legal authorities: primary authorities and secondary sources. The goal of any research task is to find the primary authorities that will determine the outcome of your legal question. And although you will not usually quote or cite secondary sources in your legal documents, you should use them to help you to identify and understand the relevant primary authorities.

There are four types of primary authorities: constitutions, statutes, cases, and regulations. Constitutions are the foundational governing documents

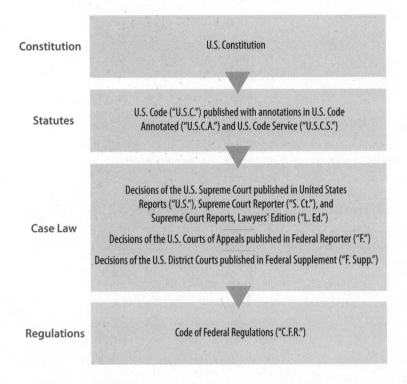

Constitution	U.S. Constitution
Statutes	U.S. Code ("U.S.C.") published with annotations in U.S. Code Annotated ("U.S.C.A.") and U.S. Code Service ("U.S.C.S.")
Case Law	Decisions of the U.S. Supreme Court published in United States Reports ("U.S."), Supreme Court Reporter ("S. Ct."), and Supreme Court Reports, Lawyers' Edition ("L. Ed.") Decisions of the U.S. Courts of Appeals published in Federal Reporter ("F.") Decisions of the U.S. District Courts published in Federal Supplement ("F. Supp.")
Regulations	Code of Federal Regulations ("C.F.R.")

Figure 39.1

for the nation and the states. Statutes are the laws passed by legislatures, which are organized and published as a code. Cases are the written opinions of courts, which are published in chronological order in books called case reporters. Regulations are rules promulgated by agencies, which may also be codified and published. Figure 39.1 shows a chart of the primary authorities under federal law.

There are many types of secondary sources, including legal encyclopedias, American Law Reports, treatises, Restatements, law review and journal articles, annotated codes, headnotes, and digests. The formats for secondary sources include books, periodicals, and electronic publications.

Some questions will require you to find only one form of primary authority—usually case law. But your research will often involve more than one type of primary authority. If you identify a constitutional provision, statute, or regulation that is relevant to your question, you will also have to look for case law that interprets that provision, statute, or regulation. Moreover, you may need to use secondary sources to understand the subject matter of the relevant primary authorities.

For example, imagine that you have been asked to research whether it is constitutional for a city to pass a law that makes it illegal to carry a gun within 50 feet of any establishment that serves alcohol. First, you would identify the Second Amendment to the U.S. Constitution as a relevant authority. But that would not be the end of your research. You would want to find secondary sources that discuss the evolution of the interpretation of the Second

Amendment. And you would look for cases interpreting and applying the Amendment.

3. WHERE TO FIND LEGAL SOURCES

A. Print Sources

Law libraries contain print versions of the legal sources that lawyers use most often: statutes and cases.

i. Statutes

Federal and state statutes are collected and organized into codes that are published as a set of books. When doing legal research, attorneys use annotated codes because the annotations include helpful information about cases and secondary sources that have interpreted and discussed the statutes.

The U.S. Code is the official version of the federal statutes. U.S. Code Annotated (West) and U.S. Code Service (Lexis) are annotated versions of the federal statutes.

ii. Cases

Cases are printed in books called reporters, which are published in sets and series. Reporters are organized by jurisdiction and court tier.[1] There are federal reporters, regional reporters, and state reporters.

The same case can be published in more than one reporter. For many courts, there is an "official" government-published reporter and an unofficial reporter published by West or Lexis. For instance, decisions of the U.S. Supreme Court appear in the United States Reports (official), the Supreme Court Reporter (West), and the United States Supreme Court Reports, Lawyers' Edition (Lexis). For some courts, including the federal courts of appeals and certain state courts, there is no government-published reporter.

a. Federal Reporters

There are separate reporters for each tier in the federal court system, but the federal reporters do not separate cases by circuit or district. The federal reporters are as follows:[2]

Federal Case Reporter	Court Tier
U.S. Reports	U.S. Supreme Court cases
Federal Reporter	U.S. Courts of Appeals cases
Federal Supplement	U.S. District Court cases

---

1. A few reporters also are organized by subject matter, including bankruptcy and tax.

2. The Federal Reporter and Federal Supplement are published by West. West also publishes the Federal Appendix, which includes decisions of the federal courts of appeals since 2001 that weren't selected for publication in the Federal Reporter.

b. Regional Reporters

West's National Reporter System groups state cases by geographic region. The regional reporters include decisions from state highest courts and some decisions of state intermediate appellate courts. The regions are divided as follows:

West Regional Reporter	States Included
Atlantic Reporter	Connecticut, Delaware, D.C., Maine, Maryland, New Hampshire, New Jersey, Pennsylvania, Rhode Island, Vermont
South Eastern Reporter	Georgia, North Carolina, South Carolina, Virginia, West Virginia
Southern Reporter	Alabama, Florida, Louisiana, Mississippi
North Eastern Reporter	Illinois, Indiana, Massachusetts, New York, Ohio
South Western Reporter	Arkansas, Kentucky, Missouri, Tennessee, Texas
North Western Reporter	Iowa, Michigan, Minnesota, Nebraska, North Dakota, South Dakota, Wisconsin
Pacific	Alaska, Arizona, California, Colorado, Hawaii, Idaho, Kansas, Montana, Nevada, New Mexico, Oklahoma, Oregon, Utah, Washington, Wyoming

West's reporters include headnotes and key numbers that correspond to the West Digests. As explained in Chapter 41, the headnotes, key numbers, and digests are useful research tools that do not appear in the official reporters.

c. State Reporters

Many state cases are also published in state-specific reporters. State reporters may divide cases by tier, publishing highest court opinions separately from intermediate appellate court opinions. For instance, Ohio Supreme Court opinions are published in Ohio State Reports, intermediate appellate court opinions are published in Ohio Appellate Reports, and select trial court opinions are published in Ohio Miscellaneous Reports. Ohio Appellate Reports and Ohio Miscellaneous Reports are printed together in a single volume, but are considered two separate publications.

B. Online Sources

Legal research used to be a process that involved using multivolume sets of leather-bound books, which were housed in grand law libraries. Now, legal research is dominated by two fee-based Internet services: Westlaw and Lexis-Nexis.

Both Westlaw and LexisNexis have recently developed new platforms in addition to their original legal research portals. Westlaw now offers Westlaw Classic and WestlawNext, and LexisNexis offers Lexis.com and Lexis Advance. In this chapter, we will use the terms "Westlaw" and "Lexis" to refer to both research platforms from each company.

Westlaw and Lexis attempt to provide the legal researcher with online access to virtually all legal research sources. Both services provide access to the same primary authorities and the same type of secondary sources; however, Westlaw and Lexis differ in the particular secondary sources they offer.

In addition to these fee-based services, there are many free online sources for legal research, which are described in Chapter 41. Also, many of the legal sources available on Westlaw and Lexis are available in print form in law libraries. In fact, many legal sources were designed to be used in print, so their physical versions can be more intuitive to use than their electronic versions. As you practice your legal research skills, you should attempt to use sources in both formats to see what makes the most sense to you.

chapter 40

Creating a Research Plan

Legal research can feel similar to searching on the Internet because both involve using search terms to look for information. And your Internet search skills will be helpful when you are doing legal research. But most people take a scattershot approach to Internet searching—entering terms at random and reviewing the results haphazardly. This undisciplined approach is not an effective legal research technique.

Instead, to ensure that your research is accurate, thorough, efficient, and economical, you must be organized. To organize your research approach, you should make a plan before you start.

> **Creating a Research Plan**
>
> 1. Formulate a research question
> 2. Identify the relevant jurisdiction
> 3. Generate search terms

1. STEP ONE: FORMULATE A RESEARCH QUESTION

The first step in planning your research is to formulate the research task as a question. Every research problem is different. And it is extremely difficult to research efficiently when you don't understand what you are looking for.

Some research tasks will require you to find a discrete answer to a simple question. For example, how many days does a party have to file a notice of appeal after a decision by a federal district court? Or, what are the elements of battery under Texas law?

Other research tasks will require you to canvass the authorities that cover a legal issue and select those that are likely to have the most relevance to your case. This type of research usually precedes preparing a legal document where you will analyze a legal question. If you have been assigned this type of research, your question will describe the legal issue that you have been asked to analyze for your client. For example, does your client's use of a music sample constitute copyright infringement? Or, is a houseboat a conveyance under the Florida trespass statute?

With these more complex research tasks, you may actually have a series of questions that you need to answer. You should isolate each question that you can identify. For example, the question above regarding copyright infringement has other questions nested within it.

- Does the client's use of a music sample constitute copyright infringement?
  - What are the elements of copyright infringement?
  - How have those elements been applied to the act of music sampling?
  - What are the defenses to copyright infringement?
  - How have those defenses been applied to the act of music sampling?

You may not be able to identify all possible questions before you begin your research. Continue to keep track of the legal questions that arise as you do your research.

2. STEP TWO: IDENTIFY THE RELEVANT JURISDICTION

The second step in planning your research is to identify the relevant jurisdiction for your research. Jurisdiction refers to what category of law (state or federal) governs the issue, which specific geographic region's laws will apply in your case, and what level of court will govern the issue in your case.

Identifying the relevant jurisdiction for your research is a three-step process:

1. Determine whether state or federal law governs your question.
2. Determine the particular state or federal circuit law that will apply in your case.
3. Determine the level of the court that will govern the issue in your case.

For example, imagine that you have been asked to research whether your client, a musician, was correctly found liable for copyright infringement by the District Court for the Northern District of California based on her sampling the song "Smokestack Lightning" for 15 seconds. First, you would determine that federal law, and, in particular, a federal statute governs copyright infringement. Second, you would determine that the law of the United States Court of Appeals for the Ninth Circuit will apply to your case because that is the federal judicial circuit where the District Court for the Northern District of California is located. Third, you would determine that the Ninth Circuit will govern the issue in your case because that is the federal intermediate appellate court that hears appeals from the District Court for the Northern District of California.

3. STEP THREE: GENERATE SEARCH TERMS

The third step in planning your research is to brainstorm possible search terms. Search terms are at the heart of any research task. No matter what sources or methods you use, at some point you will need to use search terms. Just like when you search for information on the Internet, the search terms you use determine the results you get. The following three steps will help you to brainstorm search terms:

1. Look for key words.
2. Think of synonyms.
3. Add breadth and depth.

First, you should harvest key words from the documents or information that you already have regarding your legal issue. Look for words that describe legal claims, relationships, and legally significant actions. Legal claims include the words that describe causes of action in civil cases, like "breach of contract," "negligence," and "copyright infringement," and crimes in criminal cases, like "murder," "burglary," and "drug possession." Legal relationships include the words that describe how the parties to a case are related, like "employer/employee," "landlord/tenant," and "parent/child." Legally significant actions include the words that describe the facts of a case, like "use of a 15-second music sample," "occupation of a parcel of land for six years," and "entry into a fenced yard."

After you have looked for key words, you should think of possible synonyms for those words. Different courts may use different terms to describe the same claims, relationships, and actions, and you want your research to capture all relevant results. For example, if you identify the legal claim as "gender discrimination," possible synonyms would be "sexual discrimination" and "sexual harassment." A legal dictionary may help you identify synonyms for legal terms.

Last, you should expand the breadth and depth of your search terms. You can make your search terms broader by making them more general. For example, if your case involved assault with a knife, you could expand the breadth of your search by also using "assault with a deadly weapon" or just "assault" as search terms. Conversely, you can make your search terms deeper by making them more specific. If your case involved false advertising, you could expand the depth of your search by using as a search term the specific product that had been advertised—for example, "false drug advertising," "false prescription drug advertising," or "false prescription drug acid reflux advertising."

chapter 41

Smart Research
Strategies

Because the types of questions you will be expected to research can vary so much in scope and complexity, no uniform research approach will work for every question. Instead, you will need to develop a plan that is appropriate to each research question based on the following research strategies.

Smart Research Strategies for the New Legal Writer

1. Move from general to specific
2. Use free sources first
3. Don't start from scratch
4. Browse
5. Build in redundancy
6. Run searches of the right size on fee-based platforms
7. Validate and update
8. Cite correctly

---

1. MOVE FROM GENERAL TO SPECIFIC

As a law student or new lawyer who does not have an extensive background of legal knowledge, it is best to start your research with a general inquiry and make it more specific as you gain knowledge of your topic. Starting general will provide a strong foundation for the analysis of your legal question. Moreover, your general research will point you to the more specific sources, like statutes and cases, that will determine the outcome of your particular legal question.

Often, the best place to do your general research is in secondary sources. Secondary sources are commentaries and summaries of the law. Because secondary sources are not law and can never be binding on a court, you will rarely cite them in your legal documents. But secondary sources are often the most efficient way to locate the primary authorities that will govern the outcome of your legal question.

Commonly used secondary sources include the following:

Legal encyclopedias: Legal encyclopedias are collections of brief summaries of legal topics arranged alphabetically. There are two national legal encyclopedias, *American Jurisprudence* ("AmJur") and *Corpus Juris Secundum* ("C.J.S."). Many states also have their own legal encyclopedias. These state-specific encyclopedias include, among others, *Florida Jurisprudence*, *New York Jurisprudence*, and *Pennsylvania Law Encyclopedia*. Legal encyclopedia entries include citations to primary authorities.

American Law Reports ("ALR"): ALR is a collection of in-depth articles, called annotations, which summarize and analyze specific legal issues. ALR annotations include numerous citations to primary authorities, including citations to cases organized by jurisdiction.

Treatises: A treatise is a book that provides an in-depth treatment of a broad legal subject by an expert. A treatise may be a single volume or multiple volumes. Examples of well-known treatises include Phillip E. Areeda & Herbert Hovenkamp, *Fundamentals of Antitrust Law*; David Nimmer, *Nimmer on Copyright*; and Wayne LaFave & Austin Scott, *Substantive Criminal Law*.

The category of treatises also includes practice guides, which offer pragmatic advice and often include forms and checklists. Practice guides can be particularly helpful for procedural questions. Commonly used practice guides include *Moore's Federal Practice*; Wright & Miller, *Federal Practice and Procedure*; *Trawick's Florida Practice and Procedure*; and The Rutter Group, *Federal Civil Procedure Before Trial*. Treatises and practice guides include citations to primary authorities.

Restatements of the Law: Restatements are a synthesis of the common law prepared by the American Law Institute, an organization of professors, judges, and attorneys. Restatements summarize the consensus on the state of the common law on a variety of legal topics, including contracts, torts, agency, and property. Restatements include an appendix listing the cases that have cited the Restatement.

Law review and journal articles: Law review and journal articles are scholarly publications written by law school professors, judges, lawyers, and law students that usually discuss emerging or cutting-edge legal issues. These articles are often detailed and include numerous references to both primary and secondary sources.

As you use your search terms to learn general information about your question in these secondary sources, you will find references to primary authorities that are relevant to your question. Pay careful attention to these references because they will allow you to transition your research from general background information to the specific, primary sources that will determine the outcome of your question.

For example, if you were researching the question of whether your client was liable for copyright infringement, you could begin your research by looking up copyright in the legal encyclopedia *American Jurisprudence*. The entry regarding copyright infringement describes the elements required to prove copyright infringement and includes references to the relevant sections of the copyright statute and cases that interpret the elements of copyright infringement. Your general inquiry in a secondary source, therefore, quickly provides you with specific sources that are potentially relevant to your legal question.

2. USE FREE SOURCES FIRST

Legal research can be expensive. In addition to the cost of your time, there can be a charge for every search you do on research platforms like Westlaw and Lexis. When you begin your research, you may not know enough information to formulate effective searches. To avoid unnecessary costs for your client, you should start your research using free sources, and then transition to fee-based sources once you have developed more specific research questions.

The most obvious free research source is the Internet via Google or similar search engines. Typing your research question into Google is a fine way to start your research because it can help you get a general understanding of an issue and point you in the direction of relevant sources.

Be careful, however, to verify and validate any information that you find on the Internet before relying on it for your legal analysis. There is no guarantee that information on the Internet is accurate or up to date. Secondary sources like Wikipedia can be helpful at the beginning of your research, but you cannot trust them and you cannot cite to them in a legal document. Instead, you should use them to find a primary authority that you can verify, read, and cite.

Before you use any information from the Internet to advance your research, you must evaluate the following three properties:

1. Authority: The information must be from a reputable and reliable source.
2. Accuracy: The information must be correct.
3. Currency: The information must be up to date.

For legal information, you should rely on free Internet sources only when they have some official sanction that guarantees their information is accurate and current. Further, you should use the citators on Westlaw or Lexis to validate that any authority you plan to rely on is still good law.[1]

Some of the most useful and reliable free sources on the Internet are described here:

Government websites: The text of constitutions, statutes, court rules, and regulations are available on government websites. When you need

---

1. Citators are also discussed in sections 3 and 7 of this chapter.

to read only the text of a primary authority, you should look it up on an official government website. For example, the U.S. Code is available at http://uscode.house.gov.

Legal Information Institute: The Legal Information Institute ("LII"), http://www.law.cornell.edu, provides free access to, among other things, the U.S. Code ("U.S.C."), the Federal Rules, and the Code of Federal Regulations ("C.F.R"). Like government websites, LII is a free and reliable place to get the full text of federal primary authorities.

Google Scholar: Google Scholar, http://scholar.google.com, is a free way to search for cases, scholarly articles, and patents. Google Scholar allows you to search for cases and then filter the results by date and issuing court. Once you identify a potentially relevant case in Google Scholar, you can read the full text of the opinion and see a list of cases that have cited that case.

Google Scholar also allows you to search for scholarly articles, including law review articles. Unlike the case law on Google Scholar, however, you may not be able to access the full text of the articles retrieved in response to your search if those articles appear in subscription databases like JSTOR and Hein Online.

Findlaw, Justia, and Public Library of Law: Findlaw, http://lp.findlaw.com, Justia, http://www.justia.com, and Public Library of Law, http://www.plol.org, are free sources that provide access to the text of court opinions and statutes for both state and federal law.

In addition to free Internet sources, remember that the books in the library are free. And print sources are not just available while you are in law school—many law offices have libraries with print versions of annotated codes and secondary sources. Using these print versions is a cost-effective way to begin your research.

3. DON'T START FROM SCRATCH

Rather than attempting to find relevant sources from scratch, you should use each source you find as a link to more sources. Although you may be tempted to jump into your research by immediately running searches for statutes or cases in Westlaw or Lexis (and you usually will do this type of searching later in your research process), you will likely find much of what you are looking for and find it more quickly by letting other relevant sources guide you to it.

In addition to the secondary sources described above, the best resources to use to avoid starting from scratch are as follows:

Annotated codes: Annotated codes are statutory compilations that include not only the statutory text but also references to relevant authorities, including cases and regulations, and secondary sources. When you have identified a statute that governs your legal issue, the annotated code is often the most efficient way to find cases that interpret and apply that statute. The federal statutes in the U.S. Code appear in annotated codes called U.S. Code Annotated ("U.S.C.A.") and U.S. Code Service ("U.S.C.S."). States also have annotated codes for their statutes. For example, the Florida statutes are annotated in West's Florida Statutes Annotated.[2]

Example Statute 41.1 shows an example of a statute as it appears in the U.S.C.A.[3] After the text of the statute, this annotated version references West key numbers, an ALR article, secondary sources, and a case (listed as a "Note of Decisions (1)").

Headnotes/Key Numbers/Digests: For cases published by West, editors write headnotes that summarize the major points of law in the case, and they categorize these points and other specific legal concepts according to the West Key Number System. The Key Number System is a massive outline of American law, where nearly every legal concept has been assigned a unique number. Headnotes also are assigned a number (available as a link online) that corresponds to the place in a case where a point of law is discussed. Headnotes do not have the force of law, so they cannot be quoted or cited in a legal document.[4]

To make searching for a particular legal topic easier, West compiles all of the headnotes assigned to each key number and publishes bound digests for different jurisdictions, subject matter, and date ranges. Looking up a key number in the appropriate digest will show you all of the cases that include a headnote with that same key number. The Key Number System's index is also available online through Westlaw, where you can create a custom digest from any key number. Thus, using the system is an effective way to find other cases that discuss a relevant point of law. In addition, the bound digests include a Descriptive Word Index that allows you to look up your search terms and then find matching key numbers, even if you haven't yet located a relevant case.

For example, Figure 41.1 shows the first of eight headnotes in *Light-Hawk v. Robertson*, 812 F. Supp. 1095 (W.D. Wash. 1993), the case listed in the annotated code example above as a note of decision:[5]

This headnote describes a point of law that appears in the case and relates to how a content restriction on speech is in conflict with the First Amendment. The Key Number is "Constitutional Law 90(1)."

Using this Key Number, either in the bound version of a West Digest or by clicking on the Key Number when viewing the case online

---

2. For federal statutes and many state statutes, the annotated code is not the official code for citation purposes. You should always cite the official code in your legal documents. *See Bluebook* Rule 12.2.1(a).

3. Reprinted with the permission of Thomson Reuters from the U.S. Code Annotated as available on WestlawNext.

4. Lexis also uses numbered headnotes to show the key legal points of a case.

5. Reprinted with the permission of Thomson Reuters from the U.S. Code Annotated as available on WestlawNext.

§580p-4. Injunction against unauthorized manufacture, use, or…, 16 USCA §580p-4

Example
Statute 41.1

United States Code Annotated
  Title 16. Conservation
    Chapter 3. Forests; Forest Service; Reforestation; Management
    Subchapter I. General Provisions

— Context of where statute appears in U.S. Code

16 U.S.C.A. §580p-4

§580p-4. Injunction against unauthorized manufacture, use, or reproduction

Currentness

— Text of the statute

(a) Whoever, except as provided by rules and regulations issued by the Secretary, manufactures, uses, or reproduces the character "Smokey Bear" or the name "Smokey Bear", or a facsimile or simulation of such character or name in such a manner as suggests Smokey Bear" may be enjoined from such manufacture, use, or reproduction at the suit of the Attorney General upon complaint by the Secretary.

(b) Whoever, except as provided by rules and regulations issued by the Secretary, manufactures, uses, or reproduces the character "Woodsy Owl", the name "Woodsy Owl", or the slogan "Give a Hoot, Don't Pollute", or a facsimile or simulation of such character, name, or slogan in such a manner as suggests "Woodsy Owl" may be enjoined from such manufacture, use, or reproduction at the suit of the Attorney General upon complaint by the Secretary.

CREDIT(S)
(Pub.L. 93-318, §4, June 22, 1974, 88 Stat. 245.)

LIBRARY REFERENCES
American Digest System
United States ⬤—3, 40.
Woods and Forests ⬤—5.
Key Number System Topic Nos. 393, 411.

— Key number references

RESEARCH REFERENCES
  ALR Library
  51 ALR 6th 359, Constitutionality, Construction, and Application of Statute or Regulatory Action Respecting Political Advertising — Print Media Cases.

— ALR references

Treatises and Practice Aids
Callmann on Unfair Compet., TMs, & Monopolies §2:9, The Lanham Trademark Act Limitations.
Callmann on Unfair Compet., TMs, & Monopolies §26:2, History and Constitutionality of United States' Trademark Statutes.
Callmann on Unfair Compet., TMs, & Monopolies App 40 §40:3, Excerpts from 18 U.S.C.A.

— Secondary source references

Notes of Decisions (1)
16 U.S.C.A. §580p-4, 16 USCA §580p-4
Current through P.L. 113-12 (excluding P.L. 113-4) approved 6-3-13

§580p-4. Injunction against unauthorized manufacture, use, or…, 16 USCA §580p-4

Notes Of Decisions (1)

Constitutionality

— Citation and summary of a case that cites the statute

Statute and regulation relied upon by the United States Forest Service to prohibit environmental organization's use of caricature Smokey Bear in advertisement criticizing Forest Service's management policies violated organization's First Amendment rights; organization's use of chainsaw-wielding caricature of Smokey Bear was unlikely to cause confusion or to dilute the value of Smokey Bear to help prevent forest fires. LightHawk, the Environmental Air Force v. Robertson, W.D. Wash.1993, 812 F.Supp. 1095, 25 U.S.P.Q.2d 2014. Constitutional Law ⬤—1652

> **1. Constitutional Law ●─90(1)**
>
> Statute or regulation that places burden on speakers due to content of their speech is presumptively inconsistent with First Amendment. U.S.C.A. Const.Amend. 1.

Figure 41.1

on Westlaw, you could identify other cases that editors at West have identified as discussing the same or similar points of law.

KeyCite/Shepard's: Both Westlaw and Lexis offer tools called citators that help you determine whether a case or statute is still good law.[6] KeyCite on Westlaw and Shepard's on Lexis are citators that provide a list of all subsequent primary and secondary authorities that have cited a particular case or statute. You can use a citator to learn the procedural history of a case or statute.

Citators also list citing references—primary and secondary authorities that cite the case or statute. For cases, both KeyCite and Shepard's use symbols to indicate the depth and type of treatment the case received in a later case. For example, Shepard's uses a red stop sign to indicate negative treatment; KeyCite uses a red flag. Thus, once you have identified a relevant case, you can use a citator to locate any cases that have cited that case positively or negatively. On Westlaw, you can also KeyCite a headnote to find later cases that cite a case for a particular point of law. Citators are one of the best ways to find other relevant authorities once you have located a useful case.

Attorneys used to use citators in print, but the process was cumbersome. Now, on Westlaw or Lexis you can use a citator by clicking the KeyCite or Shepard's symbols that appear on the case or statute.

Cases: Cases always cite other cases. Thus, if you have found one relevant case, you may find other cases that are relevant to your legal question by looking up the cases cited within your case and by using a citator to find all of the later cases that cited your case.

4. BROWSE

Although you will do much of your legal research using electronic sources on the Internet, you should consider, whenever feasible, browsing through sources as though you were looking at them in print. Any source that includes a table of contents or an index is a candidate for this kind of browsing.[7]

---

6. Citators are also discussed in section 7 of this chapter.

7. Case reporters, which are organized chronologically rather than topically, cannot be browsed in this way.

Westlaw and Lexis provide electronic versions of tables of contents and indexes for sources that have them in their print versions.

Encyclopedias, treatises, and statutes all have tables of contents that you should browse. A statute often has multiple sections that relate to a particular topic. By looking at the table of contents, you can identify all of the sections that may be relevant to your question.

For example, 18 U.S.C. §2333 describes civil remedies for terrorism. It states,

> Any national of the United States injured in his or her person, property, or business by reason of an act of international terrorism, or his or her estate, survivors, or heirs, may sue therefor in any appropriate district court of the United States and shall recover threefold the damages he or she sustains and the cost of the suit, including attorney's fees.

By browsing the table of contents of the U.S. Code, you would learn that 18 U.S.C. §2331 defines the terms "national of the United States," "international terrorism," and "person" that appear in §2333. You would also see that 18 U.S.C. §2335 provides a statute of limitations for actions under §2333. Thus, to have an accurate and thorough understanding of §2333, you would need to browse and read the other related sections that surround it.

Similarly, many sources, including encyclopedias, treatises, ALRs, and statutes have an index. By looking up search terms in the index, you can find all of the places in a source where your issue is discussed.

5. BUILD IN REDUNDANCY

Because your research needs to be efficient and economical while also being accurate and thorough, you should build redundancy into your research strategy. Redundancy means searching for the same information in different ways to make sure that you have found all of the relevant sources. For example, even though you should attempt to find primary authorities through links in primary and secondary sources, you should also run key word searches to make sure that you capture all relevant primary authorities in your research.

One easy way to build redundancy into your research strategy is to use a checklist. The following questions will help you determine whether you have identified all of the primary authorities relevant to your question:

1. Are there any constitutional provisions relevant to your legal question?
2. Are there any statutes relevant to your legal question?
3. Are there any cases decided by courts higher than the court in your jurisdiction that are relevant to your legal question?
4. Are there any cases decided by courts at the same level as your court in the relevant jurisdiction that are relevant to your legal question?
5. Are there any cases that are more recent than the most recent case you have found that are relevant to your legal question?
6. Are there any regulations that are relevant to your legal question?

Building redundancy into your research strategy will help you know when you are finished researching. In addition to your answers to the questions in the previous checklist, the best evidence that you have sufficiently researched a question is when you repeatedly find the same results that you have already found. If the links from relevant sources and the results of new searches all bring up authorities that you have already seen, your research has likely found everything relevant to your question.

6. RUN SEARCHES OF THE RIGHT SIZE ON FEE-BASED PLATFORMS

Tailoring the scope of your electronic searches correctly is essential to researching efficiently and economically. Whenever you run a search on West-law or Lexis, or any other fee-based platform, you want to be sure that your search is not too wide or too narrow. Running a search of the right scope ensures that you won't capture an overwhelming number of irrelevant results or inadvertently exclude potentially relevant results. Moreover, on Westlaw and Lexis, broader searches are generally more expensive than narrower searches.

Tailor the scope of your searches on Westlaw and Lexis using these four techniques:

1. Correctly limit your search to the relevant jurisdiction.
2. Avoid search terms that are too broad.
3. Use "terms and connectors" searching when possible.
4. Filter or limit your results before reviewing them.

Westlaw and Lexis always offer a way to limit the jurisdiction of your search. Make sure to identify the jurisdiction relevant to your legal question and select that specific jurisdiction when searching. For example, if you were researching a federal copyright infringement question for a case in the District Court for the Northern District of California, you would want to search for decisions from the U.S. Supreme Court and federal courts in the Ninth Circuit. Similarly, if you were researching a question involving adverse possession under Florida law for a case in the Florida Third District Court of Appeal, you would want to search for decisions from Florida state and federal courts applying Florida law.

Whenever possible, you want to avoid using search terms that are so broad that they retrieve many irrelevant results. For example, if you were looking for cases where summary judgment was granted on a gender discrimination claim, the search term "summary judgment" by itself would bring back many cases that would not be relevant. To limit your search, include more specific terms. And to find information about general topics like summary judgment, you would want to use other research methods, like free and secondary sources, rather than running case searches on fee-based platforms.

Westlaw and Lexis allow for "terms and connectors" searches, which is a form of Boolean searching. Rather than relying on an algorithm's interpretation of a natural language query, searching with terms and connectors allows you to control the relationship between your search terms. For example, with terms and connectors, such as "and" and "or," you can control whether your search results include all of your search terms or any of your search terms. You can also control how closely the terms appear in the result. For example, you can search for cases that use the term "copyright infringement" and "music sampling" within the same sentence to create a more targeted search using the connector "/s" in Westlaw and "w/sent" in Lexis. Because terms and connectors give you more control over your search, this kind of searching often excludes irrelevant results. Refer to the guides on Westlaw and Lexis for how to compose effective terms and connectors searches.

After you have run a search on Westlaw or Lexis, you can further narrow the results or run another search within the results. Filtering your results allows you to exclude irrelevant results that were captured by your original search. For example, you can narrow the results by categories including date and deciding judge, or you can search your original research results using a new search term.

7. VALIDATE AND UPDATE

The law is always evolving. Before you rely on any source in a legal document, you must validate that source using a citator. As described in section 3 of this chapter, the Westlaw citator is called KeyCite and the Lexis citator is called Shepard's. No research is complete until you have used a citator to check that your sources are still good law. At any time, a court could issue an opinion that invalidates a case, or a legislature could amend a statute that you intend to rely on for your analysis. By linking to the procedural history and citing references for every case and statute, these citators tell you whether there is negative history or treatment that may affect the validity of a case or statute that you plan to use in a legal document.

Then, even after you have validated the sources that are relevant to your question, you must continually update your research. Courts are constantly deciding new cases, and you must be vigilant to make sure that your research remains up to date.

8. CITE CORRECTLY

Ultimately, for your research to be successful, you must correctly cite the sources you rely on in your legal documents. Your readers, who may include judges, clerks, supervising attorneys, and opposing counsel, will not be able to verify your analysis if they can't find the sources you cite. Failing to cite your sources correctly will undermine the usefulness and credibility of your research. The next chapter provides detailed instructions on how to cite sources correctly.

chapter 42

Citation

1. CITATION IS A LANGUAGE

Citation is a language designed to communicate a great deal of information in a concentrated way. This language has one simple and important purpose: to concisely identify the relied-upon authorities with enough specificity that the reader can find and evaluate them. The rules of citation can be both trivial and overwhelming. But to understand how the language of citation works, remembering its purpose helps. A citation that doesn't precisely identify the source so that the reader can determine its weight, age, and relevance is not a useful citation.

> ### Citation Principles for the New Legal Writer
> 1. Citation is a language
> 2. Master the most common formats
> 3. Learn the rules that arise frequently
> 4. Use the index, tables, and quick reference for everything else
> 5. Remember local citation rules
> 6. Cite correctly as you write

You will encounter judges, supervisors, professors, and colleagues who are exacting about legal citation. For them, a writer's ability to format citations correctly demonstrates that writer's credibility, attention to detail, and professionalism. You will also encounter judges, supervisors, professors, and colleagues who believe that as long as the authorities are cited so the reader can understand what is cited and where to find it, the minute details of citation format are a distraction from a legal writer's more important tasks of research, drafting, and analysis.[1] Given these differing perspectives, knowing the expectations of your audience is critical. And if you can't know what your audience expects, assuming that your reader values the uniformity and reliability of impeccable citation format is the safest choice.

---

1. *See, e.g.*, Richard A. Posner, *The Bluebook Blues*, 120 Yale L.J. 850, 853 (2011).

2. MASTER THE MOST COMMON FORMATS

The Bluebook has rules for how to cite every imaginable type of authority.[2] But most practicing attorneys cite two types regularly: cases and statutes. If you master the long and short-citation formats for cases and statutes in the federal and state jurisdictions where you practice, you will be able to easily cite most of the authorities in most legal documents.

To master these formats, you need to understand the basic organization of the information in the citation and the format for long and short citations. A long-form citation is the complete cite for an authority. You will use long citations the first time you cite an authority in a document. For every successive citation to that same authority, you will use a short-citation format.

A. Cases: Long-Form Citations

The organization of the information in all long-form citations for published federal and state cases is the same (see Figure 42.1):

case name—comma—volume number—reporter abbreviation—first page—comma—pinpoint page—left parenthesis—court [if necessary]—year—right parenthesis—period

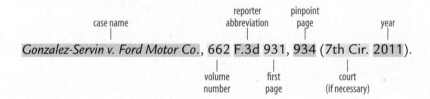

Figure 42.1

The organization of the information in citations for cases that have been published electronically is more detailed than that for published cases (see Figures 42.2 and 42.3):

case name—comma—docket number—comma—Westlaw or Lexis citation—comma—at—asterisk—pinpoint page—left parenthesis—court—full date—right parenthesis—period

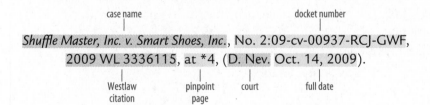

Figure 42.2

---

2. This chapter focuses on *Bluebook* citation format, but there are other citation guides, including *ALWD Citation Manual: A Professional System of Citation* (Association of Legal Writing Directors & Darby Dickerson, 4th ed. 2010) and jurisdiction-specific citation guides like the *California Style Manual* by Edward W. Jessen (4th ed. 2001).

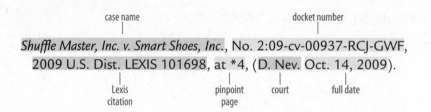

Figure 42.3

A case that is not published in a reporter may have both a Westlaw and Lexis citation; you may choose which one you use in your document. Electronically published cases all begin on page *1, so this citation format only includes the pinpoint page number (*4 in the example above).

The Bluebook has rules for citing cases within the text of a sentence and as a stand-alone citation sentence.[3] Generally, stand-alone citation sentences are preferred because they don't interrupt the writer's prose the way a citation in the text of a sentence does. When using stand-alone citation sentences, the citation should end with a period, just like a normal sentence.

The following four steps will help you write proper long-form case citations:

Long-Form Case Citations

i. Italicize and abbreviate case names
ii. Abbreviate the reporter
iii. Include the first page and pinpoint page
iv. Abbreviate the court

---

i. Step One: Italicize and Abbreviate Case Names

Every case name should be italicized. *The Bluebook* also offers the option of underlining case names, but most writers prefer italics because they look cleaner and are easier to read.

The following rules regarding the proper abbreviation of case names are the most important:[4]

* If the caption includes multiple parties, list only the first party on each side of the v.[5] If the party is a person, include only the last name of the party.[6] For example,

> Jacob Newmeyer and Stan Smith, et al., v. Golds Candlemakers
> and Goldstar Insurance
>
> ↓
>
> *Newmeyer v. Golds Candlemakers*

---

3. *Bluebook* Rule B2.
4. *See Bluebook* Rule 10.2.
5. *Bluebook* Rule B4.1.1(i).
6. *Bluebook* Rule B4.1.1(ii).

. Abbreviate the common words listed in Table 6.[7] For example,

Environmental Systems Technology, Incorporated v. Marketing
Service Corporation
↓
Envtl. Sys. Tech., Inc. v. Mktg. Serv. Corp.

American Manufacturing Company v. Regional University Society
↓
Am. Mfg. Co. v. Reg'l Univ. Soc'y

. Abbreviate the locations listed in Table 10 when the location is not the full name of the party.[8] For example,

Bank of Nova Scotia v. Pennsylvania
↓
Bank of N.S. v. Pennsylvania

Not
Bank of Nova Scotia v. Pennsylvania

or
Bank of N.S. v. Pa.

ii. Step Two: Abbreviate the Reporter

Every case reporter has an abbreviation. Writing that a case appears in the Federal Supplement Second Series would take up too much space. Instead, that case reporter is abbreviated in citations as F. Supp. 2d. Learning the abbreviations for the reporters you will cite most often will save you time.

The abbreviations for federal reporters appear in Table 1 of *The Bluebook*. The federal reporters you will cite frequently are abbreviated as follows:

Full Name	Abbreviation
U.S. Reports (U.S. Supreme Court cases)	U.S.
Federal Reporter (U.S. Courts of Appeals cases)	F. F.2d F.3d
Federal Supplement (U.S. District Court cases)	F. F. Supp. 2d

---

7. *Bluebook* Rule B4.1.1(v).
8. *Id.*

The abbreviations for state reporters also appear in Table 1. State cases often appear in more than one reporter, but *Bluebook* format includes only the regional reporter.[9] The abbreviations for the regional reporters are as follows:

Full Name	Abbreviation
Atlantic Reporter	A.
(Connecticut, Delaware, D.C., Maine,	A.2d
Maryland, New Hampshire, New Jersey,	A.3d
Pennsylvania, Rhode Island, Vermont)	
South Eastern Reporter	S.E.
(Georgia, North Carolina, South Carolina,	S.E.2d
Virginia, West Virginia)	
Southern Reporter	So.
(Alabama, Florida, Louisiana, Mississippi)	So. 2d
	So. 3d
North Eastern Reporter	N.E.
(Illinois, Indiana, Massachusetts,	N.E.2d
New York, Ohio)	
South Western Reporter	S.W.
(Arkansas, Kentucky, Missouri, Tennessee,	S.W.2d
Texas)	S.W.3d
North Western Reporter	N.W.
(Iowa, Michigan, Minnesota, Nebraska,	N.W.2d
North Dakota, South Dakota, Wisconsin)	
Pacific	P.
(Alaska, Arizona, California, Colorado,	P.2d
Hawaii, Idaho, Kansas, Montana, Nevada,	P.3d
New Mexico, Oklahoma, Oregon, Utah,	
Washington, Wyoming)	

iii. Step Three: Include the First Page and the Pinpoint Page

A long-form case citation should include the first page that the case appears in the reporter and a pinpoint page where the specific cited information appears in the case. The first page and the pinpoint page are separated by a comma and a space.

Including the first page enables the reader to find the case. Including the pinpoint page allows the reader to find the specific information being relied upon. Without both, the citation is incomplete and unhelpful to the reader.

---

9. *Bluebook* Rule B4.1.3. The regional reporters are published by West and group the states into seven geographic regions.

iv. Step Four: Abbreviate the Court

A long-form case citation ends with a parenthetical that typically includes the abbreviated name of the court that issued the decision and the year. Specific court abbreviations appear in Table 1 and general court abbreviations appear in Table 7.

Court	Abbreviations
U.S. Courts of Appeals	1st Cir., 2d Cir., 3d Cir., 4th Cir., 5th Cir., 6th Cir., 7th Cir., 8th Cir., 9th Cir., 10th Cir., 11th Cir., D.C. Cir., Fed. Cir.
U.S. District Courts *See Bluebook Table 10 for state abbreviations*	United States District Court for the Central District of California • C.D. Cal. United States District Court for the District of Massachusetts • D. Mass. United States District Court for the Southern District of New York • S.D.N.Y.
State Courts *See Bluebook Table 1*	Supreme Court of Arkansas • Ark. Tennessee Court of Appeals • Tenn. Ct. App.

When the reporter unambiguously conveys the court that decided the case, do not include the court in the citation.[10] The federal and regional reporters include cases decided by a variety of courts, so the court must be included. The U.S. Reports, however, only includes decisions of the U.S. Supreme Court. Accordingly, when citing to a U.S. Supreme Court case, you should not include the court in parentheses:

Brown v. Bd. of Educ., 347 U.S. 483, 487 (1954).

— No court included in the parentheses because the reporter unambiguously conveys that this is a decision of the U.S. Supreme Court.

B. Cases: Short-Form Citations

After providing the long citation for a case on the first reference, you should use the short-citation format for all subsequent citations to that case. Short citations are more concise than long citations, while still giving the reader all of the necessary information about the cited source.

---

10. *Bluebook* Rule B4.1.3(iv).

The following examples show the four different types of short-citation formats for cases.[11] The short form will vary depending on how much information the reader needs to identify the case and the page being cited. The following are the short formats for the citation to *Brown v. Board of Education*:

Brown, 347 U.S. at 488.

> Use this short format: one party name—comma—volume—reporter—at—page—period when the case has been cited in full earlier in the document, and the preceding citation is to a different authority.

347 U.S. at 488.

> Use this short format: volume—reporter—at—page—period when the case has been cited in full earlier in the document, the preceding citation is to a different authority, and the case name appears in the sentence.

Id. at 488.

> Use this short format: *Id.*—at—page—period when the case has been cited in full earlier in the document, and the preceding citation is to a different pinpoint page of the same case. Remember that *id.* is always italicized and should be capitalized when it begins a citation sentence.

Id.

> Use this short format: *Id.* when the case has been cited in full earlier in the document, and the preceding citation is to the same pinpoint page of the same case. Remember that *id.* is always italicized and should be capitalized when it begins a citation sentence.

For cases that have been published only on Westlaw or Lexis, use the *id.* formats above or one of the following short forms, keeping in mind that you may omit the case name if it appears in the sentence you are citing:

Shuffle Master, 2009 WL 3336115, at *4.

Shuffle Master, 2009 U.S. Dist. LEXIS 101698, at *4.

C. Federal Statutes: Long-Form Citations

A federal statute citation reflects where the statute is located in the official U.S. Code. The information in the citation is organized as follows:

title number—abbreviated name of U.S. Code—section symbol—section number—left parenthesis—year of cited code edition—right parenthesis—period

16 U.S.C. §1332(b) (2012).

---

11. *Bluebook* Rule B4.2.

There are three steps to proper long-form statute citation format:

> ### Long-Form Statute Citations
>
> i. Cite the official code
> ii. Include all subsections
> iii. Use the most recent year the code was printed

i. Step One: Cite the Official Code

Usually, you will use an annotated version of the U.S. Code to do your research. But in your legal documents, you should always cite to the official U.S. Code. Thus, your citations for federal statutes should always use the abbreviation for the official Code—U.S.C.—not the abbreviation for an annotated code.

ii. Step Two: Include All Subsections

Statute citations must be specific. Just as case citations must include a pinpoint page, statute citations must include a specific subsection. If the code section you are citing is divided into subsections and sub-subsections, include them in your citation. For example, if you were relying on 35 U.S.C. §271(e)(2)(C)(ii) (2012)—a statute with four layers of subsections—it would not be helpful to the reader to only cite 35 U.S.C. §271 (2012). The reader needs to know the specific part of that section that you are citing.

iii. Step Three: Use the Most Recent Year the Code Was Printed

According to *The Bluebook*, a long-form federal statute citation should include the most recent year that the U.S. Code was printed in parentheses.[12] The U.S. Code is printed every six years. The most recent printing was in 2012.

D. Federal Statutes: Short-Form Citations

After the first long citation for a statute, you can use short citations throughout the rest of your document. The short-citation formats for federal statutes are as follows:

16 U.S.C. §1332(b).

> Use this short format: title—code—section symbol—specific section—period when the statute has been cited in full earlier in the document.

§1332(b).

> Use this short format: section symbol—specific section—period when the statute has been cited in full earlier in the document, and there is no risk that the reader will be confused about which title is being referred to.

---

12. In practice, many attorneys omit the year from statute citations. The reader assumes that the writer is citing the most recent version of the code.

Id. §1333(a).

> Use this short format: *Id.*—section symbol—specific section—period when the statute has been cited in full earlier in the document, and the preceding citation is to a section in the same title. Remember that *id.* is always italicized and should be capitalized when it begins a citation sentence.

Id.

> Use this short format: *Id.* when the statute has been cited in full earlier in the document, and the preceding citation is to the identical section of the statute. Remember that *id.* is always italicized and should be capitalized when it begins a citation sentence.

E. State Statutes

The Bluebook citation format for each state's statutes is listed in Table 1. The long-citation formats for state statutes vary greatly because each state's code is organized differently. Some state codes are organized around numerical titles or sections while others are divided by subject area. For states that don't have an official, unannotated code, *The Bluebook* requires citation of the annotated version. For example, in Arkansas, a state statute is cited as Ark. Code Ann. §20-24-112(b)(2) (2012). Any short form that clearly identifies the specific statute being cited is acceptable after the statute has been cited in long form in the document.[13] Here are a few examples:

STATE CODE ABBREVIATION EXAMPLES
Arkansas Statute (no official version available)
↓
Ark. Code Ann. §20-24-112(b)(2) (2012).
California Statute
↓
Cal. Bus. & Prof. Code §17206(a) (2012).
Maine Statute
↓
Me. Rev. Stat. tit. 10, §1159 (2012).
Wisconsin Statute
↓
Wis. Stat. §43.15(1)(b) (2012).

---

13. *Bluebook* Rule B5.2.

3. LEARN THE RULES THAT ARISE FREQUENTLY

The Bluebook has certain rules that are not intuitive, but they arise frequently in preparing legal documents. You should learn these rules early because you will apply them often.

Rules to Learn

A. Spacing in abbreviations
B. Ordinal numbers
C. Page ranges
D. Federal Rules
E. Signals
F. String cites
G. Parentheticals

A. Spacing in Abbreviations

Single capital letters that appear next to each other in an abbreviation are not separated by a space: S.D.N.Y. Ordinal numbers are treated like single capitals for purposes of this rule: F.3d. But any abbreviation that is not a single capital letter should be separated by a space on both sides: F. Supp. 2d.[14]

B. Ordinal Numbers

Ordinal numbers should not use superscript: 11th Cir., not 11th Cir. *The Bluebook* abbreviations for second and third are unusual. They are abbreviated 2d and 3d, not 2nd and 3rd.[15]

C. Page Ranges

For a range of pages, give the first and last page separated by an en dash or hyphen. For the last page, retain the last two digits and drop any other repetitious digits: *Brown*, 347 U.S. at 490-93.[16]

D. Federal Rules

The citation formats for the Federal Rules of Procedure and Federal Rules of Evidence are as follows: Fed. R. Civ. P. 12(b)(6) and Fed. R. Evid. 408.[17]

E. Signals

Signals are short words or phrases that precede a citation and tell the reader how the cited authority relates to the proposition for which it is cited. You

---

14. *Bluebook* Rule 6.1(a).
15. *Bluebook* Rule 6.2(b)(ii).
16. *Bluebook* Rule B4.1.2.
17. *Bluebook* Rule B5.1.3.

should not use a signal when the authority directly states the proposition, is the source of a quotation, or is referred to directly.[18] All other citations should be introduced with a signal. Signals should be italicized, and, when a signal begins a citation sentence, it should be capitalized.[19]

The most common signal is *see*. Use *see* when the cited authority supports the proposition but does not state it directly. For instance, *see* is appropriate when you are inferring something about the meaning of a case, synthesizing a rule that is not stated explicitly, or using an authority to support a conclusion about your own case.

Chief Judge Alex Kozinski's decision for the Ninth Circuit Court of Appeals in *Facebook, Inc. v. Pacific Northwest Software, Inc.* provides an example of each of the ways to use *see* as an introductory signal:

> A party seeking to rescind a settlement agreement by claiming a Rule 10b-5 violation under these circumstances faces a steep uphill battle. *See* Petro-Ventures, Inc. v. Takessian, 967 F.2d 1337, 1341-42 (9th Cir. 1992)....
>
> —*See* indicates that the writer has inferred this proposition from the outcome of the cited case.
>
> An agreement meant to end a dispute between sophisticated parties cannot reasonably be interpreted as leaving open the door to litigation about the settlement negotiation process. *See* Petro-Ventures, 967 F.2d at 1342 (discussing the parties' "intent to end their various disputes...once and for all" (ellipsis in original)).
>
> —*See* indicates that the writer has synthesized this rule from the reasoning of the cited case.
>
> This agreement precludes the Winklevosses from introducing in support of their securities claims any evidence of what Facebook said, or did not say, during the mediation. *See* Johnson v. Am. Online, Inc., 280 F. Supp. 2d 1018, 1027 (N.D. Cal. 2003) (enforcing a similar agreement).[20]
>
> —*See* indicates that the writer used the cited case to support a conclusion about this case.

Other signals that show both support and contradiction are described in Rule 1.2 of *The Bluebook*.

F. String Cites

A citation sentence that includes more than one citation with the same signal is called a "string cite." A string cite can be useful when the writer wants to show that there are multiple authorities that support the stated proposition.

The citations within a string cite are separated by semicolons and ordered according to the hierarchy of authority, with the citations for higher courts appearing before the citations for lower courts.[21] When there are multiple citations from the same level of court, the citations are listed in reverse chronological order, with the most recent cases first.[22]

---

18. *Bluebook* Rule B3.1.
19. *Bluebook* Rule B3.
20. *Facebook, Inc. v. Pac. Nw. Software, Inc.*, 640 F.3d 1034, 1039-41 (9th Cir. 2011).
21. *Bluebook* Rules B3.5 and 1.4.
22. *Bluebook* Rule 1.4(d).

The Circuits were split over whether the "first sale" doctrine applied to copies made outside the United States. *See Kirtsaeng v. John Wiley & Sons, Inc.*, 654 F.3d 210 (2d Cir. 2011); *Omega S.A. v. Costco Wholesale Corp.*, 514 F.3d 982 (9th Cir. 2008); *Sebastian Int'l Inc. v. Consumer Contacts (PTY) Ltd.*, 847 F.2d 1093 (3d Cir. 1988).

G. Parentheticals

A parenthetical appears at the end of a citation sentence and gives the reader useful substantive information about the cited authority. The most common types of parentheticals are (1) those that explain the authority cited, (2) those that indicate that the authority cites or quotes an additional authority, and (3) those that describe the weight of the authority.

i. Explanatory Parentheticals

Explanatory parentheticals provide substantive information about the cited authority in a sentence or a phrase.[23] These parentheticals are useful because they allow the writer to concisely convey relevant information about a cited authority as part of the citation sentence.

An explanatory parenthetical appears after the citation and usually begins with a present participle (a verb ending in —ing). These explanatory parentheticals tell the reader how or why the cited authority supports the proposition that is being cited. In explanatory parentheticals for case citations, the —ing verb describes an action of the court, with words like holding, explaining, noting, or finding. For statutes, the —ing verb usually describes the purpose or effect of the statute, with words like requiring, mandating, describing, or listing. This form of explanatory parenthetical doesn't begin with a capital letter or include a period within the parentheses because it isn't a full sentence.

> The veterinarian's rule applies because Defendant owed no duty to Plaintiffs under the dog bite statute based on the parties' contractual relationship. *See Rosenbloom v. Hanour Corp.*, 78 Cal. Rptr. 2d 686, 689 (Ct. App. 1988) (holding that the defendant owed no duty to the plaintiff when the defendant contracted for the services of the plaintiff and entrusted a shark to the plaintiff's care and control).

Explanatory parentheticals can also contain quoted language from the cited authority. Including quoted language in a parenthetical gives the citation heft by showing how the cited authority supports the proposition through the authority's own language. If the quoted language reads as a full sentence, the parenthetical should begin with a capital letter and end with a period. This format includes a period within the parentheses to mark the end of the sentence and outside the parentheses to mark the end of the citation.

---

23. *Bluebook* Rules B4.1.5 and B11.

The hazard of being bitten and injured by dogs is an inherent risk associated with dog walking. *Priebe v. Nelson*, 47 Cal. Rptr. 3d 553, 568 (Cal. 2009) ("We therefore conclude that Priebe, by virtue of the nature of her occupation as a kennel worker, assumed the risk of being bitten or otherwise injured by the dogs under her care and control while in the custody of the commercial kennel where she worked pursuant to a contractual boarding agreement.").

Explanatory parentheticals can also be short phrases, if a short phrase is all that is needed for the reader to understand the relevance of the citation. Often, this type of explanatory parenthetical is used when the writer cites multiple authorities together and needs to highlight only one aspect of each authority.

The veterinarian's rule has been applied to a variety of professions that provide services for dogs. *See Priebe*, 47 Cal. Rptr. 3d at 556 (kennel workers); *Nelson v. Hall*, 211 Cal. Rptr. 668, 671 (Ct. App. 1985) (veterinary assistants); *Jordan v. Lusby*, 81 S.W.3d 523, 524-25 (Ky. Ct. App. 2002) (dog groomers); *Reynolds v. Lancaster Cnty. Prison*, 739 A.2d 413, 427-28 (N.J. Super. Ct. App. Div. 1999) (independent contractor who agreed to care for dogs in connection with his employment as a manager of a guard dog company).[24]

ii. Quoting/Citing Parentheticals

Quoting/citing parentheticals indicate that the authority cites or quotes an additional authority.[25] These parentheticals are useful when the source quoted or cited by an authority has some weight, relevance, or interest that would be meaningful to the reader. For example, if the cited case relies on a case from a higher court or from another jurisdiction, or if the cited case quotes an unexpected secondary source, including information in a quoting/citing parenthetical can be helpful. Only one level of quoting/citing parentheticals should be included. Additional sources quoted or cited in the cited authorities can always be included as separate citations.

A quoting or citing parenthetical follows the same format as an explanatory parenthetical that begins with an —ing verb.

"As the Supreme Court declared, '[I]t is pure fantasy to talk of 'owning' wild fish, birds, or animals. Neither the States nor the Federal Government... has title to these creatures until they are reduced to possession by skillful capture.'" *Mountain States Legal Found. v. Hodel*, 799 F.2d 1423, 1426-27 (10th Cir. 1986) (quoting *Douglas v. Seacoast Prods., Inc.*, 431 U.S. 265,

---

24. This string cite was for an issue that would be decided under California law, so all of the California cases are listed first, in reverse chronological order, before the citations for cases from non-binding jurisdictions. *See Bluebook* Rule 1.4.

25. *Bluebook* Rule 10.6.2.

284 (1977)). Unfortunately, some state courts have held that a person may kill wildlife when doing so is necessary to protect his property. *Id.* at 1428 n.8 (citing *Cross v. State*, 370 P.2d 371 (Wyo. 1962)).

iii. Weight of Authority Parentheticals

Weight of authority parentheticals provide information that affects the weight of the cited authority. These parentheticals must be included when citing a concurring or dissenting opinion. The format for parentheticals for concurrences and dissents has the judge or justice's last name followed by J. (or C.J. for Chief Justice) and the nature of the opinion, all separated by commas.[26]

> *Ledbetter v. Goodyear Tire & Rubber Co.*, 550 U.S. 618, 644 (2007) (Ginsburg, J., dissenting).

4. USE THE INDEX, TABLES, AND QUICK REFERENCE GUIDES FOR EVERYTHING ELSE

When you encounter a new citation issue, use the index, tables, or quick reference guides to find the correct format. *The Bluebook* has an extensive index that will guide you to the most helpful places in the text. In addition, the tables in the back of *The Bluebook* provide jurisdiction-specific information for federal, state, and foreign authorities. Last, inside the front and back covers, quick reference guides provide examples of the most common formats.

5. REMEMBER LOCAL CITATION RULES

Many courts have their own citation rules that trump *The Bluebook* in documents submitted to those courts. *The Bluebook* lists these types of rules in Table BT2. The citation formats for cases and statutes under local rules can differ dramatically from *Bluebook* format. Thus, follow the local citation practices for your jurisdiction when preparing any legal document.

6. CITE CORRECTLY AS YOU WRITE

Beginning legal writers are often intimidated by citation and choose to put in filler citations as they write their documents, intending to come back and fix all of the citations at the end of the writing process. But the better practice is to correctly cite each authority as you write.

---

26. *Bluebook* Rule B4.1.5.

Learning to incorporate correct citations into the flow of your writing has many advantages. In particular, it helps you to learn how to cite efficiently and avoid putting off a task that can be unexpectedly difficult and time consuming, especially if you are close to your deadline. It also ensures that you don't have to retrace your steps to find the authorities or pages that you meant to cite, which can be frustrating and create the risk of citation errors. By citing as you write, correctly citing the most common sources will become a seamless part of your legal writing process. And your early attention to detail will help you create a flawless and credible document.

Index